Race Awareness in Young Children

Race Awareness
in Young Children

MARY ELLEN GOODMAN

With an Introduction by Kenneth B. Clark, M.D.

NEW, REVISED EDITION

 COLLIER BOOKS

COLLIER-MACMILLAN LTD *London*

An ADL Freedom Book

This Collier Books edition is published by arrangement with the Anti-Defamation League of B'nai B'rith
The Macmillan Company
866 Third Avenue, New York, N.Y. 10022
Collier-Macmillan Canada Ltd., Toronto, Ontario

PRINTED IN THE UNITED STATES OF AMERICA

Preface to First Edition

WHILE THE WRITER is wholly and solely responsible for this book, she is greatly indebted to large numbers of people who have contributed to its evolution. Most of them, unfortunately, must remain nameless in the interest of protecting the identity of the families about whom I have written. It must suffice to say that I am deeply grateful to the children and to the parents who let me look into their minds and lives, and helped me do it. I am most grateful to the directors and the teachers of the three nursery schools at which the children were enrolled when the study was made. These kind and patient people not only allowed access to their charges, but provided facilities, conveniences, and a wealth of incidental information. I cannot thank them enough. Many other people helped the study along with bits of information about the community and its people —social workers, teachers, policemen, storekeepers, old residents made their contributions. To all of them I offer my thanks.

Two industrious and able graduate students in psychology aided me in collecting the data. To Doris Gilbert and Bernard Kutner, now of the staffs of the Massachusetts General Hospital and of the Commission for Community Interrelations (New York), respectively, I am most grateful for assistance of very high quality and for the most enthusiastic and harmonious collaboration. Mrs. Gilbert collected the data on twenty-one children; Dr. Kutner studied nineteen. The data on four more children were collected largely by Judith Roche while she was a senior student at Wellesley College. Her collaboration too was most helpful and very pleasant, and I am grateful for it.

5

I am indebted to still others, and to more than I can name. My students and my colleagues have played an indirect but important part. To my own teachers, now largely of the Departments of Social Relations and of Anthropology at Harvard University, I am as generally and deeply indebted as a student must forever be to conspicuously able teachers. Professors Clyde Kluckhohn and Gordon Allport have given me wise and generous direction and counsel in this particular research. I am very grateful for their contributions.

The research reported here was carried out under grants from two organizations. The study was begun in 1943 under a Fellowship from the American Association of University Women. It was concluded in 1948 with the generous assistance of the Wenner-Gren Foundation (formerly the Viking Fund) of New York. I deeply appreciate their help, their interest, and their patience.

MARY ELLEN GOODMAN

Ridgefield, Connecticut

Preface to Revised Edition

To THE ANTI-DEFAMATION LEAGUE, and particularly to its wise and able Program Director Mr. Oscar Cohen, I am indebted for long-standing interest which has led to the republication of this book. I am deeply grateful to Mr. Cohen and others of the ADL staff who have worked out so patiently and with such consideration the arrangements under which the book now appears.

The occasion provides a welcome opportunity to acknowledge also the role played by the late Mr. Joseph Kaplan of Boston, distinguished businessman, philanthropist, and humanitarian. Mr. Kaplan's love for children knew no limits of color, class, or culture; he made an avocation of encouraging studies and action designed to reduce prejudice and the blight it casts on the lives of children. His friendship and his faith in the importance of such works lent strength to my efforts and shall remain a cherished memory and inspiration.

MARY ELLEN GOODMAN

Houston, Texas

Contents

APPENDIX

Introduction

THIS BOOK by Mary Ellen Goodman is a model of systematic and objective research. It forms a part of a fascinating and important saga in the collaboration between social science and the law in the quest for a solution to one of the most important problems that has continued to plague the people of the United States. In this Introduction to *Race Awareness in Young Children* it would seem particularly appropriate to review some specifics of this collaboration which led to the historic *Brown* decision handed down by the United States Supreme Court on May 17, 1954. This decision ruled that state laws which required or permitted racial segregation in public education violated the equal protection clause of the 14th Amendment of the United States Constitution. The social science and legal core of this decision states:

> We come then to the question presented: Does segregation of children in public schools solely on the basis of race, even though the physical facilities and other "tangible" factors may be equal, deprive the children of the minority group of equal educational opportunities? We believe that it does.
>
> Such considerations apply with added force to children in grade and high schools. To separate them from others of similar age and qualifications solely because of their race generates a feeling of inferiority as to their status in the community that may affect their hearts and minds in a way unlikely ever to be undone.

We conclude that in the field of public education the doctrine of separate but equal has no place. Separate educational facilities are inherently unequal.

The implications of this decision are to be found in many areas. In addition to the legal, political, social, educational, international, and religious implications, this decision has a special significance for contemporary social psychology and social science. It has been hailed as a great judicial document because it solved the complex problem of overruling the "separate but equal" doctrine of the *Plessy* v. *Ferguson* decision which had limited progress in civil rights in America since 1896. It is an important educational document because it is an official governmental statement of the nature of democratic education and the responsibility of government for the quality of the education provided for children. It will be recognized as one of the great moral documents which stands as a milestone in the articulation and progress of the democratic ideals of western civilization. In time it might be ranked with such monumental documents as the Magna Carta, the Bill of Rights, the Declaration of Independence, and the Emancipation Proclamation. Its language has the simple, dignified eloquence inevitable in a statement of a fundamental truth. Its significance as a social science and psychological document is to be found in its analysis of the nature of racial segregation and the consequences of segregation on the motivation and personality of Negro children.

The reliance of the Court on the contributions of psychologists, sociologists, and anthropologists is indicated by these words of the decision: "Whatever may have been the extent of psychological knowledge at the time of *Plessy* v. *Ferguson*, this finding is amply supported by modern authority." The decision then cites in its famous footnote 11 a number of psychological and sociological references. This and related parts of the May 17th decision established social science data with an authority, status, and prestige reflecting a recognition and acceptance from the highest judicial body of our nation. Although data from economists had undoubtedly been previously cited by the Court, this was the first time that the social sciences had played a central role in such a historic judicial decision. It is a curious and significant fact that this productive and successful collaboration existed long before either party was aware of its existence or its inevitability.

Prior to the 1930s, much of the research in racial differences reflected the influence of the prevailing racial biases on the attitudes and hypotheses of the research workers. In the 1930s, Otto Klineberg brought a more objective approach to the study of the psychology of racial differences. His work demonstrated that racial differences in psychological traits were significantly influenced by environment.

Research on the genesis and nature of racial attitudes became more significant within this new perspective. Eugene Horowitz's continuation and systematization of Bruno Lasker's earlier studies of the racial attitudes of children is another major contribution of the psychologists in this period of predirect collaboration. Further investigations of the development of racial awareness and attitudes in very young children by Eugene and Ruth Horowitz contributed to the developing knowledge in this area.

Direct psychological research on the effects of racial rejection of the personality and emotional adjustment of Negro children developed relatively late. The work of Kenneth and Mamie Clark on the personal and emotional aspects of racial awareness and identification in Negro children was one of the first attempts among psychologists to deal with this problem systematically and empirically. Other investigators corroborated the finding that the Negro child showed symptoms of personality damage associated with his awareness of his rejected racial status.

The work of Mary Ellen Goodman may be viewed as an important bridge between those studies which were primarily seeking an understanding of the development of racial attitudes in children and those which were concerned with the personality concomitance of racial awareness and identification. On the levels of both theory and method, her work is eclectic. Her principal focus, however, is that of the cultural anthropologist. In the anthropologist's frame of reference, race attitudes are seen as patterned elements in American culture. Through a series of intensive case studies, Dr. Goodman investigates the complex processes underlying intergenerational persistence of the culturally predominant pattern of "white over brown."

In spite of the stresses and tensions that seem to have dominated the reactions to the desegregation decision, it remains that this decision marks a momentous strengthening of American democracy. The fundamental changes it demands in

American status and power dynamics can be postponed temporarily, but not avoided. Mary Ellen Goodman and the other social scientists involved in the study of various aspects of the American race problem have contributed significantly to this major pattern of social change.

It is one of those tantalizing facts, worthy of repetition, that these studies were not conceived and conducted directly for purposes of social change. They are examples of "pure" rather than "applied" research whereby social scientists seek to study a problem in social relations primarily because the problem exists and excites human curiosity. It may not have been incidental, but it certainly was not planned that the results of these studies eventually formed part of a pattern of knowledge which had some social-action significance. It may well be true that social scientists who choose this type of problem do so because of their interests and values, which include a desire for relevant and indicated social change.

The issue of the social relevance of social science research is a complex but persistent one. Mary Ellen Goodman's impatience with sterile "scientism" and her desire to avoid "trivialization" are admirable traits that are reflected in the quality and significance of her contributions to knowledge. There seems to be an increasing number of younger social scientists who dare to work on problems of social significance and controversy. Once they leave the escapist and safe haven of preoccupation with quantified irrelevance, they must accept the risks of criticism, misunderstanding, misinterpretation, and, in some cases, misuse of their findings. They cannot, however, permit these to interfere with their quest for truth and with the hope that truth will be the basis for social justice.

The first edition of *Race Awareness in Young Children* and this revision with its valuable addition of a summary of the relevant research since 1950 are monuments to the scientific integrity and social sensitivity of its author.

KENNETH B. CLARK

New York City

Author's Introduction

THE READER may or may not "know" young children—or race relations—either intimately or academically. Whether he does or does not, if he finds either or both interesting and important, this book is intended for him.

If the reader knows young children in the bittersweet way in which they are known to their parents and others who deplore and adore them, he will find in this book some familiar Johnnys and Marys. He will find them doing and saying familiar things. He will also find them doing and saying—especially the latter—some things which are probably quite unfamiliar. These have to do with race and with race differences as the children see and feel them.

There are offered here some inventories of the thoughts and feelings of young children, brown and white, and some evidence concerning the background hows and whys. These inventories focus upon a rather little-known part of the young child's thought and feeling systems—upon his awareness of race differences and his feelings about those differences.

For the reader whose concern with young children or with race relations is that of the specialist of one kind or another—teacher, social worker, psychologist, sociologist, anthropologist—there are offered here some generalizations, some hypotheses, and much of the data from which they are drawn. For the specialist, and for anyone who cares to check my conclusions or to construct his own, more of the supporting data and certain refinements of the text will be found in notes and appendixes. Since this report is deliberately nontechnical, I must ask the specialist to anticipate the lack of footnotes, specialized vocabulary, and other familiar impedimenta of technical reporting. Readability is not necessarily inconsistent with scientific canons of reliability. I have tried to achieve what I could of both.

Throughout the text, certain short-cuts are used (N) and (w) stand for Negro and white, where the racial identity of the people mentioned is significant in relation to what is being said about them. The word "Observer" designates the writer or one of her assistants. The numbered references indicate that further material, or the source of a quotation, will be found in the notes at the back of the book.

I have omitted qualifications like "in my opinion," "in the light of my evidence," "in view of the present state of knowledge." It is unnecessary and cumbersome to constantly restate what should be constantly kept in mind by the reader. All of the statements made here must be considered qualified in all these ways.

The writer is aware of the limitations of her data and of her knowledge. The sample is small but, in view of time and personnel limitations, this study could not have been more *extensive* and still have retained its *intensive* character. I would not sacrifice the latter for the former if I were to repeat the investigation. The technical literature dealing with the beginnings of race attitudes is scanty enough generally, but almost entirely lacking in materials based upon an intensive study of individual cases. To begin to fill in this gap has been my particular goal. I have been concerned not only with the nature of early race awareness and dawning race attitudes, but also with the personal and social contexts in which they develop. I have tried to get a picture of the whole child and of the whole of his little social world. We need it, I think, if we are to understand how and why he came to have his particular ideas and feelings about race. And I am interested in those hows and whys for more than academic reasons. I believe that they are keys to more democratic race relations.

Race Awareness in Young Children

Unless the promises of our civilization are soon fulfilled, the civilization will die. Mechanical cleverness will not save it. . . . The whole world watches to see whether the democratic ideal in human relationships is viable.

—GORDON W. ALLPORT

Chapter 1

"The Lord's Children—"

IN THE NORTHEASTERN PART of the United States there is a seaboard city which we shall call New Dublin. About three-quarters of a million people live here—people varying widely in respect to social and economic status, religion, national origin, and race.

New Dubliners, like people in similar American cities, are inclined to idealize the harmony and equality in which all these diverse elements live together. "We're all Americans.—America is the melting pot.—America is the land of opportunity and equality." These are still the standard themes when memorials are dedicated, historic events are commemorated, cornerstones are laid, and the graduation day speaker holds forth. They are still the expected and approved sentiments for public occasions.

But our New Dubliners come back to social realities when they leave the speechmaking. For a good many of these people the realities are quite divorced from the implications of the speeches. In the face of the realities some of our New Dubliners take comfort in the thought that "whatever we are—whatever class or nationality or race, still—we're all the Lord's children."

There is a section of New Dublin—the Dover-Harding area—where some 160,000 of "the Lord's children" are jammed into an area of less than two square miles. We shall be particularly concerned with the social realities as they are experienced by these people who live in Dover and Harding.

Anyone who knows the city will remember the Dover-Harding section as an irregular rectangle about two miles long and one-half to three-quarters of a mile wide. It lies across the city on a NE–SW axis with one end in the downtown business district and the other in a middle-class residential area. Traveling across the Dover-Harding area you see a great variety in the kinds and conditions of places in which the people live. There are the desolate tenements by the railroad tracks, the old mansions, shabby but still stately, facing on park-like streets. And there are the "projects," looking incongruously new, modern, and planned.

The Dover-Harding area is an old section of an old city. It is now what sociologists are likely to call a "transitional zone." The slow and irregular expansion of the city's commercial, industrial, and railroad facilities has increasingly encroached upon what was once a fashionable area of "town houses," many rather modest and some quite pretentious. The old residents are gone now, and their mansions taken over by institutions, broken into small apartments, or converted into rooming houses. The "blight" has descended since the turn of the century, and at an accelerating rate. As it progressed, cheap, close-packed tenements sprang up to accommodate the growing demands from immigrants for low-cost housing. These tenements are already badly decayed, and a new housing cycle has begun—government housing projects are arising where the worst of the deteriorated properties have been cleared away.

The last decade has brought improvements in housing and in general living conditions. But the Dover-Harding area remains two to three and one-half times more crowded (in terms of persons per inhabited acre) than the city as a whole. The crowding is most intense in Dover and in Lower Harding, where other indices of unfavorable living conditions reach extremes as compared with the rest of the city. High infant mortality and tuberculosis rates, high juvenile delinquency rates, high frequency of aid to dependent children and the aged, a high proportion of the population in the labor force and a low proportion at home or in school, a low median of educational achievement, a high proportion of dwelling units in need of major repairs and lacking mechanical refrigerators, central heating, and private baths—these are some of the realities of life in a blighted area.

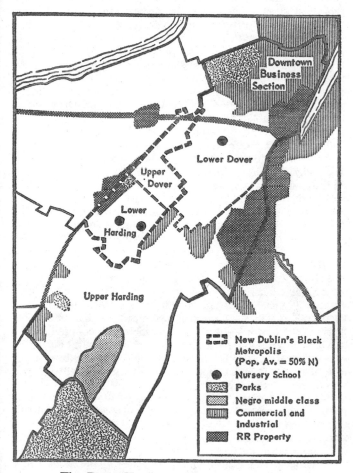

The Dover-Harding Area of New Dublin

An odd assortment of people filter into such an area. The social extremes of the population are represented by two groups of people. There are the professionals—doctors, lawyers, teachers, ministers, social workers, etc., and the students in these and other fields. They live in the area to be close to their clients or because, for the present, they can find no better quarters. At the opposite end of the status scale there are the floaters—unattached males living in the flophouses which characterize much of Lower Dover. They are often unemployed, old, ill, or alcoholic, and surviving precariously on odd jobs or public assistance. Like the first group, they are there because, for the present, they can find no better quarters. Unlike the first group, they have little hope of ever doing so.

People tend to "bog down" in Dover and Lower Harding. The lucky few pass through to Upper Harding or beyond. The undistinguished mass moves sluggishly, if at all, from a miserable tenement to one perhaps a little less miserable, or at best into a housing project. This sluggishness is due in part to the fact that in New Dublin generally neither residential nor other conditions change very rapidly for very many people. The city is old, stable, and conservative. But mobility both physical and social tends to be minimal for people whose life prospects are sharply limited by one or more socially lethal factors. The lack of general education, of vocational training, of the "100% American" racial, national, or religious identities, of individual talents or capacities, of physical health and stamina, of a stable marital relationship—all of these variables are common determinants of the Dover-Harding way of life. They tend to be self-perpetuating, despite the efforts of the people themselves and of the numerous public and private welfare agencies which "serve" the area.

It is to this essentially nonmobile group that our attention is directed. In it we will find most of the people whose children are the central characters of this book.

There are 103 of these central characters. They are the children into whose personalities and lives we shall look, and from whom we shall hope to learn something about how and why race attitudes begin.

Our 103 children have a number of things in common. They live in Dover or Harding, and most of them were born there. They are more or less personally affected by the conditions common in these areas. At best, a child does not grow up in a blighted area untouched by the blight. Our children are four-year-olds, and they are luckier than most of their age-mates in that they go to nursery school. Not many Dover-Harding children can have this opportunity. The nursery schools are good ones, and their "openings" are eagerly sought.

Some of our 103 are what Americans in New Dublin or elsewhere would call "Negroes," and the rest are, by the same token, "whites." The racial difference, biologically real or not, is for most practical purposes the most significant of the differences between our children. There are 57 who are "Negroes," according to social definition, although physically they run the gamut from markedly Negroid skin, hair, etc., to garden variety "whiteness," or very near it. The rest, the 46 who are lumped together and labeled "white," are actually almost as varied in physical type. They range from extreme blonds to brunets more heavily pigmented than some of our "Negroes."

A few of our children have traveled a bit, and travel is notoriously broadening. It can be broadening in respect to this matter of American race-categorizing. There was, for example, a little incident in Virginia when Joan M. and her brothers went bus-riding with their mother. They were newly arrived in their mother's native town, and when the bus stopped they gleefully hopped on and took the empty seats in the front. The fare paid, their mother turned and apprehensively hustled her offspring to other seats at the back of the bus. The children wondered about it, sensing a special meaning. Rosemarie wondered too, when she rode on a bus in Florida and was told that she must sit up front. Her mother explained about the laws "down south," and how they are different in the north, and Rosemarie remembered. Nobody explained to Joan and her brothers, but they could see. They figured it out, and they remembered, too.

Some others among our children get their traveling vicariously, from parents whose lives began in places more or less remote from New Dublin.[1]* There are Negro children, eight of them, who hear at home about life in the West Indies or the Cape Verde Islands. Still more of the Negro children, and one of the whites,[2] know something of life "down south," because one or both of their parents know it well.[3] Eight of our white

* References are at the back of the book.

children live with the echoes of a different social world—a world in Syria or Italy, Russia, England, or Latvia—and with the inevitable reminiscences and comparisons.

Negro and white alike, our children are exposed most of the time to the racial views and practices which are common in the Dover-Harding area. (What these views and practices are like we shall be considering later.) Most of the children are likely to grow up in this same area, since few have parents for whom the sociologist would predict "upward mobility," or even much "outward mobility." But there are six white and three Negro families whose chances are good because of a father or mother who has (or is acquiring) professional training and the status and income it can bring.[4] The rest belong to that big and essentially nonmobile group of which we have taken note before.

We have noted too, in a general way, some hallmarks of the conditions of life as it is lived by the mass of Dover-Harding people. Now we can be more specific, and see what the generalizations mean for our children and their families.

There is Joan M.'s family, for example. It was Joan and her brothers who once rode with their mother on a bus in Virginia, and thereby learned something about what it means to be brown. Joan's family has worked out a quite comfortable adjustment to race relations and other conditions of life in the urban north, but Mrs. M. still yearns for "a little home of my own, with a porch and a yard, and in a neighborhood where I felt we belonged."

Mrs. M.'s clean four-room apartment in Lower Harding boasts a radio, a telephone, and an electric refrigerator. She is used to the coal stove for cooking and heating, even though it heats best in the summer. But three flights of dark and dirty stairs separate her from the narrow, treeless street lined flush to the sidewalk with decayed tenements like her own. At either end of the block, the business section begins with its dingy grocery stores, its barbershops and pool halls and small taverns. The rent takes almost a third of their income, even though Mrs. M. "goes out by the day" quite often. When the plumbing is out of order or the roof leaks, Mr. M. has to find a way to fix things.

"There are no janitors in these buildings and the landlord lives on the other side of the city and wouldn't lift a finger if he were around. He won't put another cent into a building that will probably be condemned one of these days anyway. And he doesn't need to. If we don't like it we can get out. Plenty of other people are looking for a place as good as this.

"It could be a lot worse. There's a park only four blocks away where the children play, and Coleman House is just around the corner from the park. The boys go there to play basketball. Joan went to the nursery school there for a while so she could have a decent place to play.

"People say I keep her in too much, but she's only four and a half, and I won't let her out on the street unless I'm there to watch her every minute. I know lots of people do it, but I'm afraid of the cars and the men who hang around the tavern on the corner. And there's the talk she hears! She's very bright they tell me, and I want her to have nice manners and use good language and meet some nice children. I want her to go to a good, clean school where they have good teachers. Around here the schools are way behind the times. Her father and I finished high school—more than a lot of the people around here did. I hope Joan can do better. If we stay here—I don't know. If we could only get into a nice neighborhood she'd have a real chance."

The M.'s problems are closely paralleled by those of about 75% of our families. But many of the mothers are more indifferent or more resigned to the hazards of street play, and many are less ambitious for their offspring. Where the M.'s are high school graduates, the median for Dover-Harding adults is 8.4 school years completed. Our sample, however, includes a rather large percentage (almost a fourth) of families, Negro and white, in which one or both parents have had some formal education beyond high school. But excepting the few professional people and the students, whom we have already met, this higher education is usually a modest matter of "some" secretarial or teacher's training, nursing or trade school, art or music.

Mrs. M.'s view of the public schools is objectively verifiable, and she might have added some critical comments concerning other municipal services. The quality of the city's public services—schools, policing, street clearance and maintenance, trash and garbage disposal—varies directly with the status of the neighborhood. The people living in the most disadvantaged areas get the least efficient and "modern" of services, which are not, at best, setting records for new highs in efficiency and modernity. Complaints and pleas come to nothing, for the area has no political unity and no significant political leadership, and no "voice" in City Hall.

The people of Dover and Harding are as helpless in their dealings with the landlord as in their dealings with the lords of City Hall. In both cases they are generally facing absentee authorities and, from their point of view, quite arbitrary and absolute authorities. Toward both, they tend to feel a helpless rage which contributes to their already heavy burden of weariness and resentment. A very few join clubs which have some economic or political betterment goals. Many more join groups having "social" or religious meanings for them. But the people are not great "joiners." They lack the range of interests, the money, the time, the inclination, and the example of their neighbors.

Eighteen of our families (all of these Negro but one) have escaped from some of the disadvantages of the M.'s way of life. These people live in one of the public housing "Projects." Four such projects, largely financed by the federal government, have been erected in our area within the last decade. They are attractive, substantial, multifamily brick buildings, nicely spaced around landscaped yards and playgrounds. They replaced condemned housing and they provide a vivid contrast to the deteriorated buildings which remain around them. Indoor overcrowding characterizes the Projects as it does the private housing, but safe, attractive, and well-equipped outdoor play space considerably relieves this problem. The rentals average somewhat above those for privately owned units, but the quality to be bought with the rent dollar is much higher in the Projects. There are no more coal or oil stoves with their fire hazards and summer heat, no need to put the ice card in the window twice a week, no stumbling up and down three or four dirty, murky flights of stairs a dozen times a day, or stringing the clothesline out the window, no more sharing the ancient and uncertain plumbing facilities with the neighbors across the landing, no more narrow back windows through which comes the stench from the nearby restaurant kitchen, or narrow front ones giving a view of the bleak street and a generous measure of its dirt and noise.

The Projects have subtracted these and other hazards and annoyances from the lives of the people who live in them. They have added more than the obvious improvements in physical environment. They have added a new dimension to the social environment.

Students of the modern urban scene recognize that it creates peculiar problems in respect to the individual's sense of belonging—of having a defined and useful place in his world, and of being valued as a person by others in that world. To have a firm sense of belonging seems an essential element in personal satisfaction and security. Conversely, a sense of isolation is conducive to psychological ill-health. The staggering complexity of modern urban society, combined with the freedom and the anonymity it gives the individual, presents him with unprecedented opportunities *and* with unprecedented challenges. The city man is "on his own" to a fearful degree. Given a few breaks, and basic physical and mental health, he can find his way through the maze, affiliate himself with the persons and groups of his choice, and presumably live a reasonably happy life.

The combination of essential prerequisites—physical and mental health and a few breaks—appears to be a rarer phenomenon than we might like to believe. Certainly the conditions of life in the Dovers and Hardings of American cities are less conducive to it than are conditions in more favored neighborhoods. Mrs. M. and others like her feel, for objectively sound reasons, that they don't belong—that they play no really meaningful part. The people in the Project have some advantages in this respect. They tend to become, and feel themselves a part of, an organized community. They establish boards and councils of youth and of adults for the regulation of community affairs, they run their own play school and scout troops, sing in their own choral group, attend their own movies and dances. They develop local pride and civic-mindedness, they find constructive outlets for their energies and talents, and they practice democracy at what someone has called the "asphalt roots" level. The realities are less idyllic than this snapshot suggests. Yet some of the deep psychological needs of Harding-Dover people seem to be met, in part at least, in the Project communities.

There is one need, deeply felt by the Negro families in our sample, which the Projects fail to satisfy—the need for being a part of a representative American community. The Warner Street Project, which sixteen of our seventeen Project-living Negro families call home, is "all Negro." Less euphemistically put: racial segregation has been practiced. Our seventeenth family lives in the Forest Street Project, in which some 15% of the families are Negroes. Mrs. S. explains that

". . . our part of the Project is all for colored, but most of it is for white people. I don't think that's unfair though, because they tell us that before the Project was here there were mostly Irish in this neighborhood. Anyway, we were very glad to get in here, because most of the places that take colored are awfully run-down. . . . Last summer they had a playground here for the children. At first I didn't let Brenda go—her father didn't think she ought to. It was (racially) mixed, but I said she'd ought to learn to get along, and she did, too."

Not all our Negro parents are as tolerant as is Mrs. S. toward the public "reason" for partial segregation at Forest Street, and the similar "reasons" for total segregation at Warner Street and Abbey Hill—the latter "all white." The "Authority" has stated, as Mrs. S. reports, that its policy was simply to duplicate the color, or proportion of colors, of the pre-Project populations. The practice apears to have fallen short of the policy, since the Warner Project stands on territory previously occupied, like adjacent sections of Lower Harding, by both Negroes and whites. It is true that the whites were and are a small minority (some 10%) in this section, and that housing for Negroes was and is in more limited supply. The practice can be defended on such technicalities. Indeed it has had to be, against the spokesmen for the private welfare agencies and against the people themselves, who saw in it an implicit endorsement of segregated housing.

Like Mrs. S., most of the Negro families in our sample welcome opportunities for interracial contacts. They want their children to "learn to get along" in a varicolored world. The goal is realistic, in view of the melting pot in microcosm which surrounds them in Dover and Harding.

The Dover-Harding Microcosm

"The melting pot" here, as in much more of the U.S. than Americans often care to admit, simmers indefinitely and rarely reaches the melting point. People of great diversity of race and national origin live here for years literally on top of one another, jostle one another in the course of the routines of living, nod or smile or scowl at one another, and remain almost as distinct as they were in the beginning. Of course, there are exceptions. But contact does not necessarily bring friendship with it, not in modern urban society, where it is possible to be alone in a crowd, and often difficult not to be.

Some of our families want to be, since the crowd is largely alien. Lorraine's mother and father, who are American-born of Russian parents, separate themselves and their children as much as possible from the Italians, Irish, Syrians, and Negroes around them in Lower Dover. "We're not part of it (the neighborhood)," says Mrs. L., "so it doesn't bother me." George's Italian-born parents, tired and harassed with keeping three hungry boys fed and clothed and housed, simply have, or feel they have, no time or energy left to care about their neighbors one way or another. The G.'s are Syrian, one immigrant and the other first-generation American. They "don't mix too much. . . . There are lots of Syrian and colored here," says Mrs. G., "but I have nothing to do with them." Carl's parents (American-born of Italian immigrants) do not even admit the presence of Negroes as part of their neighborhood's citizenry, but only as transients.

Negroes are not precisely transients in Lower Dover, but most of them are relative newcomers there. They are seeping in along with a variety of other immigrants, and they are resented as newcomers by those who preceded them by only a little. In addition, they are, of course, resented for *being* Negroes. Jean's mother (of Syrian background) observes bitterly:

> "Almost all Syrians lived in this neighborhood up to now. The 'Chinks' are moving in and buying up the property. The colored are coming, too. I think they'll take over the whole neighborhood. I can't stand the sight of them anyhow. They give me the creeps. . . . People in this neighborhood don't like Chinese and still less colored people!"

Dover and Lower Harding together constitute a funnel through which New Dublin immigrants of modest status move, as we have seen, when their status becomes somewhat less modest. The process can be longer than a generation, and in the case of the Negroes it is very likely to be. Restrictive covenants and other less formal barriers to their movement are no novelties in New Dublin or its suburbs. Hence, New

Dublin, like other northern cities, has its "Negro section" in which the erstwhile immigrants bog down. In the whole city there are about 24,000 Negroes—some 3% of its population. Almost all of them (21,000) live in Dover or in Harding.

The "Negro Section"

In Upper Dover and Lower Harding—the "backbone" of the area in which our children live—the concentration of the Negro population reaches its peak for the city.[5] Of Dover's 6,000 Negroes, 5,000 live in Upper Dover. In Harding as a whole there are 15,000 Negroes (about 15% of its population). But the 15,000 are by no means evenly distributed. They cluster tightly in two areas. Over half are in Lower Harding. Most of the others enjoy the advantages of life on their island in the middle-class white zone of Upper Harding. Our children are not among these favored ones.

But even in the "Negro section" there are ample opportunities for interracial contact—or conflict. About 60% of the people of Upper Dover are white. For Lower Harding the proportions of Negro and white are just reversed. In these areas the blocks are irregularly "all Negro" or "all white," or the occupancy is "salt and pepper" patterned. That the "all Negro" blocks have slowly increased in number is a measure of the "bogging down" process noted earlier. William's mother and father (N) have seen it happening, and with some regret.

"We grew up here in Lower Harding. My, how the neighborhood has changed since we were kids. When I went to the B—— school, there were a lot of white children. Now I think there are only two or three in the whole school, and it seems too bad. I wish Willie could go to a nice mixed school like the Rodney school. Kids ought to be with all kinds. I'm glad our street is still mixed. Right next door there are two white families. We don't see very much of them because they don't have any young children. They're friendly though. One of them had a little garden out in back and they gave me some of their tomatoes. Just down the street there's an Italian family with a little girl Willie's age. They play together all the time, and they get along fine."

Willie and the rest of the T. family "get along fine," it appears, with all comers regardless of race or status. They are rather remarkable people—remarkable for their serenity, their dignity and self-respect, their healthy affection toward one another. In terms of education or job prestige, they are totally unremarkable in their neighborhood. They have those essentials—physical and mental health. They have had no really bad breaks and a few fairly good ones. They "get along," in the very general sense, where others do not.

Quentin's mother and father (N) are among those who do not get along, either with one another or with the people "on the other side of the line." Mr. M. is an angry man. Much of his anger boils over on his wife, his children, his in-laws, and his white neighbors. His wife is perhaps more frightened than angry, but she too is in battle with the whites across the street.

"Those dirty little blond brats over there! They'll yell 'nigger' when they see Quen looking out the window. He'll run and tell me, and I'll tell him not to pay any attention. I know he's probably stuck out his tongue or something. I try to get around it that way, but once they kept it up and kept it up! It just got me and I ran right out in my pajamas and grabbed one of them and shook him till his teeth rattled. . . . He was only about four, and of course I knew it was his mother's fault. She keeps out of my way you can bet. Would I just like to get my hands on her!"

There are others, brown and white, whose interracial contacts wind up in more or less open conflict. But "neighborhood relations are generally pretty friendly," in the opinion of a young social worker.

"There's a good deal of borrowing and talking over the back fence, and not too much prejudice that shows up unmistakably. There's some exchanging of social invitations, but not to any great extent. Interracial attachments do occur, of course, but they're frowned on by both groups. Interracial marriages are very few. . . . The tensions you see are mainly family and individual matters."

In New Dublin, as in northern cities generally, Negro-white contacts are primarily of a casual nature, and secondarily economic. People pass on the streets, shop in the same stores, exchange more or less polite comments while waiting at the laundromat, and mingle in the crowds coming out of the nearest movie house. The men, and sometimes the women, meet on the job. Sometimes they meet as equals. Much more often "the boss" is white. And yet the director of Coleman House (N) tells us that

"Negroes in the mid-west, where I come from, regard New Dublin as a 'garden-spot.' Compared with most places I suppose it is. We have greater civil and social liberties here than most places—maybe greater than any place else. But we still have our usual tough problems. Jobs are always hard to get, even with FEPC, though that helps. The housing problem is bad, and police discrimination is still with us."

Race relations in these much mixed areas are now and then genuinely friendly, sometimes openly antagonistic, and quite often largely indifferent. The parents of our children as a group, and even as individuals, participate in all three types. The nature of their race relations can only be crudely characterized for each family. Something close to one-half of our Negro families are primarily friendly, and the rest are more nearly antagonistic. The proportions are not much altered among the white families, but a few of these are largely indifferent.

Genuinely friendly relations—those in which the people on the two sides of the color line look *across* at one another rather than up or down—usually involve people of one of two kinds. There are the people like William T. and his family—"ordinary working people," kindhearted and friendly —who are just generally serene and agreeable. They come in all the human colors but there are rather few of them. There are remarkably few whose sense of a common humanity does not at least come to a pause at the color line. The second kind is more difficult to characterize. They are the people whom one would call, in countries less defensively democratic, the intelligentsia. In these people the sense of a common humanity may or may not be deep and strong. But they are intellectually devoted to the ideals of human brotherhood, fair play, and decent standards of living for all. Not infre-

quently they are occupationally devoted to the achieving of
these goals.

Some of the quite openly antagonistic people we have already met among the parents of our children. There are, of
course, still more, both Negro and white. But people who have
to look *up* while they throw stones inevitably assume a somewhat different posture than those who can do so looking *down*.
The quality of antagonisms varies with the postures. The one
is defensive and fearful, the other aggressive and probably
guilty. Because of the fear on the one side and the guilt on
the other, people on both sides tend to cover, or try to cover,
their real feelings.

What appears to be largely indifference in race relations may
in fact be almost anything from a very convincing cover to
genuine disinterest. Disinterest in respect to questions of race
is probably rare, however. In our sample it seemed quite
genuine in the cases of about eight white families. Patricia's
mother discusses the racial composition of the neighborhood
and mentions Negro acquaintances with an unstudied detachment. In neither what she says nor in the way she says it is
there evidence of feeling of any kind at all. "Things just are
what they are. No use getting excited about it"—this is her
way of looking at race, and at a good many other matters too.
Her outlook is one of unconcern. It is an outlook possible to
people who have neither worn a brown skin nor imagined
themselves doing so. It is hardly possible for the people who
do wear one.

Resignation, acceptance, passivity, and even neutrality are
possible. David's mother (N), having escaped from South
Carolina, has no higher hopes. She assumes that nothing better
is likely to come her way, and hence her disappointments are
little ones.

But attitudes range widely among the Negroes who have
migrated from the south. The habit of overt deference toward
whites tends to survive, usually masking degrees of hostility,
bitterness, fear, resignation, self-deception, admiration, envy,
or emulation. Sometimes there is even a comfortable acceptance of the status quo, combined with a sense of personal
dignity and security.

There is Alfred's mother, who had little interracial experience in the south and who has lived reclusively in the north.
She says she finds just as much discrimination, but of a less

open sort, in New Dublin as in Alabama. She is bitterly disappointed in her new home and, being a timid soul anyway, she has simply withdrawn. And there is Joan's mother, who has related herself very differently to white society. She admires, emulates, and likes the white family whom she has long served as a domestic. There exists between the two families an interdependence in which, though the Negro family is clearly in the subordinate position, there is mutual friendship and affection. Mrs. M. plays her subordinate role with dignity and with optimism concerning the lot of Negroes in the north. But she admits to some uneasiness: "I have a little of the inferiority complex. I've been here long enough to get rid of it —but I don't."

Still other types of adjustment are possible. There is Carol's mother, who has made her own neutrality a point of pride and self-satisfaction. Her basic confidence and security make the neutrality possible. The neutrality rewards her with satisfaction conducive to a little more confidence and security.

Feedbacks like this one are not the common type, however. More often the spiral carries morale down rather than up. Tony R.'s father, like Quentin M.'s, is an angry and frustrated man. Both are deeply insecure. They are men with a strong desire to run things but with nobody asking them to do so. Their guard is up before their families, the neighbors, and the world at large. They fight before the hat is dropped, without strategy and without skill. Their losses are heavy and they go down into a little more anger and a little more frustration. Even if they were not called "Negroes," and occasionally something less polite, these men might have much the same troubles still. But the label carries its special hazards, both because of what it means to society and because of what it means to them.

Meaningful labels abound in the "Negro Section" of New Dublin. People think of one another not only as colored or white, but also in terms of religion and national background. The habit of labeling is strongly established, often largely unconscious, and often deeply resented even as it is practiced.

What Are They?

Social classifications are not made by social scientists, or the census takers, alone. The parents of our children are not unlike the native Australians who simply do not know what to do with the stranger until they have him precisely placed in an elaborate network of interlocking clans. In New Dublin the process of getting the stranger pigeonholed may be less formal but it is almost as essential. In everyday life people ask, aloud or otherwise, "what are they?" when newcomers catch their attention. The answer may or may not come in terms that are considered proper for the census blank. Probably it will not, and possibly it will establish a classification which does not appear on the blank.

Harding and Dover people, for instance, do not always distinguish between "native-born" and "foreign-born" white. "They" are Irish (or "Micks"), Italian (or "Wops" or "Dagoes"), Syrian, Russian, English, Canadian (or "Kanuck")— if anything about them suggests that they or their ancestors once were any of these. The O'Connors may have become Conners during three generations but they are still "Irish" and maybe "Shanty" to the neighbors. If they are also "Catholics" they are therefore a little more "foreign" than the Donnellys who are "Protestants." The Greens may have been Russian-born under another name, but if they are Jews they remain not so much foreign as alien. "A Jew is a Jew" wherever he may have been born. Foreign birth is important to the degree that it shows, or is believed to show, in language, food habits, "clannishness," religious practices, manners, or about the body.

The people of our area follow the census taker in distinguishing sharply between "white" and "Negro," and in attempting to distinguish between Negro and "other nonwhite." "They" are "colored" (sometimes "Negro" or "black" or "nigger") if they are not obviously Mongoloid. The latter are probably "Chinks." Among the "colored" themselves, much finer differentiations are made. It is important to know whether a man is "American," "West Indian," or "Portuguese," and he is likely to regard it as important too. If he is West Indian he may think of himself as rather British, and indeed he may seem so to his neighbors. Certainly he seems to have some rather more formal ways, a firmer hand with his children, and a Church of England affiliation that set him somewhat apart. If he is Portuguese he is likely to be very insistent upon being called such, and to rather flaunt his command of a foreign language, foreign cookery, etc., if he can. The West Indian, too, enjoys and magnifies his differentness. To do so may not enhance his popularity but it does enhance his prestige a bit, and it serves to lift him a little toward the "foreign-born white" and away from the plain "Negro." Hence Quentin's mother, coming from a tightly-knit middle-class Portuguese family, remembers how

> ". . . they wanted me to marry one of my own kind. My husband is a colored American you know. Now I think they were right. He feels like an outsider with us—won't even visit with me at home any more. He doesn't like any of our ways. He wants plain cooking—the kind the white people have. And he gets so mad when we talk Portuguese together —thinks we're doing it to say something about him."

Joanne's mother and father are both of Portuguese background, and they yearn to move back to the community (elsewhere in the state) where they grew up with their "own kind." They are fussy about Joanne's choice of playmates, and happy when they can take her to play with "a nice little girl she knows at home." They feel that they are not wanted in Lower Harding.

Among our families there are five in which one or both parents are "Portuguese," and nine having remote or close ties with one of the West Indian islands. The rest of the Negro families are regarded as plain "American," though in two of these there is a recognition of American Indian ancestry. Mongoloid ancestry appears in two more families. On Chester's family tree there are maternal grandparents one of whom was Negroid, the other Japanese. In Irene's family there are Chinese and white forbears, with the latter so predominant that Irene is "white."

The children of the "American" Negro families tell their own story of "race mixture" back along the line. About three-quarters of them are some shade of *café au lait* or brown; some have soft wavy hair and hazel eyes. Narrowed lips and noses are quite common. Differences between the children in a given family tell the story, too, and sometimes there is trouble because of these differences.

There is trouble in two of our four "mixed marriages." James M.'s father is a Negro, his mother is a white Latin American. Mrs. M. was a lonely and glamorous foreigner, susceptible to admiration and the promise of security. When Mr. M. asked her to marry him he invited a problem with which he was not prepared to cope. His sense of inferiority has turned into such bitterness that he can tell his children he is sorry he married their mother—that he should have married someone from his own race. June's mother is of Syrian background and her father's ancestry is Portuguese Negro. There have been frequent prolonged separations, and violence when they are together.

Troubles largely outside the husband-wife relationship affect Anna P.'s family. Her parents are Puerto Ricans. Her mother's ancestry, divided between Negro and white, seemed an unimportant detail among the racially varied people they knew at home. It was not until they reached the great democracy that they discovered how crucial Anna's 25% Negro ancestry could be. Here they met discrimination and raised eyebrows. Mr. P. despises the "low calibre" American Negroes, but finds very little place on the "white side" for a man with a "Negro" wife and kids. They now feel isolated—without friends in either group. Anna and the three others will have to find their own place among the city's peoples. Being very light, they may be able to forget that Negro grandparent they left in Puerto Rico, but it will not be an easy thing to do. The people of New Dublin will not soon stop asking "what are they?"

Chapter 2

"What Am I?"

IT WAS HELEN who asked one day, "What am I?" Helen's father has a sense of humor, and it did not fail him at a rather crucial moment. "You are," he said, "a tantalizin' brown! So's your mother, and so am I."

Helen was satisfied, and happy—for the moment. She was four and a half then, but she had asked the question before. Her mother thinks she wasn't more than three the first time, and

> "She got a different answer. I said, 'You're an American, and so am I, and so's your father.' At nursery school the other day, she asked the teacher, 'What are you?' Mrs. X. said, 'I'm an American,' and Helen drew herself up very proud and said, 'I'm an American too.' . . . And then a little while back Mary said she'd rather play with David than Helen. Mary said, 'He's white and you're colored.' But Helen wasn't takin' that. She came right back with, 'Oh no I'm not. I'm a tantalizin' brown!' "

The Process of Becoming a Person

Helen's case is both like and unlike those of others of our four-year-olds. She is forthright and relatively shockproof, like her father and mother. She asks and has been lucky enough to get answers that contributed to her comfort at the moment and provided her with an answer to give to others when she needed one. She has been given reason, both at home and at school, to feel that almost anything can be asked and a satisfying answer will be forthcoming. In this way she is unlike most of our children. There are those who ask and get evasive answers or none at all. After a while they stop asking and make up their own answers.

Whatever the process of getting them, answers they must have, at four and five and even three. By three the consciousness of self is coming into focus, and inseparable from it is the consciousness of others. By the time the child can put into words the question "*Who* am I," he already has some sense of himself as a person, and a sense of mother and father, sisters and brothers and playmates, as outside the boundaries of "me." The baby had no real sense of himself, and the idea of the "me" has been a gradual growth, a result of living with people (as such), of living with people who observe a certain "style" of life, and of living with unique and individualized people. The growth of the *ego* has meant developing a sense of separateness, and this is both rewarding and painful. It is rewarding to feel separate and hence autonomous, but it is painful at times to find oneself outside others and alone.

The Four-year-old Person

The four-year-old has a strong sense of self. He has learned to enjoy his autonomy, if his growth is healthy, and,

> . . . having found a firm solution of his problem of autonomy, the child of four and five is faced with the next step—and with the next crisis. Being firmly convinced that he *is* a person, the child must now find out *what kind* of a person he is going to be. . . . He begins to make comparisons and is apt to develop untiring curiosity about differences. . . . He tries to comprehend possible future roles. . . .[1]

Our four-year-old has also a sense of others. It grows, as does the self-awareness, through making comparisons, finding likenesses and differences.

> He is beginning to sense himself as only one among many, . . . he has a definite consciousness of kind, of his

own kind, (and) a fundamental noetic attitude. . . . (He has) a dim intent to generalize and to order . . . experience.

He has social interest and

> . . . an awareness of the attitudes and opinions of others, . . . a consciousness of social milieu and . . . maturing social insight.[2]

Such being the case, the interest our children show in identifying, describing, classifying, evaluating, and comparing themselves and others is quite in line with reasonable expectations. Their interest in characteristics or behavior having to do with what adults call race, nationality, or religion is a part of these general interests and inclinations. From this point of view, Tony's flat "I'm not no girl—I'm a boy" has something in common with Elaine's "I got curly yellow hair" and with Gerry's "I had my birthday. I'm five." All of these are simple and accurate descriptions of the self. "My mother has a coat like yours"—"my baby sister wears diapers"—"my daddy goes to work at night"—"my brother got a bike too"—these are bits of what the child sees in his mind's eye when he thinks of some of the others. Again they are simple and accurate pictures, reflecting awareness of sex, age, personal attributes, family roles, clothes, time, and personal possessions. They are natural enough and unremarkable.

Considering the adult world, it is also natural enough that certain judgments of right and wrong, good and bad, pretty and ugly, etc., etc., should begin to be made. Our children are not merely exercising their eyes and ears and minds in recording the objective features of people, things, and behavior. They are at the same time learning to see, hear, and think along the lines followed by their models. Jimmie is learning the *culture* of mid-century America in the somewhat distinctive forms it takes in New Dublin, the Harding-Dover area, Morton Street, the Walker's flat, Coleman House Nursery School, and possibly a few other places. He did not arrive in the world equipped with an ego, but has had to grow his own, with the help of other people. Neither did he come equipped with a culture—with a yearning for ice-cream cones rather than toasted worms, a bike rather than a birchbark canoe, or the idea that living in a frame tenement, using the bathroom, or going to nursery school are among the "of course" things of life.

By four Jimmie has already learned a quite staggering number of the ways of his world—an amazing number in view of the fact that he came into it quite naked, culturally as well as physically. He had only a body—a body stocked with possibilities, a large number of which would appear in due course. Some of them appear almost inevitably—like the color and size and curiosity of our four-year-old. Others probably do or do not appear to a degree depending upon the nature and force of the pressures brought to bear. Some of the pressures themselves operate quite automatically and almost inevitably. If he lives in Harding or Dover, he will learn to speak English. Other pressures may operate as automatically though they are less inevitable—being denied meat on Friday or pork every day, for example. And some may be quite as effective though not at all inevitable, like having a father who breaks up furniture when he comes home drunk. Whatever the particular combination may have been, our four-year-old has already done a good deal of more or less subtly directed unfolding. In the process he has learned many of the ways *and* many of the *values* current in his world.

The learning of values, and of attitudes, means learning to want, to desire, to prefer certain kinds of things, activities, people, and personal traits or attributes. Conversely, it means learning to not want, not desire, and not prefer other things, activities, etc., or to have some "in-between" feelings.

The child's feelings, whether for, against, or in-between, are not necessarily always the same, nor do they necessarily seem to add up to a neatly logical total. Yet it is possible to see, when we know a good deal about the whole child and his life situation, that he is growing into a fitting shape. That particular combination and intensity of pressures under which he grows does not wholly determine his shaping. The pressures meet resistances of different sorts and degrees. The human material is plastic, but neither completely nor uniformly so. Still, if we knew enough about the complex properties of the material, about the intricate angles described by the mold, about the effects of degrees of pressure and the signficance of timing, *if* we knew enough about all this, we should almost surely be able to see that the shape does fit. The "if" looms very large. Here we can offer only outline drawings and estimates.

Look at William, for example. Yesterday William valued the company of girls. His attitude toward them was admiring, very friendly, and actively seeking. "I want to walk with a girl," he said firmly as Mrs. D. lined up the nursery school four-year-olds to go on a little excursion. Today William can hardly wait for John to get to school—he wants to continue a game they started on the slide just before closing time yesterday. He refuses to let Irma play with him, but he accepts Ned, at least until John arrives. This is a boy's game. Right now he values the company of boys and his attitudes towards girls are not what they were. But counting the number of times William seeks out girls as against the number recorded for Billy makes it plain that Billy's values and attitudes are different. Billy says, "I don't play with girls—I don't like girls," and generally his actions are in accord.

William's attitude toward girls has background in his experience and support from other of his attitudes. The pieces seem to fit together. Or, more accurately perhaps, we can see enough of the pieces to draw an outline and estimate dynamics.

William has a gentle father who is affectionate and kind toward his mother. She is gentle and affectionate with William, and he is devoted to her almost to the point of overdependence. For perhaps half his lifetime, his special playmate has been the only child of his age on the block, and that child happens to be a girl. William has a little sister who is "just crazy about him" and who "thinks everything he does is just right." In view of this somewhat unusual *combination* of circumstances, it is perhaps not surprising that William's orientation toward the opposite sex is favorable, and somewhat more favorable than is common among his fellows. It is relevant, too, that William is a "positive" child—he is more likely to make strong statements about the things he is "for" than about the things he is "against," and he probably has more positive than negative feelings.

Billy, on the other hand, leans toward negative attitudes and toward expressions of not-liking, not-wanting, etc. His low valuation of girls may be both an expression of his personal negativism and of an attitude common among boys his age or a little older. The background pressures are less clear in his case than in William's, though his little life has been turbulent enough to account for some negativism in him. Hence the negatives current in the culture of his world press in on soft spots. Growing up with three older children in a two-room shack on an alley, living with a careless, tired mother and with a father who is perennially out of work, drunk, or "away" (in jail) could account for some negativism. Billy, however, does not look like a young delinquent. He occasionally "blows up" at school, but he is generally quite happy, friendly, and cooperative. One might expect more than an occasional spell of temper or "moodiness," silence about home when he is at school, a sullen refusal to go to school now and then, an occasional rejection of girls—and of other "kinds of people."

Helen and William and Billy and the rest of our four-year-olds are making progress toward finding out *what* they are. In order to know what they are, they must at the same time know more about what other people are. They now know themselves to be one person—one girl or boy—among many small or large boys and girls, sons and daughters, who live with fathers and mothers, brothers and sisters. They have developed a sense of self and a sense of others, and they see more and more of the details about themselves and others. They are learning that these details have meanings, and they are learning to interpret the details "correctly," i.e., to value them as some others around them do.

Our 103 children, chattering with one another, with their parents or teachers or with Observers (the writer or an assistant), give us evidence that they are doing these kind of things:

1. They are perceiving (registering) the objective features of people, things, and behavior, and making classifications on the basis of these perceptions;

2. They are becoming used to a great number of doings and ways of doing, and are increasingly practicing these ways themselves;

3. They are learning to like the things that other people like, and to dislike the things other people dislike.

Seeing and Pigeonholing People

The first process, perceiving and classifying, inevitably extends to features and groups which the adult world calls "racial." When we speak here of "race" we are not following the anthropologist's definitions (and the plural is advisedly used). We are following the "common-sense" definition, which in fact makes rather little logical "sense" but is certainly "common" enough. It is weird logic indeed which puts into one pigeonhole labeled "Negro" people who may in *fact* have little but their humanness in common. It happens because they are *believed* to have much else in common and because those elements are *believed* to be important. The beliefs make all the difference. Cultural definitions like this common definition of race are based on *beliefs* which often bear little or no resemblance to the *facts*. But in the "real" world outside classrooms, libraries, and laboratories, it is the beliefs that count.

Young children first see the more conspicuous features of people, and the more conspicuous differences between them. They base their classifications on these. Vivien says: "this girl (white doll) belongs to this boy (white doll); this girl (brown doll) belongs to this boy (brown doll)." She is spontaneously classifying on the simple basis of the rather marked color differences between the dolls.

Most of our children made such classifications, either in respect to dolls, pictured people, or real people. The tendency to see the classificatory features is stronger, however, when the child is looking at representations than when he is looking at real people. The view is less obstructed by personality. But he does see the racial attributes of real people, including himself. Herman observes correctly: "My mother's brown-skinned." Stefan offers: "My mother's *that* white." Carol M. says: "See how colored my hands are." When Vivien informs us: "I got a white brother," she may be offering a simple description, but she is more likely making a classification. She knows that he is not literally white—like a piece of chalk, for example.

Classification was undoubtedly being made when Thomas looked thoughtfully at the children in his room at school and said: "There are two white children here and all the rest are colored." An adult would have said the same, and the "colored" ranged from very light to medium dark. Thomas called Rose "Blackie," and Rose is fair enough to make some grown-ups wonder "what is she?" So we know that Thomas classifies, and does so in a more grown-up way than most of his fellows.

Norman and Sam were sharp at color perception and classification, too. Norman started something in his group at school when he asked his teacher (teasingly she felt), "What color are you?" Sam picked up the question and answered it for her—"She's brown." Norman agreed: "She's brown and I'm brown." This was more than simple description, because Mrs. D. is very considerably browner than Norman. Sam added: "Yes, and I'm brown too," and he proceeded to name a number of children and teachers, not all of whom were present, labeling each "white," "brown," or "colored."

Hair form as well as skin color is a feature of interest, but it is a secondary basis for classification. Donald, Sam, and Norman discussed the hair of the children around them. They said some (the Negro children) had "curly" hair, and some (the white children) had "straight" hair or "curly-at-the-bottom" hair. Comments about hair—its form, color, length, and the style in which it is worn—are very common. The children stroke or finger one another's hair occasionally, when heads and hands happen to be in proximity. Deep interest is sometimes expressed by the way they do it. But when they say that so-and-so is "white" and go on to explain "why," they rarely mention hair. When they do, it is hair color rather than form that is noted. "Because he has that kind of face—hands—legs—eyes" is usual. It is the unusual child who adds "and he has white hair" (i.e., the kind whites have).

Our children are seeing physical traits and grouping people in terms of them. They do not always label the resulting groups just as their parents might, nor do they know that they are talking about what their parents would call "race." But what they are doing is otherwise very much like the "noticing" and labeling that the grown-ups do.

Learning the "Of Course" Ways of Life

We have said that there is a second important process going on in our children—the process of accepting an ever greater number of the ways of their world. The racial—and interracial—ways are no exceptions. The race-ways are, however, less obvious and more complex than a good many other kinds of ways. Hence Eddie H. has learned to eat with a fork and spoon rather than his fingers (most of the time), to put on and take off his clothes, to say "thank you" and "please" (sometimes), to ride a tricycle and use crayons and paints, and to do a thousand other things that American four-year-olds do.

So far, however, Eddie H. has not learned to do the things that older white children often do when they encounter colored children. He has not learned to say "no—I don't want to play with you—you're colored," as his six-year-old sister has. Nor has he learned, like seven-year-old John, to stop uncertainly beside the wading pool at the "Center" when he sees the colored children in it, and then go home and tell his mother he's not going there any more, "because there are too many colored." He has not learned to "gang up" with other white boys on the way home from school to "get" that colored kid who had him down in the school yard when the teacher pulled them apart. Four-year-old Eddie hasn't even learned to yell "nigger," but four-year-old Nathan and a few others have.

Our white Eddies and brown Irmas play together on the street or in nursery school with few "racial incidents." But if we were to conclude from this that they "pay no attention at all to race," we would be quite wrong. The casual visitor in the "mixed" nursery school, or the passer-by on the street, concludes just that, and goes away happily reassured that this is an age of racial innocence. Even parents and teachers are inclined to overlook the significance of the few clues they do get. They may be too busy to notice. They may also be ignoring or selectively forgetting matters which are distasteful because Americans like to believe in the "purity" of childhood. Precocious sexuality shocks them and so does precocious raciality. But the crux of the matter is that the public behavior of our Eddies and Irmas does not tell the whole story.

The whole story comes out only when these children are given repeated chances to "think out loud" just as freely as they can be encouraged to do. In the making of this study, we gave them the chances and the encouragement. We gave them time—weeks or even months—to get acquainted with us before we invited them, one by one, to "come and play with our puzzles" (or doll house, or pictures, or dolls). They accepted happily and went with us to the testing room where we had quiet and privacy. They played, and we watched, listened, recorded, and asked some carefully calculated questions. For eight months most of these children were under our eyes at least two days a week, and during that period each of them "visited" our room at least four times to play with the four different sets of materials. During those visits we learned that four-year-olds see and hear and sense much more about race than one would suppose after watching them at school or even at home.

Sarah (w) is an excellent example. At her nursery school there were a few Negro children, and one Negro teacher. But week after week her behavior at school gave no indication that she either noticed ôr cared about color. Yet the Observer's final report on her behavior during the play interviews reads as follows:

Awareness of race differences is accurate and verbalized. She is clearly aware of what she calls "black people" and has rather strong feelings about them. She shows a rather consistent rejection of Negroes. She is clearly aware that "blacks" are very different people from "whites."

The case of Joan G. (N) points up the discrepancy between what her mother knew of her awareness and what we came to know. Mothers do not necessarily tell all, of course, even to someone they have come to know fairly well and even though that someone is an eager listener with a genuine interest in mother's pride and joy. But after allowing for this factor, and for plain lapses of memory or observation, a large discrepancy appears between what Mrs. G. told us and what we knew. At home Joan had once referred to a nursery school child as "white," and she had once asked whether a certain other friend were "white." That was all of the evidence for aware-ness, and Mrs. G. was sure that "Joan makes no difference in her judgment (of people) on a basis of color." Alone with the Observer, Joan repeatedly described and labeled dolls or pictured people as "white," "brown," or "colored." She volunteered comments about real people too: "My daddy's colored. My mommy's colored." Most notable of all, this child of less than four and a half offered what strikes the adult ear as an acute commentary on American society. Joan told us:

"The people that are white, they can go up. The people that are brown, they have to go down."

The evidence is overwhelming that many of our children have developed awareness and feelings far in excess of their habits of expressing them in behavior. Those ways of expressing racialism which are common among older children and their parents are rarely a part of our four-year-old's accumulation of learned ways of doing. But much that is relevant to his later doings has already taken its place in that complex system we call his personality.

Learning the Want-and-Like Ways of Life

This is the third of the important types of development which we have noted as characteristic of our children. It is a matter of the learning of values about people and attitudes toward them. We have seen that some personal details strike the senses of our children early and forcefully—skin, hair, and eye color among them. As they become aware of such items and begin to sort people into color kinds, they also begin to value differently both the items and the kinds.

Some of this differential valuing would develop even if it were not among the life-ways of our children's people. There are uniquely personal reasons for preferring blue eyes to brown, creamy skin to coffee-colored, or straight hair to tightly curled. *Having* any of these attributes can be a reason for liking them—or for not liking them—depending upon how much you like yourself. And *not having* any of them can be a reason for liking or not liking them—depending upon how much you like the people who do have them. But it is hard to draw a line between the uniquely personal reasons and the reasons which reside in the social world and filter into the personal system after a time. How much you like yourself and certain other people is not wholly a matter of your independent and objective judgment based on your objective experience. It feels very much as though it were, but this proves only how deep culture goes. Our experience with ourselves and with others is always seen and felt in ways which are partly determined by culture.

So Joan M. (N) is not expressing a purely original point of view, based on the cold, hard facts of her experience, when she says "black people—I hate 'em." Nor has Stefan (w) been uninfluenced by culturally patterned points of view. He says he'd rather play with the white than with the brown boy (in the picture) *"because* he's white." And later: "All I like is the white one (girl in picture). *Not* the black one—the white one." Norman says of a pictured Negro boy: "He's a freshie! Look at his face—I don't like that kind of face." The face in question is hardly to be seen, and what does show looks to the casual observer quite an unremarkable medium brown. Vivien (w) says that the white lady "is better than the colored lady" in the same picture. The opinion is not that of a neutral judge. Billy (w) is not neutral either when he looks at two pictured men, both ordinary and unremarkable, and says: *"A good man—and a black one."*

Here are expressions of positive or negative *valuing,* and in no uncertain terms. To "hate" black people, and to not like the "kind" of face a brown boy is assumed to have; to choose the white over the brown boy to play with "because" he's white, and to like only the white boy; to see the white woman as "better" than the brown; to set "black" against "good"—these are expressions of strong feelings. Nor are they the only evaluations made by these particular children. If we had nothing more in the way of evidence concerning their individual feeling tones, we might question the significance of the single statement. But there is much else on the record for Joan M., Stefan, Norman, Vivien, Billy, and a good many others. The value-laden comments from each of them add up to an unmistakable total. Not all our children feel so strongly, or perhaps they are not so much given to putting their feelings into words. But a fourth of them said enough to make it clear that, among our four-year-olds, their systems of race-related values are strongly entrenched.

The process of learning how other people place Negroes and whites on various scales of value is well under way. But *attitudes,* we have said, are involved in our four-year-old's learning too. Having an attitude means being "ready" and "set" to act in a particular way, when and if you meet a certain kind of situation. Acquiring an attitude is like cocking a gun—the person and the gun are thereafter poised for action. Triggering comes for the person when the appropriate situation is met. There will be no shooting until and unless all of the necessary elements have accumulated: the person, his values, his attitudes—and a situation. Values are an indispensable part of the ensemble. They supply the push—the feeling power which carries the individual into action. Some recurrent actions become so automatic that little or no emotional steam goes into them. The more common daily habits of a people are of this sort. Life-ways of a less recurrent and less unanimously accepted sort involve more feeling, and race-ways are among them.

Our children are "building up steam" about race. Simultaneously they are getting "ready" and "set" to go into action one day. They seldom go into action now (beyond the talking-about-it kind of action) for one or both of two reasons: (1) the steam is not yet up, i.e., they don't yet feel strongly enough, however vehement their statements, to do anything about it; (2) they have not yet learned to go through certain motions, like yelling "nigger" when the other kids do it, simply as one of the relatively automatic gestures copied from others around them. In either case the necessary attitude (or attitudes) is missing.

The necessary attitudes may be missing, in spite of firmly held and strongly felt values about colored and white. They may be missing in spite of opportunities for copying. This can happen when some other values, like fair play, politeness, kindness, etc., are strong enough to block the development of antagonistic race attitudes, or to block the copying of actions which depend upon antagonistic attitudes. The child may have built up strong feelings—out of his personal experience as he has learned to see it, out of what he sees and hears of other people's feelings, and in response to his particular needs. Yet these may be kept in check by countercurrents pouring from the same wells—from his perceptions of personal experience, from his sample of culturally patterned attitudes and values, and from his own psychic imperatives.

We—and They

Our four-year-olds have come a long way. The possibilities packed in each of these erstwhile blobs of protoplasm have unfolded, as the blobs themselves expanded. Both processes have meanwhile been affected by the push and pull of a great variety of forces outside them. So each child has come to feel himself a separate person, but close to other persons, as an "I" within the "We." He has also come to sense the existence of persons a greater distance away, the existence of "They." "They" may be the people in the next flat or on the next block, the children next door or in another school, or any one of a hundred other kinds, with their reciprocal "we's." But here our interest is focused upon racial "we's" and "they's." We have already seen a little of the making of "we-they" thinking and feeling. Now we will look to the nature of that thinking and feeling in Negro children and in white.

Chapter 3

"The People That Are Brown—"

FIFTY-SEVEN LITTLE PEOPLE, more or less brown, can teach us something about the meaning of color. Nine of them will teach us rather little; they are the ones who do not yet see it very clearly or very often. Twenty-six will teach us a good deal. They see it quite clearly and quite often. Twenty-two have much to offer. They are sensitive to this cue a large part of the time.

It must be remembered that our conclusions about all these children are based largely on their "private" behavior. It was what they did and said while they played with our toys and looked at our pictures that gave us most of our insights. But these were sometimes very importantly illuminated by evidence from home and school behavior.

Children of Low Awareness

William is one of those children whose awareness of race is relatively low. Like others whom we put in this category, his interest in color is erratic. When it does appear, he often uses the wrong words. He calls white clay and white paper "blue," but he knows the right word. Sometimes he even uses it at the right moment, but he is just as likely to call the brown clay "white" one moment and "brown" the next. He tries to describe people in color terms. He sees that there are differences and he knows that "white," "brown," and "colored" are words which can be used in talking about the differences. But he has difficulty in making up his mind how to use the words. "All of these are colored—all of these people are brown. These and these and these are white," he volunteers, waving vaguely toward the assorted browns and whites.

This kind of impartial tossing about of words is a transitional phase between having none to use and using them consistently and correctly. The pleasure of hearing oneself say new words is not limited to four-year-olds. But in them it adds impetus to the process of learning to see new things. It gives them a handle by which to take hold, and until the handles get firmly attached, it is doubtful whether the ideas that go with them can be very clear. William is rather vague about what property of a thing or a person he is abstracting when he applies a color word. He is experimenting when he does so. The experiment is a success (in terms of learning) if he gets a response that clarifies things for him. If the Observer had corrected his mistakes in using color words, William would have learned something. This we did not do, of course, since we were the learners and the children the teachers in this situation. We tried hard to avoid doing any teaching.

William is experimenting with ideas more complex than those that go with color words. "Best," "nicer," and "prettier" are in his vocabulary, and they have some meaning for him. He says a dark brown doll is "best" (as compared with light brown and white). And then again he chooses a white one as nicer than a matching brown. He can't make up his mind which is prettier of another matching pair.

These inconsistencies suggest either uncertainty about the meaning of what he is saying, or uncertainty about what he wants to mean. But comparative terms are commonly used and understood by four-year-olds. "This is the best tricycle," or "my mommy is nicer than anybody"—usages of this sort are frequent. Hence, William's problem is more likely to be one of uncertainty about what he wants to mean. He may, of course, be quite certain now about the brown being "best" and equally certain later about the white being "nicer." However, until his certainties show some consistency, we can only conclude that he has none of the general sort. He is not saying that brown dolls are best, but only that this particular brown doll is best at this moment. It might be so for reasons having nothing to do with its brownness, but this is unlikely, in view of the fact that the dolls are alike except for color.

William is uncertain too about himself. Does he look most like the brown or the white boy doll? (He is in fact a medium dark brown.) He indicates the white—the one he had earlier said was nicer. But perhaps he isn't sure. It may even be that he doesn't quite want to be sure. He thinks that when he was a baby he looked like the medium brown and the light brown babies. He is positive about only one thing—he didn't look like the dark brown baby. "I wasn't no colored baby like that (dark brown)! I was a red baby like this (light brown)." (He is quite right.) He certainly means that he was not the color of the dark brown. He probably is not using "colored" as a group label. But of this we cannot be sure, since he had tried earlier to use it as a label. We can be sure of the vehemence and at least momentary certainty with which he disavowed that dark brown doll. It is the only strong statement he ever made to us.

William's low level of race awareness is thus made up of occasional perceptions, of faulty attempts to pigeonhole, of minor evidence for differential valuing, and perhaps even uncertainty about the attributes of his own person. It is important to note, however, that he may be more certain about what that self is, or was, than he likes to indicate. We know that he is very certain about what it was not—very certain that it was not "colored" like that dark brown doll. We know that he was thinking of himself, and comparing himself with the dolls, in terms of color.

Where William is an open kind of child—responsive, trusting, and generally buoyant—Sharon is in contrast. She looks and acts somber, scared, or defiant, she is inhibited and silent. Sharon withholds more, and her exploring and experimenting are more covert. But she gives us some clues and they add up to this:

(1) She knows her "colors" better than William, and she applies them accurately to "brown" skin, "black" hair, and "white people."

(2) Like other low awareness children, she uses color terms rather seldom. Sharon uses them only in response to a question (for example, her father asking "what color is your teacher?").

(3) She sees personal color as an important thing about real people, pictured people, and dolls.

(4) She does not put it into words, but she tells us by consistent gesture responses (to our questions "which is

nicer," etc.) that she prefers those having white coloring, and finds them prettier.

(5) Her gestures tell us too that she thinks of herself, and of her favorite teacher (N), as wearing this preferred coloring. Sometimes her mother is included, but her little brother is emphatically identified with a pictured Negro boy.

Sharon is sparing with words. In her case there are special and personal reasons for being so (partial deafness, large tonsils and adenoids, and others). But it tends to be true of our low awareness children that they are either experimenting with words (like William), or wary of them. Sharon is wary of them. But she conveys meanings through gesture and expression.

Sharon's sights and feelings are rather focused on whiteness. We do not know that she thinks of people who have it as making up a group—even that she thinks of them as having certain other characteristics, or as being set apart from people who are brown. We do not know that she dislikes brownness, but we do know that she likes whiteness. Her self-image is white, possibly both because she likes it that way and because she is in fact a rather light brown. But the image of her favorite teacher as white can be only wishful—perhaps a way of saying "to me she's nice and pretty."

Sharon shows us a mind rather sparsely furnished with ideas about color, but more orderly than William's. There are striking differences between them as persons and as personalities. But they both build self-images about which they feel strongly. Sharon is light brown and sees herself like the white dolls. William is medium brown and sees himself as *not* like the dark brown doll. Sharon is quite certain of what she likes and wants to be, within the rather narrow range of her vision of possibilities. William is sure only of what he does not want to be.

Some others of the low awareness children show a tendency to see the self, or want to see it, as lighter than it is. Of David W. (who is medium dark), the Observer concludes:

> Pretty clear realization of self and family as brown— marked progression during period of observation. Early inconsistent brown preference, but with dislike of N hair and heads, gives way to identification with w's, and w preference.

James F., a medium brown child, puts his feelings about himself into unambiguous words. It is noted on his record that

> . . . on early tests he shows a covert, nonverbal white identification, both as a baby and as a boy. On later tests he identified with Negroes. When asked "is this boy (N) like you?" he replied: "No, *'cause I don't want him to be. But he looks like me.*"

Children of Medium Awareness

The children whom we have grouped together in the medium awareness category are more intent and vigorous in their exploration of the social world. They want to know "what am I?" and "what are they?" Having found some answers, they can even go on to the quite abstract thinking involved in Irma's question: "Why are some people brown and some white?"

The children in this category are perceiving more details about people and they are using more adjectives to report and order these details. They do not always use them accurately, however. Malcolm, David H., Paul B., Estelle, and Charles often use color terms inaccurately. Genuine confusions are sometimes involved, and the kind of experimentation we saw in low awareness children. But with Malcolm and the others, there is evidence of greater general sophistication. Sometimes, too, there is good reason to believe that the Observer was being "kidded"—a piece of sophistication which is quite meaningful in itself. Charles, for example, cheerfully and randomly labeled people and dolls "red" or "blue." This seemed a rather naive business until his mother told us that at home he calls Negroes "black,"—or sometimes "blue" or "red"—"just for fun."

"Kidding" the Observer was sometimes "just for fun" and it sometimes had deeper meanings. It must be remembered that the Observers were white and these subjects brown. In spite of well-established friendly relations there was, in a few cases, evidence of a residue of mistrust, which may have had some racial basis. Mistrust in a child like Estelle would be almost inevitable, however, probably irrespective of the color of the Observer. Estelle is used to untrustworthy people and she has learned to reciprocate. When she describes the white baby doll as "green" and the dark brown one as "white," we can afford to be skeptical—in view of her entirely accurate labeling when some mixed brown and white dolls were brought into her schoolroom one day. That response was spontaneous. Her responses to the Observer had a guarded quality.

There is sometimes aggression in the misuse of color terms too. Herman knows very well that his mother and sister are "brown-skinned." He knows about his schoolmates and sometimes about their parents. "Gerry's father is white," he tells us spontaneously. But Rosemarie, with her blue eyes and pale blonde curls, he describes as "brown." There is a reason. Rosemarie and Herman have tangled in the school yard. Nadine shows aggression, too, and it is directed toward her sister. She says that her sister is like a brown doll and she herself is like a white one. We know that she speaks often of the fact that her sister is "lighter," and that this awareness does not make her love her sister more.

Inaccuracies in the use of descriptive terms, whatever the meanings of the inaccuracies, are less frequent than faulty racial identifications (of the self or of others). But in these medium awareness children, the errors are less a matter of naiveté than of wishfulness. These children know that they are brown, and often they know whether they are light, medium, or dark. Some of them know exactly the color of their own hair, its length and form, and the color of their eyes. Less frequently, they know equally well what their parents and siblings and friends are like in these respects. But the knowledge is often unwelcome. The realities are faced grudgingly and discontinuously.

Gerard is one of those who has trouble facing reality. He has been using "colored" and "white" accurately for a year now, and he makes fine distinctions. He speaks of "the light one" to describe Negroes fairer than himself. He puts the light brown doll in the group of brown dolls and not, as most of our children do, with the white ones. But he has unpleasant associations built around brownness and pleasant ones around whiteness. Whites are "prettier" and "nicer." The brown doll is the "dirty one," and he uses "black nigger" as a weapon against other children (regardless of color). He is aware of two color kinds and he values them quite differently. It is not surprising that in the test situations he identifies himself with whites, and stumbles unhappily in the process. "I'm like that one (brown boy)—no, that one (white boy). This (w) is Gerard now," he asserts. "I thought you said this one (brown)," the Observer suggests. "No!" he says belligerently, "it ain't now!"

The idea that whites are "prettier" is a majority opinion. Eighteen of our twenty-six medium awareness children state this value more or less explicitly, and in a variety of ways. Malcolm (medium brown) says wistfully to the white Observer: "I'd like to be like you." Paul B. (very dark) vehemently rejects the brown doll: "I don't like that father. He's got a black head.—I don't like that one (another brown doll). I don't like black hair. I like that one (white)." Paul manages just one identification with a Negro ("He's got a face like me"), and for the rest he likens himself to whites. Nadine finds the white doll "pretty" and "clean" and "nice." The brown doll's hair "doesn't look good." Nadine knows herself to be very dark. "My big sister is lighter," she observes, and she has wondered aloud to her mother when she will become lighter too.

That the child's value system can be in painful contrast with his knowledge of himself is most clearly illustrated in the case of Dianne. She is a dark brown child, even darker than her mother, and she likes whiteness to a rather extreme degree. There are only a few colored children in her nursery school. She is conspicuous among the assorted whites, and conscious of the fact. She went home one day and asked her mother "am I colored?" The affirmative answer was followed by the explanation that "some people are black and some are white." Dianne, like most of our four-year-olds, was most concerned about herself. "I don't *want* to be colored," she declared. Back at nursery school again one day, Carol (w) took a good look at Dianne and asked her if she were colored. "Yes, I am. Don't touch me! Don't sit near me!" And Dianne sat away by herself looking unhappily at her arms. Then there were days when she vigorously lathered her arms and face with soap. After one of these efforts, she said triumphantly to Peter: "This morning I scrubbed and scrubbed and it came almost white." But she knew it had not really done so. Looking at pictures with the Observer, she stopped pretending. They talked about the white girl in the picture, and Dianne faced the fact that the white girl looked like Dorothy, "Because Dorothy's white and I'm brown."

Dianne's problem in self-identification is complicated

mainly by her values. This is not to say that the complication is an insignificant one for her. But it can be even more acute. Very light children face the value problem with its "so near and yet so far" implications. They have also to try to understand the meaning of "colored" as applied to themselves and to others who are not conspicuously colored.

Gail has almost succeeded. She has asked and been told (by her parents) that she is colored. Her skin is a pale brown which could be matched among so-called whites. So could her eyes, though they are very black. But her hair is an unmistakable attribute. Gail is keenly aware of hair—her own and that of others. She comments on its color and length. Hair is "yellow," "brown," or "black," "short" or "long." People are alike or different depending upon their hair; Rosemarie is like the pictured white girl " 'cause they both got yellow hair." A Negro girl is like Gail " 'cause she has hair like mine." The baby dolls remind her that "I didn't have any hair when I was a baby." There were many more such comments, and her parents report her admiration for long and "light" hair.

In order to establish her own identity, Gail has had to go beyond skin color. She sees herself as "colored" not because of her skin but because of her hair. She comes close to having a concept of racial kind, whereas most of our medium awareness children think in terms of simple color kinds. Nadine makes this thinking very clear. She was asked: "What *kind* are the people in this picture?" She answered: "I don't know. *—But I do know what color.*"

We have seen that the growing sense of color kinds is accompanied by a growing set of values. The child's values are sometimes stated quite unmistakably. Sometimes they can be inferred from the way in which he makes associations between color and other kinds of things. We have seen that Gerard thinks of brown and dirt, Nadine of white and clean. David H. refers to people as "light," "dark," or "chocolate." This last is unusual, and probably a pleasant association. It suggests a positive valuing. So does "light," which is fairly common. "Light" carries the tone of the pleasant and desirable in connection with race and also in a more general way. Grown-ups use phrases like "light and sunny." Sunshine, cleanliness, and even safety tend to be associated with lightness, whereas "dark" conveys quite opposite meanings. So too does "black," a term which our Negro children are often forbidden (by their parents) to use in respect to people. It is almost as "loaded" as the most vicious of epithets. John shows us something of the process of association, as it works in his mind. He volunteers that there are "ghosts and giants," who "scare or hurt people. . . . They are in *dark* places, . . . and their faces are *black*."

Our children are learning to use as weapons words which have unfavorable connotations. David H. says "I don't like your old black head,"—"shut your black mouth." He knows exactly what he says, and says exactly what he means, even to his mother: "You're Boogey—you're dark-skinned. But I'm not, 'cuz I'm light." (He is in fact very light, much lighter than his mother.) Malcolm and Leslie and James S. apply a long list of unpleasant adjectives to Negro figures among our play materials. They are "rough," "funny," "stupid," "silly," "smelly," "stinky,"—and "dirty." "Dirty nigger" is one of Leslie's favorite retorts. He may, of course, have learned the phrase, like the child whose big sister came home with a report of the battle she had *finished* because of it. But he may have put it together himself. "Dirty" is a word used often by our children. It may be used descriptively, as Gerard referred to the brown doll as "the dirty one." But Gerard also uses it as part of an epithet ("'shut your dirty mouth"). Since he knows and uses "black nigger" as an epithet, he sometimes substitutes "dirty" for "black," as Leslie does. James' descriptive use of "rough" is so unusual that we can assume it to be his own idea. It carries rather unpleasant overtones in the general application, and James is simply transferring from the general to the specific

Words which carry negative valuing are becoming associated, in the minds of our children, with Negroes and their physical characteristics. And this is happening in minds working under a thatch of more or less "Negroid" hair. In these same minds, as we have seen, there is growing the idea that the physical characteristics of whites are "prettier." And the whiteness preference goes still further. Estelle says that if we are going to make a figure of a little girl out of clay, we should use the white clay rather than the brown. Why? "Because *it will make a better girl*." And she adds: "I like to play together more. . . . I like to play with the white ones." James M. tells us that "People won't like her if she's black. . . . Only (even?) her friends won't like her." Charles' mother

says: "He don't care what kind of children he plays with—
but he'd rather play with the white."

They don't care—but then again, they do. This tells very
well what color means to these medium awareness children.
They care, a part of the time, what the self is like. Some of
them care very much, a good part of the time. Others care
less, or less frequently. They care how the self "got that
way." "Did God make me this color?" Nadine asks. "Will the
black (brown) soap make my hands black?" James M. wants
to know. And they care about the whys and hows of the color
business in general. "Black lady—maybe she's got paint on,"
says James M. "Or maybe she's got ink. She's so black—
maybe she's full of ink." They care about relative prettiness
and general niceness and social attractiveness. They are often
confused, about many of these things. They are often ambivalent, both liking and not-liking, choosing and rejecting, drawn
to and repelled by the same things almost at the same time.

Children of High Awareness

We have put into this category the twenty-two Negro children who perceive racial attributes very often, speak of them
often, and have a consistent (or nearly consistent) idea of
race or color kind. This does not mean that they invariably
see the social world as divided between Negroes (or browns)
and whites. Even in the test situations, they sometimes lose
sight of the cues or clues to race or color identity. But the
significant thing is that they *lose* sight, temporarily, of something they are accustomed to see.

Joan G. shows exactly this kind of variability. She was
putting together a picture puzzle in which there are ten
figures to be fitted into two rows of five each. There are five
brown ones and five white—two families identical save for
color. You can finish the picture with mixed or with homogeneous families. Joan put the pieces briskly into place, quite
unconcerned with the color of the figures. She finished with
two mixed families, and surveyed her handiwork. Then color
came into focus. "Take this one out of here, and this one out
of here," she says, pointing to the two whites in the row with
three browns. She does it all over again, and this time the
picture shows five browns in a row—the bottom row—and
five whites on the top.

These twenty-two are not only more consistently aware and more "kind-minded," than our other brown children. They are also more sophisticated. Like Joan with the picture puzzle, they show us that they know about the separation and differentiation of the color kinds in the social world. Viola reproduces it in clay. She makes "the three white and two browns" (strings of clay), and says: "All the browns be by theirself and all the whites by theirself." She moves the brown ones away from the white ones. There can be no doubt that she is thinking about people, because she continues: "All the brown ones are skinny people, and all the white ones are fat people."

Along with the sense of separation there goes a feeling for uniformity in groupings. These children segregate the dolls, as Viola did with the strings of clay. Often they do not insist upon homogeneous groupings of dolls representing family members as Joan did. But they indicate their sense of the usualness, and sometimes even the rightness, of homogeneous families. They sometimes put the feeling into words. Tony A. murmurs to himself: "The black boy—he got a black mother." Joanne observes that her own doll is "just like me—I'm my child's mother." They may even comment upon the unusualness of a mixed family. Karen makes such a family with the dolls, and explains, "It's a white man married to a colored woman."

In these children, as in our medium awareness group, there is evidence of a great deal of wishful thinking about the attributes of the self and those others who are important. There is the same difficulty in facing reality, and the same value conflict at the basis of it all. These trends are even more marked and more emotionally disturbing, and for two very good and closely related reasons. First, the high awareness child sees more clearly the physical characteristics of the kind of which he more surely knows himself to be. Second, he has a stronger set of values, and most of them are negative in respect to his kind.

Our high awareness children are almost conscious of the dilemma in which they are placed by being unable to like some of the most striking aspects of themselves, their families, and their friends. At a subconscious level, they are strongly affected by their problems. They squirm, literally and figuratively, as they talk with us about matters which clearly focus on race and color. We do not use the pointed words, but they do, and they recognize the nature of the topic to which we have led them. Sometimes they make us feel mean and cruel, as though we had not only put the knife in but even turned it.

There is a kind of desperation in Tony's cry of "Brown—brown—brown!!" as he throws down the picture about which we have been talking, and talking too long for his peace of mind. The matter is becoming more and more personal and personally threatening. He and others must have felt like Barbara, who was obviously unhappy. She did not enjoy being asked to tell which doll or picture looked most like herself, and her parents. And finally she said so, with intensity and exasperation: "Don't ask too many questions!—*I can't stand it*."

Intense feeling is not always apparent, however. A child can be objective and unemotional, like Joanne. She states matter-of-factly that the brown doll "is named Joanne, and is just like me." She is one of the few who seem not to be of two minds about the fact of being "colored." But even she, toward the end of our acquaintance, begins to show the usual signs of ambivalence. She now acknowledges whites as "prettier" or "nicer," but in a hesitant and unhappy fashion.

Each of our highly aware Negro children deals with his dilemma in ways which are natural—or possible—for him. Eddie T. faces it stubbornly: "I'm brown," he asserts, and "I like him (brown boy) better than her (white girl)—*because I wanta like him*." This is the tenor of his responses: I know what I am and I'm going to like it. He needs to like it, but in fact he cannot do so. He shows a marked preference for whites and whiteness. Eddie T. is a good strong brown. He cannot "kid" himself about what he is. Colin, and some other very light children, can and do, finding some temporary comfort this way. "I like the white one," says Colin. And he adds firmly: "*I'm* the white one." He insistently restates this identification in different contexts. June is darker than Colin, and she finds it easier to pretend about the past than about the present. She *was*, she says, like the white baby doll. "I wasn't black like that (the brown one). I was like that (another white). I was like that *before*."

There are still other ways of meeting the dilemma—rationalizations, justifications, and a variety of subtle implications. Tony A. admits that his parents look like the pictured Negro couple, but finds it necessary to add, about his father and mother, "they're *good* people." Viola likes the white doll better " 'cause it's cuter than the other one" (the brown doll, to which she has given scarcely a glance). Tony R. evades self-identification, as a good many of these children do occasionally. He says that he was like neither of the baby dolls, when he was a baby. But he adds wistfully: "I was called 'Butch' when I was a baby. Is that one (white) 'Butch'?" Joan G. says of the matching boy dolls that the brown one is nicer because "the white one is too heavy." But her resolution to like brown fails her when we come to the girl dolls. She fondles the white one, and then—briefly—the brown one. "This one," she says, "this one I'm holding (brown)—*it just gets on my nerves.*"

Shadows

These brown children are not all tense and unhappy, though much of what has been said might seem to suggest that they are. They run a wide gamut of personality types, and they react to color in terms of their personalities. Some take it in their stride, either because they are as yet little aware of it, or because they are able to take most things in that fashion. The specific ways in which they take it, fitting this piece into their own particular configurations, we shall examine later (Chapter 10). For the moment, we have seen enough to know that color casts a shadow, faint or strong, over the lives of all these children. It "gets on the nerves" of many. There is trouble brewing, and they have a sense of it.

The people that are brown—they have to go down.

Chapter 4

"The People That Are White—"

THERE ARE FORTY-SIX four-year-old "people that are white" in our sample. There are many differences between them, differences both physical and social. There are shadows of one sort or another over the lives of many of them, but they share a freedom from the shadow cast by color. They belong to the "right" race, if not to the most right religion or national background. They are looking down at the people under the shadow of color, and the view is likely to be quite different from this vantage point.

The view is different too, of course, when the eyes are accustomed to it. Our white children, like our brown ones, are not equally aware that there is a color line on their horizon. Seven are but faintly aware of the fact. Twenty-eight have the line in focus some part of the time, and eleven see it clearly and are not inclined to forget that it is there.

Low Awareness

Marvin shows us how very limited can be the range of vocabulary and of perception having to do with race, and how strong the tendency to see isolated and unique items without arriving at generalizations. These are, in fact, the hallmarks of our low awareness children.

Marvin has a very sparse color vocabulary, and he is quite

casual about the use of it. Orange is "green" and yellow is "white" if he happens to remember those adjectives at the moment when he happens to notice that the thing *has* a color. He is equally casual about people and their attributes. Sometimes he notices their clothes, and observes that "the little boy in the picture (N)—he hasn't got a sunsuit on like me." Therefore, that little boy doesn't look like Marvin. But then again he notices eyes or hair, and it dawns upon him that "he (brown boy) is the brother of her (brown girl) because they have the same kind of eyes." And again, while affirming that the white girl and the brown girl are "both pretty," he notes that "they both haven't got the same hair." On the whole, he finds himself most like white boys, but he never remotely approaches putting this idea into words. Physical attributes are not very important to Marvin, anyway, either in respect to himself or to other people.

Marvin is impartial, as well as indifferent and unperceptive. He tells us that he would be perfectly happy to play with the mixed group of children in the picture. But he adds ruefully, "Nobody plays with me." He is concerned about his very real inability to establish close social contacts. This is *the* social problem, so far as Marvin senses any problem at all. The color of the children is a dim and unimportant trifle. He has some notion that brothers and sisters look alike, but certainly playmates don't have to.

Peter Q. is not quite so oblivious. He does not consistently notice racial attributes, or even age and sex attributes. But upon occasion he describes pictured brown people as "dark" or "black." One of his dark brown schoolfellows is "the boy with the dirty hands and face." This description suggests that Peter's response to color may not be entirely neutral, and some other comments reinforce the impression. The Negro boy in the picture looks "like an old man," the Negro man is an "old guy." Peter says "I'm scared of that little boy (brown—breaks everything—I don't like him—'sposed not be up our house." The Negro woman in the picture Peter emphatically doesn't like. Conversely, he does like nearly all the whites. So, though he does not say "I like white people—I don't like dark (or black) people," it appears that his values are building in that direction. Peter is, in this respect, like William K. and Paul C. Of Paul the Observer concluded: "The incipient rejection (of Negroes) is inconsistent, unverbalized, and probably unconscious, but nevertheless, it is present." It does not appear to be present in our four other children of low awareness.

Medium Awareness

These twenty-eight are the children who see clearly, though sporadically, that people are "black" and "white." These are the color kinds that nearly all of them recognize. Half of them see a "brown" kind as well as—or instead of—a black kind, and three sometimes call this kind "colored." "Negro" is never used, and "nigger" very rarely.

To describe as "black" what is actually brown, and sometimes a very light brown at that, is a significant mistake. These children generally "know their colors" quite well. They are not likely to call black shoes, or a black coat, or a black crayon "brown." And some of them, by their alternation between "brown" and "black" in reference to people, make it perfectly apparent that they are not *seeing* black when they *say* "black." Hence, this word has become for them a color-kind name rather than a literal description. They have learned the kind name which is current in their social circles. Along with the name, they have developed some degree of feeling for the distance between "black" and "white" people, and for the sharpness of difference between them. These feelings are, of course, also current in their circles. But even the general meaning of the phrase "black and white" is conducive to polar thinking about people. It is meaningful that this particular pair of labels, rather than the less uncompromising "colored" (or "brown") and "white," should have become the common expression among these children, and among their parents as well. The currency of the labels is both cause and effect of the value system of the whites.

The symbolism of black-white labeling is closely paralleled by the "dark-light" usage. Seven of these children occasionally use one or both of the latter terms. As we have noted earlier, we can expect "dark" (or "darky"), like "black," to carry unfavorable connotations. Sometimes our children are quite aware that it does. Pamela tells us that "you shouldn't say 'darky'—it's not a sweet word." But this kind of self-consciousness is rare. Diane describes the Negroes in the pictures as "dark" or "black," and adds that they are "nasty," they "look awful," they are "fresh kids." What is more, "They're strangers. I would push them out (if they came to visit)." The whites, however, are "beautiful." Lilita assures us about Eddie T. (N), whom she knows at nursery school, "He's not a pretty one." "I want a cute boy (in a picture)," says Ronald, "I want a white boy."

The unfavorable associations building around the attributes of Negroes are implicit in the tendency to see Negroes as "dirty." This is a tendency we have met before (among Negro children themselves), but it appears more frequently in this white group. "There are two boys like that (N) in school," says Lilita. "Their faces (are) not clean." Paul P. describes Negroes as "black," or "dark," or "brown." And he sees the brown child in the picture as "a dirty little boy." Yvonne thinks the brown boy looks like her little brother "because he (brother) gets dirty so quick." Carl studied the Negro woman as she passed through his schoolroom. "I don't like her," he concluded. "She's dirty." The brown doll has "filthy hands," says Peter, adding emphatically, "black—is *black*" (meaning, apparently, "black is filthy").

Such unpleasant associations can develop in the child's mind quite independently. He need not have copied anyone else's set of associations. This is demonstrated in Hester's case, among others, but Hester also demonstrates how such spontaneous associations can be displaced by copying a different sort. Her mother reports that Hester's first reaction to a Negro child was: "Dirty little boy." "No he isn't, he's brown, like chocolate," her mother pointed out. "Chocolate" sounded fine to Hester, who took to referring fondly to her brown friends as "little chocolate girls—with lots of pigtails. Brown —like chocolate pudding." She even reached the point of wanting, temporarily at least, to be like them. "I want to be a little chocolate girl with lots of pigtails."

To wish to be like a colored child, or even to admire any of his distinctive physical attributes, is a very rare thing among these whites. Pamela thought "these black ones (dolls) are better." Yet even she felt it necessary to emphasize the lightness of her good friend Jane (N). "Jane's colored, isn't she?" Pam inquired of her mother, adding hastily: "But she's very light colored. She's pretty—*very light*." David thinks the brown dolls are prettier and generally nicer, and his associations with brown people are reminiscent of Hester. David sees a Negro as "a gingerbread man." So does Joseph, on one occasion, but his pleasant associations end right there.

Most of these children express preferences for whites or whiteness. A few give almost no evidence of having acquired color likes or dislikes. The white preference may be quite vague and generalized. Eddie R., for example, says broadly: "I like white." Or it may be more or less specific, and mainly a matter of personal esthetics: "I like blue eyes," "yellow hair is best," "the white ones are prettier." It may be stated in terms of social participation, as it was by Lilita. We asked her which of the children at nursery school she liked best to play with. The answer was immediate and unqualified: "The white ones."

In these medium awareness children, preferences tend to be somewhat inconsistent, and they are not always verbalized. To put the matter the other way around, these tendencies are two of our reasons for putting a given child into the "medium" category. It is often clear that the inconsistency means a limited awareness of the racial aspects of people and situations. Looking at the child's sequence of responses in the testing situations, and elsewhere, it is often plain that he perceives in a piecemeal fashion. He looks at pictures, and sees only sex or age, or details of clothing in some. In others he immediately sees race. His habits of seeing, and of thinking, are not yet "jelled." His attention moves from one to another of the salient features of people and situations. It sometimes moves at a rate quite bewildering to the less flexible adult. His interest fluctuates rapidly too, and his failure to note racial aspects sometimes means a loss of interest in the situation generally.

On the whole, however, the child's interest in matters having to do with race is high. He expresses it in the frequency with which he comments on color of hair and eyes, faces, and other body parts. Sometimes when he does so he is thinking out loud about the color unity of these parts. David, for example, concludes after thoughtful scrutiny that "the man is all black—every bit. Face is too." On other occasions he remarks on "brown face and hands, black hair," and on "white face and hands." Interest is also expressed through readiness to make comparisons. Diane says that she is like the white girl in the picture, "because she has blond hair and so do I." She notes too that the brown boy and girl

dolls are brother and sister "because they're both black."
Lilita informs us in no uncertain terms that her father does
not look like the Negro man in the picture. "He's *not* brown
—he's *white!* He's light."

Strong curiosity, as well as general interest, is conveyed by
what these children say and do. Parents report questions, and
we heard a good many ourselves. Pamela's mother tells us
that her daughter is "always asking about color. For example,
she knows that Jane (N) is colored. When she met Bobby
(w), she asked if he were colored too. When I said 'no,' she
was off on some more questions, because Bobby, just as she
said, 'is darker than Jane.' " Subtleties like this are beyond
the range of most of our children. Their questions are generally more like Ronald's: "Why they (N's) colored? Why
they look like that?" Or Burton's "Why is her hand black?"
Or Eddie R.'s "Miss W. and George are black. Why?" Or
Velma's "Why is she that color? Is she sunburned? Can she
change?"

These questions and more have come from our children.
They are conspicuously uniform in one respect. These white
children do not ask about themselves—*why* their own color,
or the lack of it. They take it completely for granted, in the
fashion of "primitive" tribesmen, that they are "the people."
The others, those under the shadow of color, "they're different," as Paul P. explicitly puts it. Being different, they
are, as Diane says, "strangers." Strangers among the tribesmen are at best objects of curiosity, at worst, objects of
hostility.

Our little tribesmen give evidence of a great deal of curiosity toward the "stranger," considerable hospitality, and considerable hostility. They prove their social acceptance on the
playground, and often state the appropriate values during
testing. "I would like to play with all of them" (mixed group
in the picture). "I would ask this little boy (N) to come in
and play with me and have supper at my house." "I would
like all of these (N and w dolls) to come to my birthday
party." "He (brown boy) and I would divide the lollipop.
We would swing together." Responses like these are usual.
Burton gives hospitality and acceptance an unusual twist when
he says: "The little boy is brown. Goin' to make him white.
Goin' to take him to my house too." It may not mean "when
he is white he will be acceptable," but it sounds very much
as though it did.

Hostility and rejection appear rather seldom in "real life" and very often in the testing room. These feelings are sometimes sharply stated in color terms, sometimes only implied. Paul P. reacts to the brown doll with "bad girl—I hit her!" Ronald is more vehement, and less polite: "I don't like dat boy (N). He stinks.—I don't like Juny (N schoolmate). She's a smelly girl. She hits me." And when we show him the picture of the Negro man and woman, he is through for the day. He grimaces at the picture, and turns his face away. "I don't want any more," he states firmly, and departs. Carl, referring to the same picture, says, "I don't like this man, and the lady neither." Joseph is moved to ideas of violence: "I don't like that man (N). I make an axe. I bang his head off." Peter S. assures us proudly that "there are no black people at *my* house." Roland and Patsy are general, but explicit: "I don't like little black boys—nor my mother neither"; "I hate them that way, I hate black."

These children are faintly aware of other "strangers" in their midst, or of being just a little strange themselves. Ian, who has personal reasons for wanting to know, asks: "Jews are Americans too, aren't they?" Diane has heard about "Catholics," and Nancy about "Chinese." Vesta knows that she is "part-Polish," Lilita that she is "Latvian." These references were incidental and largely neutral. It is the Negro who is the conspicuous stranger in their little worlds.

"Medium awareness" in our white four-year-old consists in the naming, associating, and differential valuing which we have seen him acting out or stating for us. Basic to all of this is the awareness of what "I" am, and of what "we" are. With it goes the comfortable (though largely subconscious) feeling that "we" stand on firm ground and, relatively speaking, on high ground. From our vantage point "they" can be surveyed and their measure taken.

High Awareness

Eleven of our white children give evidence of a quite adult degree of clarity about matters of race. It is true that color is their focus of interest and the major basis upon which they classify. But they are also highly perceptive of other differentiating physical traits and of how these cluster with color differences. Danny notes the "rosy cheeks" as well as the "white skin" of the white doll. Debbie observes the "funny hair" of the "brown ones," and the "light brown," "dark brown," or even "black" hair of the "white" people she knows. These children not only see the gross color kinds, but also some details about each of the kinds. They approach, and a few of them achieve, a genuine idea of racial kinds.

High awareness also involves near-consistency in seeing and reacting to racial attributes, a high frequency of accurate racial descriptions and labelings, and evidence for a quite consistent set of race-related values. Relative clarity, consistency, and certainty distinguish the thought and speech of these high awareness children.

Racial identity has become for them a significant matter. The frequency and spontaneity with which they comment upon it are proof enough. It is significant and it is to them quite obvious. They have no doubts whatever about who is "white" and who is not, and they do not leave us to infer this fact. They are highly explicit about it. They are able to be, because they command a race vocabulary with which they are no longer experimenting. They know precisely what they are saying when they use it.

There are, of course, differences between these eleven high awareness children. In respect to vocabulary there is unanimity in the use of just one term, "white." They all use this label, and no other, for the "we-group." The other group—"they"—are "black" or "brown" or "colored." Nearly all of the eleven command all three terms, but they do not all limit themselves to such polite reference. Three of them use an epithet which they know to be highly impolite. They use it because they do know it to be just that.

Differences among the eleven become most striking when we examine the values they state or strongly imply. In this respect there is a very wide range. More accurately, perhaps, there are two ranges: first, there is the range of values having to do with white people and, second, the range having to do with brown people. The white-related values range from mild and slightly inconsistent white preference to very strong and very consistent white preference. The brown-related values range from nearly consistent acceptance to highly consistent rejection. There are strong "for" and "against" feelings in some of these children. When the two are combined in a given child, we find something very nearly like full-fledged race prejudice.

In David J. there is just such a combination of strong "for" and "against" feelings. David likes *only* the white people (in the pictures) and the white dolls. We know this not simply because he never chooses a brown as prettier, or nicer, or more desirable to play with, but also because he puts it into words, and emphatically. He is not satisfied with saying, "I like the white one." He must add, "I like it better than the black one." Again, "I like the white one—it's my favorite." And later, "I like the white one—I *don't* like the black one—it's black." This last ("it's black") appears to be by way of explanation. He is saying: "It's black—*therefore* I don't like it." In another instance the white doll "has prettier hair."

Whenever a choice is asked for (or volunteered), David states *both* his preference and his rejection, as though to underscore the former. Sometimes, however, there is no question of choice. This is the case when he is shown the picture of a solitary brown boy. Under these circumstances, David turns to stronger statements of rejection to convey the nature of his feeling. He multiplies his rejections, lest we be in doubt: "He's black! He's a stinky little boy.—He's a stinker—he sh——! Take it away! I want another little boy." Then, as though to make it clear to us that his reactions to this particular "black" boy are no exception, he adds: "I don't like colored boys." We show him another picture (the third in a series of six). In this one there are Negro and white children happily playing "London Bridge" together. It is too much for David. He takes one look at the picture, shouts "they look like sh——!" and runs out of the room.

David is unlike most of the children in that he gives us only his stark, terse, unqualified reactions. The others are likely to offer something substantial in the way of "reasons," justifications, or rationalizations. David seems to have taken it entirely for granted that the Observer would understand and share his point of view. This confident expectation is conveyed in the comment we have noted: "I don't like the black one—it's black." He is giving what he regards as a reason, and he expects the Observer to regard it as such. The same assumption is apparent in this statement: "I like the white girl (doll) because, —— you know—." The Observer was expected to "know" that its being white was reason enough for liking it. David's assumptions, and his undefended opinions, suggest a mind quite simply furnished. The simplicity has nothing to do with intelligence (with which David is in fact well supplied). It has rather to do with a lack of shadings or conflicts in his value systems. He is all "for" whites and all "against" Negroes. He apparently conceives no "in-between" possibilities nor is he aware that other people do—or might. Neither is he in conflict within himself. He appears to harbor no general "ethical" or "democratic" values which might move him to feel a need to justify his race values. In the either-or quality of his value system he has much in common with prejudiced adults. But his immaturity is conspicuous in his unawareness that the Observer might not be entirely of the same mind, and in his lack of internal conflict as well.

Debbie is very unlike David J. Where he is at the extreme in respect to strong, unqualified, and consistent white preferences and brown rejections, Debbie's values are relatively weak, qualified, and inconsistent. She is alert to race differences, and too regularly so to be classed with the medium awareness children. But her awareness is a much more complex affair than is David's.

David sees black and white, both group-wise and value-wise, but Debbie sees a wide variety of in-betweens. She knows about kinds of people other than "colored" and "white." There are the "English," and there are "Jewish" (who are "white, of course"), and "Catholic." There are boys and girls, men and women, and sometimes these sex and age factors loom larger than race in her perceptions of people. She sees the races not so much in absolute categories as in relative ones. They are "lighter" and "darker," and within each there are variations. Hair can be "yellow," "light brown," "dark brown,"—even "light black" or "dark black."

Debbie, in fact, sees a great deal more about the world of people than does David. Her perception of detail is much finer, and it is matched by her ability to capture detail and nuance in words. She is keenly aware of both the racial and personal attributes which identify herself and others whom she knows well. Debbie knows that her sister is white, and she also knows that her sister does not look like the white girl in the picture. The latter "haven't got the same color hair" (as her sister), and "she doesn't walk like my sister." The pictured brown boy looks "a *little bit* like Georgie (N), because he's black." She sees individuality as well as racial category.

Debbie expresses marked preferences for whites and explicit rejections of Negroes. She would rather play with the white boy "because he's lighter," and she tells us firmly "I don't like the brown ones." But she feels some uneasiness about this kind of statement, and usually she finds a subtle way to defend it. She decides that she should tell us that the white baby doll she prefers is "the sweet one," and the dark brown one (which she has not explicitly rejected) is "the funny one." She likes the white mother doll (better than the brown one) "because she has a flower dress."

Debbie does not just prefer whites and reject browns—it is not so simple a matter. Her reactions are complicated by the fact that she also prefers to be polite, kind, and fair. She uses no impolite epithets, and she wants to see fair play if there is only one lollipop or one swing to divide between herself and the brown girl. She would "cut the lollipop in half" and "have the teacher get another swing." These are solutions more ingenious than David's. They also reflect the operation of a value system applying to *people*—to people divorced from their color. There can be no divorce in David's scheme of things, nor is he well supplied with "democratic" values to apply in any case.

Consensus

From the point of view of a truly objective observer, these white children about whom we have been talking might well be called "bleached." It would be a term more appropriate than "white" as the opposite of "colored," and in terms of realities and of the history of the species, it would be more accurate. But our children are not objective observers, nor do they hear objective labeling. They hear little of an objective order which has to do with race. What they do hear is the consensus, and in widely differing degrees and fashions they build its overtones into their own little personal systems.

It is the consensus that "we" are on the comfortable side of the color line. "We" are on the side where people are pretty, and clean, and good, relatively if not absolutely. This is the burden of what these white children have told us.

The people that are white—they can go up.

Chapter 5

We—and They

IN THE TWO PRECEDING CHAPTERS we have seen something of the nature of race awareness in our Negro children and in our white ones. In Table 1 there is presented a brief summary of the more conspicuous aspects of low, medium, and high awareness as these aspects appear in both racial groups.

Negro and White—The Common Variations

We have found in these four-year-olds variations such as one might expect to find in any sizable group in respect to any particular kind of social awareness. Looking across Table 1 from left to right the range is apparent.

To describe this range in terms of three points—low, medium, and high—may seem to be like describing a one-foot rule by saying that on it there are marks for one inch, six inches, and twelve inches. What is intended is rather to indicate the kinds of marks to be found in the lower, middle, and upper thirds of a race awareness scale established for us by these children. The fact is that our children show degrees of awareness falling all along the scale from one inch to twelve, that is, from low to high awareness. But in the interest of simplifying our description of the range of variation we have grouped together those whose awareness is of the same general degree. The low awareness cases show, as it were, a one to four inch range of variation, the medium a four to eight inch range, and the high an eight to twelve inch range.

The generalizations about each of the three levels of awareness should be understood as indicating the nature of the low, medium, and high thirds of the scale rather than as descriptions of discrete points on the scale.

To clarify the summary of what we have found, we have in fact represented our data on three scales rather than on one. In Table 1 we have summarized in terms of a "Perception" scale, a "Vocabulary" scale, and a "Concept" scale.

A given case may fall at somewhat different points on these three scales, but the discrepancies between degree or nature of perception, extent or content of vocabulary, and extent or nature of conceptualization were seldom very striking. This lack of sharp discrepancy within a given case is as much to be expected as is a range of variation between the cases in our sample. Perception, vocabulary, and conceptualization are facets of a general process and depend upon one another. As we have observed earlier, the child must have word handles to attach to perceived things before he can do very much complex thinking about his perceptions. Conversely, he must be able to see discrete items—to pick them out of perceptual masses—before he will have much need for words in which to talk or think about what he sees. The three processes develop together, though not always at uniform rates.

In the top row of boxes in Table 1 we have generalized about the differing degrees in which our children *see* (register, attend to, take note of) the physical clues which mean "Negro" or "white" to the adult. The range is great. At the low end there is the tendency to only occasionally register personal features which have racial significance. These are sometimes sensed as having more than ordinary significance or as being like or unlike the features possessed by other people. On the whole the attention paid to color (or other racial features) comes and goes, alternating with attention to sex and age features. At the high end of the scale the racial attributes have come into focus as a cluster built around color. They are personal features which stand out in high relief in the mind's eye, and which seldom fail to do so.

In the second horizontal row of boxes we have generalized about the degree to which our children command a race vocabulary. Down along the lower end of the scale there are children for whom the command of words is as limited and uncertain as is their vision. Sometimes they are conspicuously searching for words and experimenting with the process of

TABLE 1
Summary—Nature of Awareness in Negro and in White Children

	Low Awareness (15% of Ns) (15% of ws)	Medium Awareness (45% of Ns) (61% of ws)	High Awareness (40% of Ns) (24% of ws)
Perception (Noticing)	*N and w:* 1. Erratic interest in and attention to personal color (primarily) or other racial attributes. 2. See isolated and unique items about individuals.	*N and w:* 1. See color and other physical attributes clearly but not consistently. 2. Interest, attention, and curiosity strong but fluctuating.	*N and w:* 1. Clear perception of color and other racial attributes. 2. Nearly consistent attention to these items. 3. Color, etc., both obvious and significant features.
Vocabulary (Describing and Labeling)	*N and w:* 1. Race terms used infrequently, and often inaccurately. 2. Experimentation in use of. 3. Some associational terms used (dark, dirty).	*N and w:* 1. Race terms used fairly often but not always accurately. 2. Associational terms frequent (black, dirty, dark). 3. Epithets and depreciatory terms fairly frequent. *N:* Race terms used in "kidding" fashion, or as expressions of mistrust or of aggression.	*N and w:* 1. Race terms numerous and accurately used. 2. Associational terms and epithets frequent.

TABLE 1 (con't.)

	N and w:	N and w:	N and w:
Concepts (Ideas and modes of thought)	1. Little generalization or abstraction. Think in terms of the specific and concrete. 2. Some idea of color kinds—attempts at classifications in these terms. Uncertainty. 3. Some differential valuing of race attributes and the people possessing them. N: Some rejection of N attributes, focus on and favoring of lightness or whiteness. w: Impartial or somewhat favorably oriented toward ws and unfavorably oriented toward Ns—dirty, dark, old, don't like, scared.	1. Think in terms of color kinds (black and white usually). 2. Concerned with "hows" and "whys" of kinds. 3. Regard these kinds as polar extremes. 4. Concerned with social meaning of kinds. 5. Differential valuing of kinds. Whiteness positively valued. Negro-ness negatively valued. N: 1. Wishful identification of self or others (ws none). 2. Reality evasions. Reality faced grudgingly and discontinuously. 3. Value conflicts. 4. Self-involvement. w: 1. Sense of social distance and differentiation. 2. "I" and "we" awareness and sense of status assurance. 3. Some hostility toward and rejection of Ns. "Stranger" orientation, but with interest.	1. Think in terms of color and/or race kinds. 2. Sense racial differentiation and separation. 3. Sense for rightness of racial uniformity in social groupings. 4. Wide range of differential values. 5. Values strongly held. N: 1. Value conflicts strong. 2. Wishfulness and reality evasions near consciousness. 3. Race status sensed as a threat. w: Wide variation in degree of complexity of value system, but strong for and against values.

tying words and perceptions together. They make mistakes, but some of them have settled upon a few tie-ups which are quite commonly made by their elders. At the high end of the scale there are children who use as many racial terms as do most of their elders and who use them in much the same ways. They do so without fumbling. Their periods of experimentation have passed. The words are not toys, they are tools, and some of them are weapons, single or double-edged, as well.

In the third of the rows of boxes in Table 1 are generalizations about the varieties of racial concepts we have found grown or growing in the minds of our children. At the lower segment of the scale, do they think in terms of classes or categories rather than in terms of individuals A, B, C, etc.? Do they think in terms of brownness or whiteness as traits common to A, B, and C, X, Y, and Z respectively? To a very limited degree, they do. In flashes they do, but their occasional notions about classes and abstracted attributes are uncertain and wavering. Do the low awareness children feel differently about people whom they do perceive as brown or white (or possibly as dark or dirty)? Yes, they are likely to, again in a vague and uncertain fashion.

But their fellows clustered along the high third of the scale are quite a different lot when considered in terms of their ideas and modes of thought about race. For them the world is peopled by different "kinds," and color kinds are likely to be among the three or four kinds of which they are most clearly and continuously aware. When they talk about "colored" or "black" or "brown" or "white" people, they are likely to be indicating a *kind* which is for them distinguished by a number of physical traits in addition to skin color. Furthermore, they are likely to speak of these kinds in words heavily laden with value judgments and with the notion that the kinds are not only separate but also separated. Vague and uncertain about these matters they distinctly are not. They may not be in the least happy about the nature of the judgments and opinions they themselves make, but they feel impelled to make them just the same.

Negro and White—The Uncommon Variations

Scattered through Table 1 there are references to developments in one racial group which are not paralleled in the other. We sometimes find not only a lack of parallel developments, but developments which seem to run quite counter to one another.

Even among our low awareness children notable differences appear. Negro children may be in general rather nonperceptive, but upon occasion they not only see color but are quite forcefully struck by it. For reasons certainly below the level of consciousness they sense that this item is important *and* that it has something to do with themselves. Our low awareness white children, on the other hand, perceive color in a sporadic and offhand fashion. It is one of those things about people of which they take note occasionally but which sets up no widening ripples in their emotional reservoirs. It is of some general interest, but it is not a matter felt intimately and personally.

In the low awareness whites the perception of color may, however, touch off a chain of associations at the end of which the child is left with something like a faint and generalized sense of distaste for the *presence* of the attribute. Our low awareness Negro children may experience much the same associational sequences and much the same distaste. But in the Negro children there is the suggestion of an accompanying preoccupation with the *absence* of color, whereas for the whites this is the unexamined ground upon which they stand.

Among the medium awareness children there are more striking differences. The Negro children are clearly the more uneasy in company with the topic of race the more they see and know about it. They are at once compulsively interested in the topic and extremely uncomfortable with it. They are personally involved, evasive of the realities and wishful about the unrealities. Not so the white children, whose emotions are little involved and who do not feel themselves personally implicated in any case. Insofar as they perceive white and black they sense them as quite separate and differentiated. "Black people" as a type are strange, unlovely, and unloved, if not actively rejected.

Children of high awareness exhibit precisely the same trends in more intensified forms. In the white children keener awareness brings a greater sense of security in their racial status. It also brings stronger pro-white and anti-Negro feelings. For the Negro children high awareness brings an increasing sense of insecurity in respect to racial status, heightened emotionality, and a greater sense of personal involvement and personal threat.

We and They Across the Line

Clearly our children have, in varying degrees, a sense of a "we" group and of a "they" group, different sorts of feelings about these two groups, and some inclination to look across the sensed line between them.

The racial identity of We and of They is, of course, a function of the side of the color line from which you view things. Looking from the brown side We are brown and They are white, and looking from the white side the colors of We and They are reversed. Logically, a number of other features ought to be reversed, too. If the people on the white side have a sense of belonging with whites, of preferring whites and whiteness, of withdrawing from or rejecting browns and brownness, and of superiority to browns—if these ideas develop on the white side, the same ideas in reverse color should logically develop on the brown side. We should be able to find on the brown side the reciprocals of the ideas on the white side: browns should feel that they belong with browns, they should prefer browns and often reject whites, and they should feel superior to them.

Such orderly reciprocality is not what reality is made of— not in any significant segment of American adult society. Neither is it reality in our little segment of New Dublin child society. It is the realities of the "across-the-line" *orientations* which occupy our attention here.

A Sense of Direction

To be "oriented" is to have a *sense of direction,* and this our children have, in varying degrees. Orientation toward We and They race groups is something short of, and different from, fully developed race attitude, which we have defined as *readiness for action.* The line between orientation and attitude is a tenuous one to be sure. It is not necessarily coincident with the line between childhood and adulthood, or even between early and late childhood. But the infrequency with which our young children go into action shows that they are not yet equipped with fully developed attitudes. And the frequency with which they express points of view about race indicates a more or less marked sense of direction. What we know of their older brothers and sisters, and of their parents, suggests a different distribution of attitudes and orientations.

In these older people there are more of the former, while the latter remain as background.

On the basis of what our children have expressed in the way of perception and classification, familiarity with race-ways, and acceptance of race-related value systems, we have arrived at some conclusions about their general orientations. These conclusions are summarized in Table 2.

When we compare the figures in the column for Negro children with those in the column for whites, it appears that there are indeed some radical departures from the perfect symmetry which evenly reciprocal relations would bring about. Here are the nonreciprocal realities in respect to group affinity, group preference, superiority-inferiority, and friendliness-antagonism. These are the particular kinds of orientations which we have assessed in our children.

We-group Affinity

In respect to strength of orientation toward one's "own kind," Negroes fall somewhat short of whites. About three-fourths of our brown children, as against nearly all of the whites, give evidence of a sense of belonging with or to the people on their own side of the line. They feel at home and comfortable with these "same-side" people, and vaguely at one with them.

Those children who do not feel so about the We are either genuinely in error about the self and its biological or social bonds, or they are genuinely correct but other-oriented nevertheless. Alfred (N) is so little aware of the whole business of race that he shows no affinity with either group. Children like this we have not counted in making up the table. Neither have we counted children who, like June (N), though highly aware, are also highly divided in their minds about where they belong. Dianne (N) is one of those whom we counted among the children genuinely correct about the self and its actual bonds but oriented toward whites in spite of that. Dianne knows her biological and social "own-kind" very well indeed. But she has little sense of belonging with them, and some sense of belonging with whites. Nor has Colin much sense of belonging with browns. Colin might conceivably be one of those who is in error about his biological identity, since he is very light. He can hardly be in error about his social identity, however, in view of his high level

TABLE 2

Summary—Nature of Orientations in Negro and in White Children

Type of Orientation	N		W	
	No.*	%	No.*	%
In-group Affinity	37	72	35	97
Out-group Affinity	14	28	1	3
	51	100	36	100
In-group Preference	13	26	36	92
Out-group Preference	37	74	3	8
	50	100	39	100
Superiority toward Out-group	0	0	21	48
Neutrality toward Out-group	23	43	23	52
Inferiority toward Out-group	31	57	0	0
	54	100	44	100
Friendly toward Out-group	47	84	26	56
Indifferent toward Out-group	4	7	5	11
Antagonistic toward Out-group	5	9	15	33
	56	100	46	100
Friendly toward In-group	31	56	43	93
Indifferent toward In-group	11	20	3	7
Antagonistic toward In-group	13	24	0	0
	55	100	46	100

* Not all subjects committed themselves sufficiently to allow of conclusions concerning all of their orientations. Percentages are calculated on a basis of the total number who committed themselves on a given orientation.

of awareness and the almost totally Negro society in which he moves. Colin, like Dianne and a dozen other Negro children, feels that he belongs with whites. He also feels, as do the others, that he prefers whites.

We-group Preference[1]

That there is a correlation between a sense of out-group affinity and a feeling of out-group preference is hardly surprising. The correlation appears in David, who is the sole white child seeming to have something close to a sense of belonging with brown people. It also appears, as we have seen, in Colin, Dianne, and the other Negro children who have a sense of belonging with the out-group. But the preference for the out-group does not always depend upon having an affinity for it.

We have thirty-seven Negro children—three-quarters of those who express any preference at all—who are preference-oriented toward whites. This group is markedly larger (nearly three times) than the group of Negroes who are affinity-oriented toward whites. Among our whites there is a negligible proportion (three) who prefer the brown group.

Our conclusions concerning preference rest on expressions having to do with social partisanship and participation, general or abstract preferences ("nicer," "better," "good," etc.), and personal esthetics. A comparison of the points of view expressed by two children of high awareness will indicate the cumulative nature of the evidence. Sections from our summary records on Tony R. and on Danny are presented below.

(1) *Tony R.* (*N*)

(a) *Partisanship:* Rather marked w partisanship (6 responses of this type to 3 responses which might be called nonpartisan). E.g., when he has finished the "family puzzle" (5 white and 5 brown family members, all in bathing suits), he examines the picture and volunteers: "I'm going to let the white people out. I'm not going to let the brown people out. The white people are goin' swimmin'. The brown people are goin' home."

(b) *Social participation:* Gives 5 responses showing w preference and/or N rejection, 2 nonpreferential responses and 1 N participation preference response.
Example 1. w preference and N rejection

"I wouldn't invite him (brown boy in picture) to my house. Only white boys could come, 'cause I like the white boys."
Example 2. w preference

"I like all the white boys and all the white babies and all the white girls (to play with)."

(c) *General preference:* Strong w preference and N rejection, with considerable ambivalence (11 w preferences, 9 N rejections, 8 ambivalent responses, i.e., "both" or "all").

One statement "I like black people—is this black?" (pointing to brown doll), his only indication of an N leaning. His "I don't like them" (*re* white man and woman) the only indication of a w rejection.

Gives repeated explicit statements of w preference, e.g., "I like white people. I don't like colored people."

(d) *Personal esthetics:* Strong w preference; some N and w rejection. E.g., affirms brown boy is good-looking, adds, "but I don't like him."

Says both N and w couples are "ugly people" (N first).

One unusual self-reference response: He rubs some of the w clay on his face and fingers. Asks "Could this come off?" (Note: Tony is medium brown. Identifies strongly with whites. Rejects N identification. Knows own attributes. Strongly wishful *re* whiteness.)

(e) *Summary on preference:* w partisanship, w participation preference, w general preference, w esthetic preference (and probably wishfulness concerning own color attributes). Also N rejection and some ambivalence. Highly explicit and vigorous expressions.

(2) *Danny* (w)

(a) *Partisanship:* Marked tendency to be, or attempt to be, nonpartisan (4 nonpartisan to 2 w partisan responses). W partisanship tends to appear when he is pressed for a definitive response. E.g., his responses to the story about white boy (himself) and the brown boy (both greatly want the *only* lollipop; what to do?). He said first, "I don't know." Asked again, he said: "Push down (in) the pocket and get (find) another lollipop." Question repeated; he said: "Just one boy came for it (w) and the other boy would have to be in school." Q. "Which boy in school?" D. "The colored boy, 'cause I never saw a colored boy eating a lollipop, and I never saw a colored boy (person) before Miss W——— (his N teacher)."

(b) *Social participation:* w participation preference (5 w, 1 N, and 2 nonpreferential responses). Again shows initial tendency to avoid outright declaration of w preference. *Example 1.* Asked which boy he would rather play with (N or w in puzzle picture), he points to N and then w. But adds: "This one (w) because this one (same) has brown hair. I have brown hair and my sister has brown hair. She might play with this one too."

Example 2. Asked whether he would rather play with girl (w) or boy (N). Replies: "Both. The girl more. I saw her first."

(c) *General preference:* w preference (responses divided 7 w, 2 N, 2 nonpreferential). Strong tendency to elaborate rationalization of w choices (tendency also in responses noted above).

Example 1. Which woman in the picture (N and w) do you like best? Danny points to w. Q. "Why?" D. " 'Cause I looked at her first, and I didn't see this one (N) for a little."

Example 2. Which woman in the picture (N and w) is nicer? Danny points to w. " 'Cause I don't like people that carry flowers so much (N woman wearing corsage). They waste flowers—carry people's flowers away. If you pick your own flowers, it's all right."

Example 3. Which of these women to visit you? "That one (w), because this one (N) steals flowers." Implicit N rejection in this last comment.

(d) *Personal esthetics:* Strong and explicit w preference (6 w and 1 nonpreferential response). Again hesitant declaration and tendency to justify choices, e.g., "These dolls (N and w babies) are pretty." Q. "Which is prettier?" D. "This one (w) is prettier in the skin, and this one (N) is prettier in the dress." (Note: dresses identical.)

Implicit esthetic N rejection: "This one (the w of another pair of babies) is prettier in the skin. This one (N) is colored."

Explicit N rejection finally comes out, tied up with esthetics: "I don't like colored people so much. They aren't so pretty."

(e) *Summary on preference:* Tends to be and tries to be equalitarian, basically w partisan; w participation preference but uneasy in declaring it; w general preference more or less elaborately rationalized; w esthetic preference, implicit N esthetic rejection. Expressions subtle. Anxious about own preferences. Not comfortable with them.

Tony R. and Danny are "high awareness" children. Their responses show a degree of consistency and explicitness which is missing from those of children less aware. But these records serve to demonstrate what the phrase "out-group preference" can represent, in the mind of a brown four-year-old, and what "in-group preference" can represent in the mind of a white one.

Superiority-Inferiority

Our conclusions concerning orientations of a superiority-inferiority sort are highly inferential. We cannot support them with any particular set of responses (such as those just reviewed), but only with our impressions of the over-all "tone," or "posture," or "inclination" suggested by the child's responses.

A sense of superiority is conveyed in the way a child phrases statements, and in the way he delivers them. "I would *let* him (brown boy) come in my house and play with my toys." "*My* brother's not black!" "They (Negro children) are *all right*." It is difficult to convey the lift of the head, the vehemence, the shrug of the shoulder, all of which told the listener as much as did the words. A sense of superiority is implicit, too, in the judgmental tone of much that our white children say and do in reference to browns. They dispose of the browns with the finality and assurance of their "I don't like—" or "I don't want—" or "That's ugly—dirty—black—naughty—bad—nasty."

Our white children never indicate a sense of inferiority in relation to browns. Neutrality—a kind of lukewarm midpoint on the superiority-inferiority continuum—does appear frequently. About half of our white children give us no reason to suppose that they feel anything more marked than a passive neutrality. The other half falls close to the superiority end of the scale.

Our Negro children feel superior only to one another and never, in our experience, do they assume a posture of superiority toward whites. The subtleties of expression which spelled superiority orientation among the whites are missing in these children. They express neutrality (some 40% of them), but over half of our Negro children convey a sense of inferiority to whites. They convey this orientation primarily through their implicit acceptance of the judgments which are made on the other side of the line. They agree that whites are "prettier," "nicer," more desirable playmates, and even that Negroes are "dirty," "ugly," and generally undesirable. In rare instances this kind of acceptance leads to a depreciation, not only of the We-group, but even of the self. Andrew uses "black" as a general epithet, and then turns it on himself, "I'm black—black—black." (He is in fact no more than medium brown.) Herman carries self-depreciation to the extreme, though possibly with personal as well as group reference involved. Herman tells us: "I'm not no good."

Friendly-Antagonistic

The child's position on a friendship-antagonism continuum has also to be inferred from the over-all tone and quality of his responses. We have, in fact, assessed his position on two such scales. We have estimated the degree to which he is friendly, indifferent, or antagonistic toward members of the We-group and made this same estimate for his orientation toward the "opposite" group. Some striking differences between the Negro and the white children appear here, as they have elsewhere.

The whites are always either friendly or indifferent toward whites as a kind, with the latter orientation very rare (three cases). The Negroes, on the other hand, indicate a truly friendly orientation toward Negroes in only a little over half of our cases. The Negroes, more often than the whites, are indifferent toward the We-group, and in about a fourth of our Negro children we observed something very close to antagonism toward "own-kind."

Among whites the orientation toward Negroes is of a friendly order in over half of our cases. It is seldom indifferent, and about a third of our white children seem to us more or less antagonistic toward browns. Negroes, too, are seldom indifferent toward the opposite group, but they are much more frequently friendly—nearly always so in fact. Antagonism toward whites may be present, but it is not often expressed.

Thomas (N) gave us our most striking demonstration of a strong anti-white inclination. There were numbers of incidents at school when he vehemently rejected teachers and children—all of them white. He never made his reasons explicit, but his reactions in the testing situation made his basic mistrust and resistance very clear. Thomas showed more "fight" than any other of our Negro children. He even turned the weapons back against the customary wielders. Invite the little white boy to his house? Certainly not! "I wouldn't," said Thomas. "I wouldn't have him. He's too nasty—and he's too dirty."

The Basic Orientations

We have arrived at some generalizations about particular kinds of We-They orientation in our children, and about the nature of their awareness of the We and They race groups. Having done so we can abstract the most basic common elements which run through the thinking and feeling of the children in each racial group.

Basically our Negro children are out-group oriented. Through all the individual variations there runs this common thread. It is a thin thread in some, a stout one in others; in some it appears only sporadically, in others it is quite continuously in view. But it is there. These children share a fundamental orientation—a sense of direction *away* from Negroes and *toward* whites. Graphically speaking, the orientation describes a straight line.

Our whites are in-group oriented. Individual variations among them are as great as among the Negroes, but this they have in common. Among them there is none of the self-reference, the deeply personal involvement which is in our Negro children. The whites look across the line with varying degrees and kinds of emotion, but without emotions of self-doubt and self-concern. Racially speaking they are complacent about the self. Their basic orientation—their sense of direction—is *around* within the orbit of the white world. The orientation is, graphically speaking, a circle. They touch the color line, but they are not directed across it.

Chapter 6

White Over Brown

WHAT OUR FOUR-YEAR-OLDS have taught us about the meaning of color, or about the meaning of its absence, has now to be looked at in context. We shall see something of the backgrounds in which these meanings have developed. Without knowing more about what lies behind and beside the race feelings of our children, we can hardly understand how these feelings came to be what they are. And it is important to know the *how*, if we are to learn from these children things which will help us to understand and to deal with other children.

We have seen that there are race-related value systems growing in the four-year-old, and that the value systems lead to a set of racial orientations. This is one particular part of the whole process through which the child is going while he acquires the culture—the life-ways—of his people. Starting culturally naked he eventually covers that nakedness with a mantle woven from those life-ways. But the life-ways of a people, whether American, Japanese, or Eskimo, are very many. No child can use them all, nor does he have an opportunity to do so. The external setting in which he grows does not offer him all of the culture, nor are its particular offerings made with equal vigor. There are degrees of pressure exerted upon him to accept this or that item or pattern of culture.

In this and in successive chapters we shall be concerned

with two matters: (1) with the *nature* of the race-related cultural offerings to which our children have been exposed, and (2) with the *ways* in which these offerings have been made (by whom, and under what conditions). These are the *cultural* and *social* aspects, respectively, of the settings in which our children are developing their racial values and orientations. To know more about these aspects will help us to understand the *how* of acquiring racial values.

The Cultural Aspect

What is the nature of the race-related cultural patterns to which our children have been exposed?

First and most importantly, they have been exposed to a master concept and a master belief about race relations. They have been exposed to a very basic idea which finds myriad expressions throughout the United States. If the idea were to be described in one terse and oversimple formula, it might well read $\dfrac{\text{White}}{\text{Brown}}$.

White over brown, with the line between, is an oversimple description of race relations in New Dublin or elsewhere in the country. It is even an oversimplification of the race-related value system current among the parents of our children, but it gets at the heart of the matter. It is precisely this superposition of the whites, tacitly recognized by all and deeply resented by the subordinated browns, which constitutes the biggest single fact about race relations, and the most comprehensive idea to which our children are exposed. The idea is pervasive and it pervades silently, like a creeping fog, and is just about as difficult to stop. It has seeped through the nation and along the line of the generations, and we can see it now seeping into our children, white and brown.

We have already observed something of the forms it assumes. We noted (in Chapter 1) that the parents of our children experience a variety of feelings about intergroup relations. There are the Negroes who have migrated from the south partly in search of an escape from the white-over-brown formula. They have not found it, and the failure lies in a private pool of disappointment more or less hidden behind a tangle of public words and attitudes. The migrants are not alone in this. There is in some degree the same disappointment in all our Negro parents, and with it bitterness, hostility, resignation, envy, or emulation in varying degrees. In the white parents we found friendliness, disinterest, or antagonism. Even friendliness can be consistent with adherence to the white-over-brown formula. One can feel very friendly toward an inferior, or even especially friendly toward him, if he is not regarded as potential competition. One can also feel disinterested until the inferior is seen as a threat, but at that point antagonisms rise. The typically American emphasis upon competition, therefore, plays a part in the preservation of white-over-brown.

As we came to know them, the parents of our children told us a great deal about their own attitudes. Frequently they told us more than they realized or intended, just as they often tell their children more than they realize or intend to tell. Here are some of the things we heard about that master formula for race relations and how it figures in the lives and in the thinking of the parents. Having considered some fairly typical views, we will be able to see what picture of a race-divided world these people are likely to have offered to their children.

White Over Brown: As the Brown Parents Know It

1. Donald's Parents: "An inferiority feeling—"

Mr. and Mrs. K. are lively, intelligent, gregarious people. They have social grace and charm, and they enjoy exercising these endowments. They get on well with people generally and with each other. Mrs. K. stays at home most of the time. She keeps house beautifully and plays mother competently. Mr. K. works very hard and comes happily home to his family when he has finished. Father and mother love each other and love their children, who reciprocate the feeling.

The K.'s, with their two sturdy and attractive sons, make up a firm little unit which looks to the bystander like something close to the ideal American family. In terms of the personalities of its members, and of their relations with one another, it is rather ideal. This is the more remarkable in view of the special problems the K.'s have to meet because of their race.

The job problem and the housing problem are the most conspicuously racial problems with which the K.'s have to contend. A man of Mr. K.'s sort, with a degree from a reputable local college, would not likely be a janitor if he were white. And no one is more painfully aware of that fact than the K.'s themselves. If the K.'s were white, and Mr. K. had the kind of job for which he was trained, they would be able to find and to afford something better than the dismal tenement flat in which the family lives in Lower Harding. They are keenly aware of this fact, too. Mrs. K. has painted and scrubbed the flat until it shines, and made pretty drapes and slipcovers, but nothing can conceal the cheapness of the structure, its general state of disrepair, or the pinched look of the little rooms. "We'd like to move," says Mrs. K. wistfully, "but we don't want to until we can make a good move. We've had tough sledding financially ever since we were married, and we're only just now getting out of the red."

The school problem is another of the special hazards in the lives of the K.'s. Their Bill, who is two years older than Donald, went to the Rodney Nursery School when he was Donald's age. Those years were fine, but Bill's parents regretfully saw him go on to the local public school which is "nearly all colored," when they had hoped "to get him in a school that is mixed." They had cherished this hope for two reasons: they wanted Bill to go to a good school, and they wanted him to have normal schoolboy relations across the color line. The K.'s are quite right in regarding the "nearly all colored" schools in Lower Harding as often inferior to the racially mixed or the all-white schools. And they are quite American in wanting freedom for their child—freedom to choose his friends from among the members of a racially mixed group. Bill is not happy at school, for reasons which are partly racial. His parents are keenly aware both of his unhappiness and of the racial reasons.

Then there is the social problem. The K.'s, being very sociable people, would like to move in a cozy clique made up of people like themselves. These would be people sharing their urban middle-class standards, tastes, and habits. The color of their friends would be relatively unimportant, but the K.'s would like the same social freedom they want for their children. They would like to choose friends and to be chosen on the basis of their qualities as people, without the constant interference of racial identity to deflect the choices parallel to the color line. While they are tied to the Lower Harding area, the K.'s will find few congenial friends among

Negroes and almost none among whites in Harding or most other places. Mr. K.

> ". . . gets along pretty well with most of the white fellows he knows, but it's like a school affair when they get together bowling or something like that. He made a lot of friends at school that he still sees once in a while, but they never bring their wives when they get together. The wives seem to think that we don't want them—and they certainly don't seem to want us. I guess they don't understand what an inferiority feeling you can get. Anyway, we have no close friends who are white."

Job, home, school, and friends—these vital aspects of the K.'s lives, and more, are deeply affected by the white-over-brown formula. The K.'s are psychically healthy people, but their racial identity is a constant source of irritation, pain, and deprivation. There is an open sore in these otherwise healthy people. In the intimacy of family living one cannot forever cover up one's sores.

A child in Donald's family gets a picture of a white world largely separated from the world in which he finds himself. This white world rarely admits his kind, and its good jobs, good houses, and good schools are not for him, even though he wants and deserves them. The picture is done in somber tones, and it is quite accurate. The K.'s do not present a distorted picture. They are strong enough to see their chances for just what they are. They are as dissatisfied with what they see as able and ambitious people who can be honest with themselves must be. To be so honest with oneself takes strength, too, and more than most of our able and ambitious Negro parents possess. Most important of all, the K.'s are able to think of themselves first and foremostly as *people*, and as Negroes only secondarily and when forced to it by circumstances. They are race-conscious but not race-obsessed.

2. Winona's Parents: "No particular trouble—"

The V.'s assure themselves that they have had "no particular trouble with white people, and never expect to have." They hold that "if you don't go lookin' for trouble you're not likely to get it."

The kind of trouble to which Winona's father and mother refer is the noisy and showy kind—brawls on the street corner or namecalling over the back fence. Having largely escaped this kind, they feel they are getting along with whites very nicely. They think in terms of white-over-brown, and while they may be irked by it, they are not in revolt against the formula.

The V.'s think of themselves primarily as Negroes, and as inevitably functioning largely in a Negro world. They tend to be satisfied with avoiding "particular trouble" with whites and getting along without competing for "white" jobs, housing, schools, or friends. The general trouble that comes with being brown bothers them less than it bothers the K.'s because they do not conceive of a world very different from the one in which they live. "As short as life is," says Mrs. V., "why harp on a thing like race."

Mr. and Mrs. V. live with their four children in two rooms, while renting out the rest of their house. The lack of order and attractiveness in their surroundings bothers them not at all. The rusty hand-me-downs they wear may be pinned together, but nobody worries about appearances. Keeping fairly comfortable and decently covered is the important thing, just as a comfortable supply of plain food, a roof over one's head, and a yard for the children are important things.

Mr. V. supplies these important things quite adequately. He is an industrious, enterprising, and acquisitive man who is constantly involved in a variety of small business deals. These are carried on largely in the Negro community. Both Mr. and Mrs. V. are very thrifty. Their income goes only into those things which they regard as important. If there is any left over, it goes into some mysterious cache and apparently stays there. This middle-class thrift is not accompanied by middle-class pride. They will turn for help to a social agency, in case of an emergency illness or operation, rather than dip into the cache.

The V.'s are accustomed to deal rather brusquely with the world and with one another. Father fancies himself an iron-fisted patriarch rather like the ideal family head of the West Indian island where he grew up. Mother has no such pretentions, but she in fact rules the domestic establishment quite as firmly as he likes to think he does. The children are kept in line with the strap if necessary, but they are not without genuine affection.

Money is the keystone of the social arch so far as the

V.'s are concerned. Browns may be on one side and whites on the other, but this aspect of the structure is less important than whether you have or have not money. It is money that keeps the parts of the structure in place. They propose to get it if they can, and the sheer having of it is the goal. They have no dreams of college education for the children, a nice little house in a nice neighborhood, or of living more with and like middle-class Negroes or whites. The prospect of having some accumulated money promises a sense of security which they lack. We cannot know how much of their general sense of insecurity stems from insecurity in their racial status. Certainly it is not toward a change in that status that they consciously yearn.

So the children in the V. family, Winona and the other three, get a rather different picture of white-over-brown than do the children in the K. family. For the V.'s the color line is, in fact, stronger. They hardly think of the possibility of its being erased, either for themselves or others, in small or in large matters. Rather it is wise to concentrate on the achievement of financial security, meanwhile staying largely on one's own side of the line and out of trouble with those on the other side.

In both these families, the children are being introduced to their parents' well-organized adjustments to race, and to other matters as well, of course. The K.'s and the V.'s deal with the race issue in ways which add up to a fairly consistent pattern for each family. There is some comfort, if no real solution, in this.

3. Andrew's Parents: "Nothing but trouble—"

There is no solution and there is scant comfort in Andrew's family. The R.'s have "nothing but trouble." Their troubles are not all racial, to be sure. The marital bond in this family is weak, but there are five children, of whom Andrew is the youngest. All of them are "problem children," one way or another. Both parents are handsome and self-centered people. They have grudgingly given up their respective visions of personal independence and gay and glamorous lives as the children were added to the family. Mr. R. grubs away at a semiskilled labor job while he yearns for the jazz band and the night lights he once knew. Mrs. R. escapes from the children she never wanted to temporary factory jobs and extended visits with her own Portuguese family in another town.

Both the R.'s are preoccupied with their own problems. Both are bitter, hostile, and suspicious toward a world which not only has failed to reward their individual attributes but which also penalizes them for being Negroes.

Mrs. R. could, in fact, have "passed," but with a brown-skinned husband and a brown-skinned brood of children her chance is gone. She never seized it when she might have done so, but in retrospect it looks like the opportunity of a lifetime thrown away, and thrown away for a man she can barely tolerate and for children who are one long series of headaches. She is gloomy, jumpy, erratic, and thoroughly unhappy. She sees color, and a man of color, as a major wave in her sea of trouble.

Mr. R. might have worked out an adjustment to the color problem if it were not for this bitterness in his wife. He gave up the career he loved and wanted because his wife

". . . hated being left at home alone nights when the children were little, and she hated what she called the 'artificiality of the people who hung around night clubs.'— Maybe she was jealous.—Anyway," says Mr. R. grimly, "she got her way. And now I suppose I'm too old to go back."

The R.'s have worked out no patterns of effective adjustment at all. They have none between each other, none between themselves and their children, and none with which to face the race relations formula. They make hasty and ill-considered moves from one experiment to another. Nothing works out right for them, and their children can get from them no sense of order or peace in the world. The picture they give is of the armed camp, with hostilities inevitable. It is a picture of man against woman, parents against children, and browns in a losing fight against whites.[1]

White Over Brown: As the White Parents Know It

1. Ian's Parents: "Nothing to do with them—"

The M.'s are in a number of ways the white counterparts of Donald's family. Ian's parents, too, are alert, informed, and gregarious people, vigorous participators in the world that touches them. Ian's family, too, is a very closely knit group in which affection and mutual interests unite the members.

The striking differences between the two families have racial implications. The M.'s though they are Jewish, have little sense of minority group status and no sense of inferiority. They are realistic but confident about their position in the middle-class society of Upper Harding. They know people more affluent or better educated than themselves, but none whom they really envy. A sound marriage, a comfortable home, three bright, happy children—this is their good life achieved and they see no one who has a better.

All this the M.'s have, and their personal intelligence, luck, and industry have much to do with it. Mrs. M. has deserted professional nursing to devote herself to home and family. Mr. M. has built his own modest little business around his craftsman's skills, and these same skills have helped to furnish a comfortable home tastefully. Both have given the best of their attention and judgment to the rearing of children who are the joy of their teachers as well as their parents.

But there is intelligence, industry, and some luck in Donald's family too. All of it together has not brought the K.'s what the M.'s have. It has not brought the K.'s an adequate income or an attractive home on a quiet, tree-shaded street in a "nice" neighborhood, with good schools and congenial friends nearby. It has brought these conditions of life to Ian's family, and the fact that they are white accounts for no small part of the difference.

Where Donald's parents were sharply aware of their racial limitations, Ian's parents take their racial privileges entirely for granted. They have no sense whatever of being privileged people, but they have a strong sense of being superior people. If they were to compare themselves with Donald's family, they would assume the difference in life conditions to be the quite natural outcome as between superior and inferior people. But it would never occur to the M.'s to make such a comparison, or to speculate about reasons for the differences. Donald's family, from the viewpoint of Ian's, is too socially remote to be thought of as comparable.

The M.'s make their sense of racial superiority and of racial distance quite explicit. They exhibit interest in "the race problem" in a degree appropriate to people who feel a personal and social affinity for intellectuals and intellectualism. They profess the appropriate sentiments about democracy and equality, and then they get to the heart of the matter.

Equality is one thing, but Mr. M. has to admit that about some other things he feels pretty strongly. He would not, for example, dance with a Negro as he once saw some white people doing.

"It was very interesting," he reports, "and I suppose those people do believe in freedom and in everybody being equal. But, you know, things just aren't that way. Why, if a Negro tried to get into the R—— Ballroom where we used to go, he'd be thrown out in a hurry!"

Mrs. M. has to admit that she's "not very keen about being around them" herself.

"I don't know where I got the feeling, but it's there. I don't know why exactly—I'm just not very keen about it, that's all. . . . When I went to the Mother's Club meetings at the Rodney Nursery School and found myself among almost all Negroes, I felt out of place. What could I say to them? We have nothing in common. I decided I wouldn't go any more. . . Of course I'm nice to them. I speak to them at school, but I have nothing to do with them, that's all."

The M.'s are explicit too about children and matters of race.

"We want our children to be democratic and know how to get along with all kinds of people," says Mrs. M. "Then later on they can choose their own friends. . . . So it's good for them to be at the Rodney School, but still, the school isn't what it used to be before they started taking such a rough group—so many lower class families. . . . There used to be hardly any Negroes there. Our children haven't associated with colored except at the nursery school. There aren't any in our neighborhood and we've had them in our home only in the capacity of servants—a cleaning woman now and then. Of course, when they're here like that, the children and I have lunch with them.

I wouldn't hurt their feelings and beside I wouldn't have the children get the idea that I minded. We certainly don't want our children to be prejudiced."

The M.'s sincerely do not want their children to be prejudiced. They are kindly people who would not hurt the cleaning woman's feelings, and they are enlightened Americans among whom prejudice is as unfashionable as it is prevalent. So they steer an erratic course, sending their children to a mixed nursery school and praising the democratic values implicit therein. Meanwhile, they deplore the presence of "rough" and "lower class" children in the school, and its many Negroes. The M.'s are experiencing some value conflicts, but none which are seriously disturbing. Their democratic values are easily served by making the culturally standardized verbal gestures, and just a little more. Their prejudiced attitudes are not often triggered into action. In each of the M.'s, logically incompatible value systems are not too uncomfortably accommodated within one personality. They are by no means exceptional among our parents in this respect.

The M.'s assure us that they "have no occasion to discuss race in front of the children." They are embarrassed when their friends and neighbors do so. The embarrassment arises largely, however, because these people wonder why the M.'s send their children to a racially mixed nursery school. They, in fact, do so because the school has an excellent reputation and because it is inexpensive. Their praise of its democratic admissions policy is a defense to their friends and an afterthought.

For all the complexity of the value systems which Mr. and Mrs. M. presumably do not discuss before the children, their vigorous support of the white-over-brown formula is crystal clear. Their assumption of racial superiority, their strong sense of a yawning gulf between themselves and the people with whom they "have nothing in common" and with whom they choose to have nothing to do—these are the major facets of the picture they present to their children.

2. Ronald's Parents: "All right in their place—"

The white G.'s of Lower Dover have something in common with the brown V.'s of Harding. Both families are made up of unremarkable people joined in rather unremarkable groups. The parents get on well enough with each other and with the children, with considerable amounts of yelling and brawling regarded as a necessary element in holding your own. Both the V.'s and the G.'s are responsible parents. They keep their children fed, sheltered, schooled, and in reasonably good health. They work hard to do so, having to depend more upon ingenuity and the breaks than upon specialized training to bring in the necessary money.

The G.'s, like the V.'s, live in quarters which are too small for them and which are barren of all save the minimum essentials. Frills are important to neither family, whether in the home or on the person. Frivolity is out too, no parties, no "socializing." The movies and even church-going are rare, though the G.'s profess themselves to be Catholic. They find life hard. The other fellow will cheat you out of your eyeteeth if you don't beat him to it. You have to be sharp and you have to plug at it, and you have to stay out of trouble.

You have to keep your children out of trouble, too, and this problem looms large to the G.'s. They are not concerned, like the V.'s with keeping themselves out of racial trouble. The G.'s do not have to worry about that, since they know who would come off second best. But their big boy runs with a gang of Syrian kids like himself, and the gangs of "nigger" kids fight them with no holds barred. Even four-year-old Ronnie is always out of the house and on the streets, usually with bigger boys and their gangs. The G.'s have less control over their offspring than do the V.'s partly because Lower Dover is a happy hunting ground for the gangs of boys bent on diversion and the working off of their accumulated gripes against their dismal lives. The G. boys, like the others, "swear and lie and smoke and fight." Their parents storm and threaten them with God's wrath or whatever else they can think of, and the boys storm back and race out on the streets again.

If the boys have accumulated gripes to work off, their parents are not very different. Besides their general gripes about the toughness and dullness of life, there are some particular ones having to do with the neighborhood. It was already packed with Syrian and Italian families when the Negroes began to move in.

"Now," says Mrs. G., "they live in swarms around us. This section is low now that they've moved in. There's something about colored in a neighborhood that lowers it.

It don't seem right that they should move into a white neighborhood—they're gettin' very independent. And the colored boys so bold! Hittin' white boys—that's what they do."

The G.'s, however, "have nothin' against the colored." Mrs. G.

". . . knows them," she tells us. "After all, I've worked with 'em. I'm not against 'em—everybody's as good as everybody else is what I say. And many's the time I've given it to the boys for yellin' 'nigger' an' things like that. That's a real bad word to use around here you know. Still you can't blame the boys too much. That's what they are around here—'niggers.' . . . It's the way I said—they ought to know enough to stay in their own neighborhood. They're all right with me as long as they stay in their right place."

"Their right place," so far as the G.'s are concerned, is not only another neighborhood but also a "lower" one. Being a Negro neighborhood, it would inevitably be a lower one. And when "they" came out of that neighborhood, they should not be so bold or independent as to trade blows with whites as though the two were equals. Nor should they have the boldness to fight back when they are called "what they are." There may be trouble, the boys may get into it and get hurt or picked up by the cops, and none of these things would happen if "they" had stayed in their right place.

In respect to the picture of race relations which they offer to their children, the G.'s are not so different from the V.'s. Neither family has much inclination to broach the color line. It is a hard and immutable fact of life, like the high cost of living and the crookedness of the politicians. The G.'s and the V.'s are given to cursing rather than to intellectualizing about the immutables of life, and to avoiding as much trouble as they can. They would agree that there will be less trouble if Negroes and whites stay—both of them—in their right places on their respective sides of the line. The V.'s, however, would like to see the axis of the line rotated through 180 degrees. The V.'s would settle for white *parallel to* brown, as a race relations formula. But the G.'s are quite satisfied with white-over-brown.

3. Nathan's Parents: "You never can tell—"

Nathan's family is rather like Andrew's. Nathan's father and mother, like Andrew's, are at swords' points with each other. Like Andrew, Nathan and his big sister are sadly in need of being loved and of being led, with a firm hand constantly within reach. Andrew's father, however, sticks it out with his family, while Nathan's was quick to find an escape via the U.S. Navy.

Mr. T. comes home for a visit now and then when his ship docks, and there may be a brief reconciliation during which the T.'s dream of getting out of Lower Harding and into a nice suburb where they would live happily ever after in their own little house. But father soon runs off again and mother soon goes out again. Both of them, like Andrew's parents, are overgrown children quite unable to cope with children of their own and with grown-up responsibilities. In Nathan's home, as in Andrew's, there is no order and no peace.

Nathan's mother, like Andrew's, regards her marriage as a "big blunder." But Mrs. T. has no color issue upon which to pin her trouble. Mr. T. is of Irish parentage like herself. If either feels any sensitivity concerning this background it is deeply hidden.

Mrs. T. has some problems involving race, however. In her search after gaiety she gets about the neighborhood a bit after dark, and occasionally there is a colored man in sight. She is of the opinion that

". . . the colored people are different than we are. They don't act the same, and it gives you the creeps. . . . Why, there was a woman I knew—lived over here a ways—she was coming home down a dark street one night and this Negro sailor come up and attacked her, and she was carryin' at the time. He held a razor at her throat! Well she got to the police and described him, and you know it's hard to tell them apart, but I guess she knew him—and the police found him and now he's doin' time. Maybe she knew him—maybe there was somethin' more to it. . . . Anyways they've never bothered me, and I guess if you leave them alone they probably won't. Just the same, I never did like bein' around them, like when I was in high school and it was all mixed and I never did like goin' to the washroom with them and all that. I just never did like the idea, that's all. They're different, and you never can tell what they might do."

In view of Mrs. T.'s convictions along these lines, it is hardly surprising that

"Nathan and Mary are just like me about it. Mary, she's terrible. Always talkin' about the 'niggers' that go to her school and how she don't like mixin' with 'em. Nate don't like mixin' either. He don't like to play with the colored children, but I told him plenty, and I think he knows how to behave now. He used to go around talkin' about 'niggers' and I told him he had got to stop it or I was goin' to beat it out of him. He might say that and you can't tell what they might do to him! Besides, like I told him, he shouldn't call them names because he wouldn't like it if they called him names. They got feelin's too, and as long as we live in this neighborhood we got to be nice to 'em and get along the best we can."

Mrs. T.'s particular focus on white and brown is consistent with her more general preoccupations. She has a childish fear of the strange and the "different," and a lack of confidence in her own ability to cope with the unfamiliar. She is susceptible to this implication of contrast between white and brown and to the corollary notion that it is unpleasant to "mix" with strangers whose ways must surely be different and unpredictable. Her concern with sexuality finds its expression too in her thinking about brown and white. So does her naive kindliness and her general yearning to like and to be liked. The picture she holds up to her children brings these particular matters clearly into view.

White and Brown

In these six families we have seen a range of responses to the idea of white-over-brown. Although the idea is culturally patterned, and has some place in the thinking of all our parents, it is of course somewhat differently seen and interpreted in each family. Those we have discussed above are representative of three general and recurrent types of response. For all their differences, our parents are given to viewing race *rationalistically, conventionally,* or *egocentrically.*

This is to say, first, that they are given to viewing it *primarily*, though probably never exclusively, in one of these ways. Second, it is to say that we are considering types of *thought-ways*, and not of attitudes. Any one of these types of thought-ways can be the vehicle for friendliness, indifference, antagonism, aggression, hostility, fear, or any other of the many possible racial attitudes.

1. *The Rationalistic View*

Donald K. and Ian M. have parents who view race rationalistically. So have about a dozen others of our Negro children and about the same number of white ones.

We use the term *rationalistic* to suggest a certain intellectualism, detachment, or social consciousness about race, or a kind of realism based upon some knowledge and information. Any or all of these tendencies may be weakly developed, but in people who have something of them in their thinking, there is less blind acceptance of the status quo, and often more complex and involved value systems, than in the people who do not have them. The people who take a rationalistic view are often people who have had some education beyond high school, but not necessarily so. In any case, they are people who have learned to think somewhat independently, to handle abstractions, to deal with social issues on a problem-solving basis.

They may go through all of these processes and still wind up quite openly prejudiced about race, like Ian's parents. But prejudice in people like this has less certainty, less dogmatism, less of cultural orthodoxy in it. Sometimes they wind up quite genuinely emancipated from the white-over-brown idea. This can happen to either Negroes or whites, but it does not happen to Negroes so readily as one might suppose.

Negroes, too, being Americans and therefore saturated with American culture, find it difficult to escape from the standard race formula in their own thinking. Donald's parents have done it. This was what we meant when we said that they are strong enough to face the realities. The realities are not just matters of poor housing, a poor job, and so on. The realities are also intangibles, matters of being told, usually by implication but repeatedly and unmistakably, "you are inferior people, you belong apart and below." People must be strong who can face years of these realities, tangible and intangible, and retain their faith in themselves and their conviction that the race formula is fallacious. Few of our Negro parents have been able to do it.

Few of our white parents have been able to achieve their emancipation either. Basically they have the same problem that the Negroes have—that is, they are Americans, culturally as well as politically speaking. Brown or white, one does not easily unlearn a fundamental part of one's culture. But the whites have another difficulty which the browns do not. Put oversimply, the whites have much to lose in renouncing their inherent right to a position above the line. Those same realities which make life harder for the Negro and remind him of his inferiority work in reverse for the white. So it takes a strong white man, as well as a strong Negro, to unlearn the formula. It has happened in seven or eight of our white families.

2. *The Conventional View*

Winona V. and Ronald G. have parents who view race in highly conventional terms. So have over half of the rest of our children, brown and white.

By *conventional* we mean that the race-related thought patterns of these people tend to run along the well-worn tracks. The people may or may not feel comfortable in these tracks, and they may or may not like the standard race formula as it applies to themselves or to others, but in a very fundamental sense they are tied to it. They may have occasional glimpses of different possibilities or even a strong yearning for them, but they have no experience of these possibilities either personally or vicariously.

We saw this mode of adjustment among Negroes in Winona's family, and we saw it among whites in Ronald's. The conventionally minded Negroes see themselves as Negroes primarily and permanently, and work out some kind of *modus vivendi* in these terms. The whites see the Negroes in the same way, and assume their own superposition as immutable. There is little social consciousness, little perspective and vision among these racially conventional people of either race, but the whites tend to show such thought-ways in lesser degree than do Negroes.

Conventionality in matters of race is likely to go hand in hand with inflexibilities of other sorts. New ideas, departures from habitual ways and viewpoints, imaginative and original moves tend to be greeted with suspicion, noncomprehension, and offhand rejection. The habitual thought-ways of conventionally minded people are likely to be cast in the either-or mold. Matters are seen as black or white, and not only in respect to race. One is "for" or "against." Shadings, nuances, and complexities are unfamiliar and rather alarming. These people are disinclined to become confused by value conflicts, such as the conflict between democratic-humanitarian values and racial values. They do not really sense the logical incompatibilities among these ways and views, but habitually apply a given set in particular concrete situations. It is not among these conventionally minded people that we find consistent or significant rejection of the white-over-brown formula.

3. *The Egocentric View*

We have met the *egocentric* view in the families of Andrew R. and Nathan T. It is characteristic of perhaps seven of our white families and twice as many Negro families.

The egocentric view of race consists essentially in having no view at all, or no established mode of responding to race and race difference. It consists in poorly organized value systems and in a residual awareness after one's perceptions have been filtered through a dense screen of personal preoccupations. Hence this view tends to characterize the most psychologically disturbed of our parents and the adult members of our most disorganized families. People like Andrew's parents and Nathan's mother are too lost in a fog of personal troubles to be able to see very much beyond the immediate moment and situation. Their energies are concentrated upon immediate and intimate matters. When race becomes involved in these matters, they see it, and they may see it rationalistically or conventionally, but they see it only secondarily, and in a narrow and intensely personalized framework.

Negroes almost inevitably see it more importantly and more frequently than do whites, however. Their personal preoccupations are likely to have, all of them, a marked racial facet. It can hardly be otherwise, since it is quite impossible for them to escape those status realities about which we have talked before. The difference between these Negroes and the conventionally or rationalistically minded lies in the degree to which the egocentrically minded personalize race problems—see them as parts of their personal problems.

People given to the egocentric view are not likely to be in revolt against the cultural patterns having to do with race. They are often in revolt, but rather against particular limitations upon their particularly cherished freedoms than against any general social limitation. They are concerned with the "me."

Chapter 7

"Such Nice People—"

IN THIS CHAPTER we continue our consideration of the race-related cultural patterns to which our children are being exposed in their homes.

We have seen that they are being exposed to varied interpretations of the white-over-brown formula. But there are other culturally patterned ideas which are relevant to the making of race attitudes. These others bear less directly, but very importantly, upon attitudes about race. We will look now to the nature of these ideas and to the nature of their bearing upon matters of race.

Nice People

All of the race-relevant ideas have something to do with decisions about whether people are or are not "nice." Negroes are often seen by whites as not-nice, and this not simply because they *are* Negroes and because whites have learned to see Negroes in this fashion. Negroes, as individuals, *could* be seen as people, rather than as members of a racial group, and still be seen as not-nice. That is, they could be measured against a set of standards for "niceness" in people and accepted or rejected in terms of those standards alone. In such a case acceptance or rejection would be no matter of racial prejudice, though it might be a matter of other kinds of prejudice. Acceptance or rejection of Negroes solely in terms of nonracial standards is probably very rare. But to be aware of it as a possibility helps us to understand that judgments of people across the line can be made in other than purely racial terms. The judgers may, of course, drag in the nonracial values as afterthoughts, using them to support, defend, or conceal judgments already made in racial terms. We are not concerned here with such conscious or unconscious tricks of the mind. We are concerned rather with the nature of the values which make them possible.

To be importantly concerned with the "niceness" of people, and of things too, is itself a conspicuous feature of American middleclass thinking. Hence it is not surprising that the common American standards for niceness reflect conspicuously middle-class values. Neither the standards nor the values are limited, however, to people whom the sociologist might label "middle class."

The idea of niceness admits of degrees. If it is said that "they are *such* nice people," or "*very* nice people," the people in question are being placed toward the "nicest" end of the scale. But if they are "rather nice," or "nice enough," they are being pegged somewhere down around the middle. When the people under inspection are judged to be close to the not-nice end of the scale, they are "not particularly nice" or even "impossible" or "awful" people.

Blanket judgments like these represent summations of a series of particular judgments made in terms of values which are also ranged along scales. The polar extremes of some of these scales are:

good (straight, decent, steady, clean)—bad (crooked, mean, wild, dirty)

fine (respectable, refined)—coarse (disreputable, crude)

wise (sensible, learned)—foolish (not sensible, ignorant)

polite (courteous, polished, or smooth)—impolite (discourteous, rough)

attractive (pretty or handsome, well-groomed, clean)—unattractive (ugly, messy, dirty)

friendly (sociable, warm-hearted)—unfriendly (unsociable, cold)

careful (reliable, trustworthy)—careless (unreliable, untrustworthy)

thoughtful (considerate, kind)—thoughtless (inconsiderate, unkind)

ambitious (industrious)—shiftless (lazy)

When "they" are said to be "such nice people," it is likely that "they" will already have been found relatively good, fine, wise, polite, attractive, friendly, careful, thoughtful, ambitious —some or all of these.

Returning to our consideration of the families of our children, we shall see how much emphasis they put upon these culturally patterned criteria for niceness in people and even in things (clothes, furniture, houses, etc.). We shall see, too, how niceness judgments are involved with their racial judgments, and what in the way of social orientations these people exhibit.

Niceness—As Brown People See It

1. Joyce's Parents: "Nothing but the best—"

It is the general opinion in her nursery school that Joyce I. is a very pretty child—pretty and sophisticated and charming. It is also agreed that she is something of the "spoiled only child," a little vain and quite self-centered. In spite of that she is a great favorite.

When Joyce arrives at school in the morning hand-in-hand with her mother people are inclined to stop what they are doing and enjoy the sight. The two are much alike in looks anyway, and their common perfection of clothes and grooming makes them more alike and conspicuously attractive. They walk straight and with their heads high. They both know that their clothes are right, that they smell sweet and look lovely, and that Joyce's father is very proud of them.

The pride is quite mutual in Joyce's family. Personal appearance is a matter of intense concern to all of them, and they satisfy one another's quite exacting requirements. Mr. I. is rather on the dark brown side, as Mrs. I. is keenly aware in view of her own very light skin and Joyce's medium brown. But he takes great pains about his appearance too, and when he leaves for work in the morning he looks more like the college student he used to be than like the skilled worker he now is.

Mr. I. is not quite happy, though, with merely looking like a college man. He would be much happier if he could actually be one again, and get that degree he would have had by now except for the war. It could be managed, with G.I. benefits, but it would be hard on them all to get along on so much less than they have. The degree probably would mean rather little more income in the long run anyway than his present job. It would be different if Joyce's mother worked too. She could do secretarial work as she used to before she had Joyce, but she just cannot face the idea of leaving her daughter to anyone else's care for more than an hour or two.

Mrs. I. wants "nothing but the best" for Joyce, so far as her parents can provide it for her, and her father is in complete agreement.

"A college education if we can possibly swing it. Right now we're thankful enough for nursery school! It was hard to get her in there you know—their waiting list and all that. And it costs more than most of the others pay because fees are adjusted to income. It's worth it though to get her education off to a good start and give her that little extra advantage over the others when she gets into public school. There are disadvantages of course. We're *very* careful about the children she plays with at home—just the children of our close friends, and they're all fine people. You can't help her getting in with some rather rough kids at nursery school, but fortunately some of her friends are there and I think she pretty much plays with them. For her age she has a lot of sense about people—she seems to know which ones are nice and which aren't.

"That's what matters to us of course—having friends— attractive people—who have good, sound qualities. We like nice things—we haven't much but when we add another piece of furniture in the apartment, for example, we give it some thought and we buy something good. We hope we have pretty good taste, and we like to be around other people who have it, and people who read a good book now and then and can talk about something beside the weather and each other! We like to be sociable—small as this place is we do have a few people in now and then and we go to their places occasionally, and we enjoy it. The only thing is it's not easy to meet the kind of people we like.

"We have no white friends now. We both had, when we went to mixed schools. But somehow those things don't last. After schooldays we went our own way and they went theirs. We've both worked mostly with white people, and we get along fine. Right now Joyce's father is the only Negro on his job. He's friendly with the fellows—they talk about getting together off the job sometimes—maybe dropping in to see us, but they never do, and we never go to their homes. The church Brotherhood is mixed, but somehow we don't get well acquainted there either.

"It isn't that we care what color our friends are. We feel we're as good as anybody—we just don't feel inferior. But we think the colored are just as wrong to practice self-segregation as the whites are to segregate them. We would mix more with the nice class of whites, but we just don't meet them.

"Having ideas like ours, why naturally we get called 'snobs,' and especially among our own people. They would think I was a snob no matter what I did of course—I'm just too light not to have that kind of trouble. At least I never tried to 'pass'—they don't have that to hold against me. I don't believe in it that's all. I'll not deny being a Negro. But you just don't know what it's like—being called a 'nigger.'

"I'm as much for the race as the next fellow, but they won't believe it if you're not ready to take on just any old uneducated, shiftless person for your best friend because he happens to be colored. And if you maybe see a white person once in a while and act friendly—then you're a snob! Well, then we're snobs I guess, because we like nice people, even if they happen to be white."

2. Tony R.'s Parents: "Away from trash—"

Tony R. is a big, sturdy boy, and you seldom meet a brighter one. He is quick—quick with words, and quick with his fists and his footwork. He should be all these things, since his father and mother and big sister and brother are much the same. They stick close to one another and to their aunts and uncles and cousins. Brains and brawn run in the family, and both have come in very handy.

It is a fighting family—the R.'s "don't take it lying down." Mr. R. has fought and talked his way from a rural slum in Puerto Rico to an urban slum in New Dublin. He has come a long way geographically speaking, and he has made some progress socially speaking, but nothing comparable to what he would have liked. For an ambitious man, being a butcher is nothing to brag about, even though he has seen very little of the inside of a schoolhouse. For a man who has brains and knows it, and who very much wants other people to know it and reward him with the good things of life, there are too few satisfactions in his situation. New Dublin doesn't appreciate him and he hates New Dublin for it. He would "just like to show them something!"

Through his wife, and through his children, Mr. R. does in fact manage to show them something. A man with a handsome wife and three strapping and handsome children has something to brag about, especially when they all pay him the respect due the head of the family and behave themselves the way the wife and children of a West Indian should. The wife is a strong, smart woman who keeps a clean house and knows how to cook and sew and look after her part of the job. The kids don't talk back to their parents, they mind their teachers, get their lessons fast, and know how to take care of themselves in a "tough" neighborhood.

Tough neighborhoods are no novelty to Mr. and Mrs. R. Mr. R. has passed through a good many in his travels, and Mrs. R. grew up in one a good bit tougher than the one in which she now lives. She remembers

". . . how my dad taught my sisters and me to fight—not scratching and hair pulling, but with our fists, like boys. We did, too. You had to in those days, to keep your doll or your all-day sucker or whatever it was. Later on you had to fight sometimes to keep what my dad called 'your honor.' He wanted us to be able to take care of ourselves, but we'd better keep clean and know how to act like ladies too, or we'd get plenty from him! These days things aren't so bad, but still we've had to teach our kids to fight too. I can't keep them dressed nice the way I'd like to—they'd wreck their clothes running around this neighborhood, and anyhow the other kids would call them 'sissies.' I keep them away from the gangs as much as I can. They play together or with their cousins, or I take them to the park or to the beach in the summer. Still they're at school and they get loose around here part of the time, and come home swearing and saying things their father and I won't stand for. When they're outside, they're bound to go in for some rough stuff, but in our home we won't have it. We keep our home as decent as we can.

"One thing the kids have got to learn, and that is to tell right from wrong and what's good from what's bad. They've got to learn to act right themselves and not get mixed up with bad people or wrong things. I tell them if they don't know about a person or something that's happened, they're to ask me—or their father—and we'll straighten them out. I don't want them givin' dirt or takin' dirt from anybody—white or colored, and I make it my business to see that they don't.

"Sometimes down at the nursery school things have happened that made me wonder, and I just went right down and had it out. Like the time Tony came home with a story about how his teacher gave him a good crack. He might have needed it, sure, but I'm not crazy about a teacher cracking my kids, and I'm not afraid to say so. Her being white doesn't cut any ice with me. Of course it turned out that the whole business was one of Tony's big jokes—he just loves to make up a tall story and get somebody excited about it.

"I got plenty excited when I found out one of the kids at nursery school had yelled 'shut up, you big black nigger!' That was no story, that much I found out, but I never did find out which one it was—I would have wrung his nasty little white neck. And what made me maddest was that he didn't do it just once, but he kept it up, and the teacher let him! She should have put a stop to that so fast! In a mixed school I suppose those things are bound to happen once in a while—there are good and bad in all races and some bad white ones are bound to get in. It's their parents of course —they wouldn't act like that if they didn't get it at home.

"Well, I think the nursery school ought to be more careful. It's a good school and they ought to keep it that way. No matter if it's white or if it's some other color—we want to keep our kids away from trash."

3. Thomas J. and His Mother: "Doin' what's right—"

Thomas is big and loud and rough. When he first came to nursery school he had no idea how to play with the other children. He grabbed their toys and threw things at them, but after a while he made some friends and learned to get along with them a part of the time.

Thomas has been alone with his mother most of his life. His father belongs to some mysterious past about which nobody talks. His mother doesn't even talk about that with the Negro social worker who has helped her solve the problems of keeping a roof over her head and food in the mouth of a growing boy. Mrs. J. is the quiet kind anyway, quiet and lonely and shrinking. If anyone but herself and Thomas get into that little third floor tenement room and kitchenette, only she and Thomas know about it.

Neither of them tells very much about what goes on in their lonely little world, or in their minds, but a few things are clear. It is clear that for Mrs. J. her son and his welfare are almost the only things that matter. She speaks at all freely only about Thomas, and when for a minute or two she loses herself in talking about him, there is a wise, kind, and self-respecting woman sitting where before there was a tired, frightened Negro.

For Thomas Mrs. J. was able to go out and ask people— white people—for something because she had decided he needed it.

"He'd never had the chance to play with other kids 'till I got him into nursery school—I thought it would do him a lot of good.—I kept goin' back, and so then after a while they said they'd got a place for him. I couldn't pay very much. I thought for a while maybe they didn't want him. But I guess that wasn't it at all. They're so nice at school— they've been so nice to Tom and I. I guess it don't matter about how much you can pay—or who you are. They want all the children to play and get along nice and learn how to do things right. That's what I want—I want Tom to get along and be doin' what's right.

"He's a good boy—he's kinda rough and a little fresh sometimes—but he's a good boy. He learns things fast too. —I like to be alone and read a lot—he's like that too. When he wasn't three yet I had a little book of alphabet stories I used to read him. He learned his letters that way before he got in school. He learned the Lord's Prayer too, and some Sunday school stories. . . . I tried to send him to the Baptist Church for a while. He learned the stories and come home and told them to me, and he don't forget 'em.

"Tom don't miss a thing. He notices things, but he don't let on. He keeps things inside—he holds things. Like at school—you'd never know how much he notices. Maybe for a long time he won't let out a peep—and then all of a sudden he will. . . He must have heard somebody talkin' about the Japs and the Indians. He ask me one day who they are. I says 'they're people—just like us. Some of 'em are bad—but they're people like us too.'

"Since's he's been goin' to school he's been noticin' people—little things about the way they look and how they act. He's awful fussy about his clothes—and bein' clean and all—and he notices things like that a lot. He likes pretty people and pretty clothes and clean things. Now he's noticin' colored and white. I tell him not to say a person is colored or white—just tell me their name, and if they're nice and pretty and all like that. . . . It's not that he likes one better than the other. It's just that he knows the difference.

"Sometimes he says some funny things about it too. The other day when I was washin' Tom—gettin' him ready for school, he says to me: 'Wash me good Mamma, because some of the children don't wash up so good, especially the colored boys.'—If I was a sensitive person I might have took it different from the way he meant it. I s'pose somethin' happened about it at school. I s'pose his teacher said some child didn't wash up very good, and maybe it just happened to be one of the colored boys."

Niceness—As White People See It

1. Diane T. and Her Mother: "Aim high—"

Diane is as blond as her mother, and she has her mother's devotion to the enhancing of her porcelain prettiness with pretty clothes, appropriately ladylike manners, and coy, feminine ways. Children who don't "play nice" are to be avoided. Mother wouldn't like them.

Mother *didn't* like them, and mother didn't like the nursery school. Diane sometimes came home with her clothes in a mess and wearing the marks of most unladylike battles. A woman alone in the world, a woman who has given her husband to the defense of his country, sees her first obligation to herself and her child. She cannot afford to jeopardize a precarious grip on the ways and the society of "the nicer class of people" by unnecessary contacts with the less-nice class, or by allowing her daughter to develop any undesirable attachments or any peculiar ideas. Furthermore, the nursery school staff proved itself quite unappreciative of the benefits of having people of the T.'s calibre associated with the institution. They not only made no special concessions but behaved as though they had quite failed to recognize superior people when they saw them. It was a really intolerable situation!

It is not, of course, that Mrs. T. is a snob. It is just that the T.'s, mother and daughter, "expect nice things, and aim high."

It was not the interracial character of the nursery school milieu so much as its lower class character which made it impossible for them. But Mrs. T. concludes that

"Naturally, when you have so many Negroes, it is not going to be a very high class group. . . . Now to Diane a colored child is no different than a white child, and I don't mind her playing with the colored children. They're the cutest things when they're young! . . . She plays with them at school and even in our neighborhood she sees a little colored girl now and then. Of course our neighborhood is white—some rather nice old homes and a few apartment houses like ours that aren't pretentious, but better than what you find anywhere else in Lower Harding. I suppose this colored child lives a few streets away. Anyway Diane is very sweet to her when we meet her on the street, but one day the child asked to come upstairs with us and Diane said 'no, no, honey—don't come up.'

"Now of course I wouldn't want my child to treat them any differently. She knows that I stop and chat a little with the colored mothers at the nursery school myself. We'll talk about school and so on and I'll even walk up to the corner with them, but it stops right there. I don't know why— I just don't have any interests with those mothers. I certainly wouldn't encourage them. I don't mind chatting but socially I draw the line. The colored should stay with the colored and the white with the white.—Of course at the nursery school they uphold the colored race—the Director herself leans to the colored! It's hardly the way to run a nice school.

"As I said, I don't mind Diane playing with the colored children, so long as they're clean and decently behaved, and she doesn't either. She can't stand being dirty you know, and I can see that even some of the white children aren't as clean as they might be nor as nice as they might be either. That's what you get when you have such a mixture. But it isn't so much the mixture that I mind, not now, while Diane is little. But I must say that I feel in my own heart that I *hope* she will never find companionship with them after she leaves high school. I can't imagine being attracted to a colored man myself and I don't think my daughter ever would be, but I wouldn't want her to get interested. I certainly wouldn't sanction a mixed marriage! Diane would say to me—Which side am I on?—Where do I belong?—Her child would be very unhappy—only Negroes would accept her. It isn't so bad for the parents as it is for the children. It's very unfair for them.

"The whole thing is to know your own kind and stay with them, white with white and colored with colored, and the better class of whites together. Now we may not be in the social register, but we know some nice people and we're at home with them. They're the kind we should be with. You know you have to be very careful—especially a woman alone—not to lower yourself. And when you have a nice child like Diane, you owe it to her to see that she has the right associations. I've been giving these things a lot of thought lately, and I know one thing I'm going to do. I'm going to take Diane out of that nursery school."

2. Yvonne's Parents: "People like us—"

"She's the funniest child," says Mrs. G. of her daughter, "She's little and skinny and kind of mousy—don't have much to do with the other kids, but she likes them all right. Comes home and chatters on to me like a magpie about this one and that one, but to see her at school you wouldn't think she knew from nothin'.

"And clumsy! What with bein' such a little thing, you wouldn't think so, but as my mother says, she has two left feet. I wouldn't be bothered with it myself, but this friend of mine takes her little girl some place for dancin' lessons and I've let her take Vonnie a couple of times. Thought it might be good for her, but she don't like it much.

"Maybe it's because she's been with me so much, but she gets along with grown-ups better. She's never paid much attention to her little brother. Thinks he's too fresh and rough and he musses up her hair—I curl it sometimes and boy does she love herself with curls! The neighbors think she's wonderful. Such a little lady! Well they don't know her as well as I do—but I don't mean to say she's not a good kid. Vonnie's all right, but I don't know where she gets some of her ideas.

"She gets around and talks to people, of course, that's part of it. She chins with all the women around here and brings me the news—in case I've missed anything. I get around and do some chinning myself of course. Sure, I like to talk—my husband's the quiet type—he says he don't get in a word edgeways, but gee, I'd go crazy if I couldn't get out and see people. He comes home dead tired from drivin' the truck all day and he don't even pay much attention to the kids. Me—I like to be sociable, sit down and have a cup of coffee with one of the other mothers on the way home from nursery school—have a beer and relax in the afternoon—enjoy life a little. I keep my place clean and I make the kids pick up their stuff and not throw magazines around all over the place and so on, but I don't see no point in knockin' yourself out. Life's too short. As my mother says—if you don't have a little fun while you're young, you never will.

"My mother lives just a little way from us you know. I grew up right here in this neighborhood—right where my mother lives now. It used to be kinda nice around here but now everybody's poor like us. Houses all fallin' down around our ears, and a lotta new people comin' in. The priest was tellin' me the other day that it's not just us Irish around here now—everything else you can think of, even 'niggers' comin' in, but not right around us yet.

"Well I'm used to them from down at the nursery school. Of course most of the mothers there are all right, and I can be nice to them, but I wouldn't go any farther. I always say there are 'niggers' an' then there are Negroes. Now people like Vonnie's teacher and most of those mothers—they're Negroes. Why Helen's mother—I've been real friendly with her and what if she didn't go and get huffy one day about some little thing I said—she and that Jewish woman she pals around with. That's the way they are—ready to take offense. I didn't mean nothing—all I did was tell them about what happened the other day when Vonnie and me were goin' home from school. We passed this black man, and he just about butted me off the sidewalk. Well I was so mad—I guess I said somethin' to him —not very loud, but when we got home, Vonnie wanted to know what I said. So I tried to pass it off and told her I hadn't said anything much. Well she's pretty sharp some-times—I had to laugh. She says 'Oh yes you did say some-thing mama, you said "nigger." At school we don't say that—we say "colored people." ' Well now, I ask you—wasn't that one for the book—and the funny part is I didn't even know she knew the word 'colored' but I knew she saw the difference all right, and I thought sometimes she stood back a little.

"Well anyways these two mothers acted like I'd com-mitted a crime after I told 'em this story. It just goes to show you can't get along with 'em—not people like me anyways. Of course the lower classes—people who don't care *what* they do—will intermarry and associate. And then the upper classes—people who've been to college and so on—they will associate. They find a Negro who's been educated and speaks their language, and they can get along with him all right. But the middle classes—and I don't know, but I think that's people like us—they just don't mix. That's all there is to it—mixin' is no good for people like us."

3. Patsy's Parents: "Other people's feelin's—"

People are inclined to feel sorry for Patsy G., and to try to be kind to her. Patsy has so little. If she were a more attractive child it would be easier to give her the extra atten-tion and loving she wants and needs so much. But she is a big, lumbering child who squints badly behind the round glasses on her big, round face. Her babyish whining, her way of clinging to the teachers at nursery school and to strangers —especially to men—is hardly winning. But she tries to please, and when she sings and dances with the other chil-dren, she can be quite animated and surprisingly pleasant to watch.

Seeing her at home, it is not hard to understand why Patsy whines and clings to grown-ups and plays up to the occa-sional male visitor at school. At home she is an incidental item among the five other children, all of them but one bigger and overpoweringly noisy. They tumble over one an-other in the crowded disorder of the G.'s tenement flat in Lower Dover where Mrs. G. tries to keep some kind of home together on the monthly "relief" check. She is too tired, too worried, or too busy to pay Patsy any particular attention.

She tries to keep the three big boys and the big girl from heckling the child too unmercifully or kicking her around. And she does whatever else she can manage. Somebody gets Patsy to nursery school dressed in whatever is reasonably whole, reasonably clean, and something like her size. Somebody brings her home again, and Mrs. G. keeps her "off the streets" sometimes when it occurs to her to wonder about Patsy's comings and goings. Otherwise Patsy plays with the Syrian or Italian children on the block, or by herself if nobody wants her around.

Times are hard for the G.'s, but in some ways better than before Mr. G. moved out. They should have had more money before—cab drivers sometimes make a decent week's pay—but the wife and kids don't necessarily see much of it. There are dozens of dingy bars on the streets around the G.'s place, and it was the barkeeps who saw most of the pay and who had most of Mr. G.'s company, such as it was. Even they, and the boys around the bar, got tired of hearing about what a fine country is old England, and about what a big man Mr. G. would have been had he not made the mistake of wandering far away and eventually into a hole like Lower Dover. But the boys didn't have to take it when "the old man" staggered home to work off his bitterness on the wife and kids, or listen through the night to his exhausted snoring when the beatings were over.

It is better to get along on what the city provides. No beatings now—Mrs. G. hasn't the heart for more than spankings, even when she thinks a good beating might be in order. Even so Patsy pines for a father, and vaguely hopes the next grown man she sees will be the one.

Patsy's mother does what has to be done, or just a little more. She thinks about what has to be thought about, or what she can't help thinking about. The future is uncertain and better not thought about.

"It would be nice if all the kids could finish high school. —They oughta get to the Baptist Sunday School once in a while—teach 'em to be quiet and read the Bible—that's good for 'em. . . They shouldn't get into fights on the streets—the cops'll be after 'em again. Fightin'—plenty of fightin'. Fightin' in the house an' fightin' on the street. . . . Gangs after each other—whites against the colored from a coupla blocks away. But my biggest boy has colored

friends. . . . Funny, they're friends, but they don't get
along. I tell 'em—maybe they'd get along better if they'd
stop yellin' dirty names at each other. They don't call no
such names in this house—we got some respect for other
people's feelin's. We ain't got much, but we got that. My
friend Mrs. P., with that colored husband and those half-
colored kids, they've got plenty of feelin's. Can't do nothin'
much about it—the race business. It's tough for 'em—they
got it awful hard. I'm not goin' to make it no harder,
nor my kids neither, not if I c'n help it. . . . Be a lot less
trouble in this world if people cared sumthin' about other
people's feelin's."

Niceness Standards and Social Orientations

We have met six families differing from one another in
many ways. The variations in which we are chiefly interested
here, however, are matters of race and matters of standards
for niceness in people and in things.

Our six families fall into three groups to which the sociologist would at once attach labels having to do with their
position in the social class hierarchy of the community. These
families might well be tagged "lower-middle," "upper-lower,"
and "lower-lower" class, although they do not conform in all
respects to the usual criteria for these class groups. But we
are not primarily concerned here with establishing class
identity. Rather we are concerned with the nature of *social
orientations*. We shall label our three types of families in
terms of social orientations in order to focus attention on
their "niceness" standards and on the relation between these
and their race attitudes.

The distinctive social orientations which recur among the
families of our children we shall call the *choosing*, the *avoiding*, and the *accepting* orientations.

1. *The Choosing Orientation*

Joyce I. and Diane T. are children whose parents are in a
position to be somewhat "choosy" about their own and their
children's associates and surroundings. The I.'s and Mrs. T.
have security and a body of ideas which allow them to be
selective. They are "better off" financially and socially than
many of their associates and highly conscious of the fact.

Their social advantage lies in their own possession of a number of the more highly valued "niceness" traits. They have social "know-how," at any rate, and are themselves socially desirable people, from the viewpoint of their immediate neighbors. These and others of our parents who incline to *choosing* are people highly conscious of what they are doing now and of what they wish to do in the future. They have some perspective on their social status in relation to that of other people, and an awareness of their long-range social direction.

The I.'s are quite representative of our *choosing* Negro families. The I.'s want "nothing but the best" for their Joyce, within their present and future limitations. They plan, scheme, consider, and scrutinize possibilities and opportunities for reducing those limitations. They cultivate the appearance, the living conditions, the social habits, and the aspirations of the people whom they have chosen as their kind—that is, as the kind they are and want to be. They know very surely the nature of that social kind, and they speedily recognize examples of it when they meet them. So does Joyce, whose selective orientation is as nearly that of her parents as her relative maturity allows.

The social kind chosen by the I.'s has no color. They know it to be a kind more commonly associated with white people, and to that extent they are drawn toward whites. Moreover, they have a sense of racial insecurity which can be relieved only by acceptance by white people. For these reasons they would choose whites of their kind as friends if they could, but they find almost no opportunity to do so. Neither their contacts nor the attitudes of the whites allow them to exercise this choice.

Mrs. T. is an example of the choosing orientation in our white families. She "aims high" and "expects nice things." She plans, schemes, cultivates, etc., just as do the I.'s. She too has chosen a social kind, and has communicated the choice to her child. Diane is in this respect a remarkable carbon copy of her mother. There are no major differences save one between Mrs. T.'s niceness standards and those of the I.'s. The difference is all-important in respect to race relations, for Mrs. T., unlike the I.'s, sees her social kind as having but one possible color—her own. She sees nice people as white and not-nice ones as colored. Since niceness is to her of such importance, the people who do not have it, or whom she believes to be without it, are beyond the pale. Her emphasis on niceness reenforces her anti-Negro orientation.

For others of our white parents it does not work that way, or does not do so to the same extent. But on the whole our choice-oriented white families (about eleven, all told) are among those Harding and Dover people who do not stay in the area too long or who are even less intimately a part of it than is Mrs. T. The others either are on the way out, into a "nicer" neighborhood, or else feel reasonably sure of getting out when and if they want to. Their Negro neighbors may look a little nicer to them on the eve of their ceasing to be such. At any rate, these whites, who are often also people of rationalistic race views, tend to be able, at least upon occasion, to see niceness first and a brown skin second. They tend to exercise some conscious choice in respect to Negroes, using the same yardsticks they use against whites.

Our Negro families who are choice-oriented (about thirteen) are not always quite so happy about association with whites as are Joyce I.'s parents. Five or six of them are rather too overcome by feelings of racial insecurity, inferiority, and defensiveness to be able to apply their "everyday" niceness standards to whites. The rest, like the I.'s, would like nothing better than to be able to pick and choose on a basis of niceness as they see it, with race as a very secondary matter.

The children in both the white and Negro families are inclined to be concerned with niceness, and to be selective about people and things in terms of niceness standards.[1] But they exhibit less inclination than their parents to see color first and niceness second. It is true, however, that they *see* things in this order more frequently than one would judge after observing what they *do*. We have noted earlier the marked discrepancy between the four-year-old's ideas about race and his actions concerning it. Whether brown or white himself he is in fact learning to associate color with non-niceness (especially with uncleanness and unprettiness). But still, even the white child, when he meets a particular colored person, is likely to be most struck by the qualities and attributes which are individual matters. If he finds these "nice," there are likely to be few reservations in his dealings with the person of color.

In short, our children of choosing families are learning to

choose, and to choose as their parents do. As yet, however, they choose with less tendency to see color first and niceness second, or to see less niceness, or none, where there is color.

2. *The Avoiding Orientation*

In Tony R.'s family, and in Yvonne G.'s, there exists a social orientation which is primarily of an *avoiding* type. These people have a sense of social direction, not so much *toward* selected kinds of persons and things, as *away from* certain kinds. Their concern is less with what they want than with what they do not want. They have less general security than the *choosers*, and less inclination to map out a road to a well-defined goal. It may be that the two conditions tend to go together quite naturally. When there are no very good reasons for "expecting nice things" (or things much better than one has), it is probably more comforting not to think too much about future roads or goals. The avoider is primarily concerned with keeping what he has—with staying "away from trash" and its possible contaminations—and hanging on to such relatively nice people and things as he has.

The value systems having to do with niceness are fairly clear-cut and uncomplicated. Good and bad, right and wrong are sharply different and largely either-or matters, as Mrs. R.'s comments suggest. Furthermore, there are, as Mrs. G. says, people above and people below the "people like us," and modes of behavior appropriate to each group. As the R.'s avoid "trash," Mrs. G. avoids situations inappropriate to people like herself. But the R.'s find that there are people and behaviors on both sides of the color line which they wish to avoid. Mrs. G. is most concerned with avoiding the people on the other side of the line. Her avoidance orientations reenforce her adherence to the white-over-brown formula just as did Mrs. T.'s choosing orientations.

About one-half of our 103 children, among both browns and whites, have parents who are primarily oriented along avoidance lines. This orientation goes along with a more or less marked interracial friendliness in the cases of about half of the white avoiders and two-thirds of the Negroes. These differences between the race groups are not particularly striking. It appears that in either group avoidance may or may not support interracial withdrawal or antagonism. But it is of interest to find white avoiders more frequently nonfriendly than are white choosers. Among Negroes the choosing or avoiding orientation seems to be less significant in relation to race attitudes.

The whites of the avoiding type are about evenly divided between people like Yvonne's parents, whose general avoidance supports Negro avoidance, and people in whom this combination does not operate. At least it does not operate strongly enough to produce clearly nonfriendly attitudes toward Negroes. With few exceptions the children in these white families exhibit across-the-line orientations much like those of their parents.

The Negroes who are avoidance-oriented show, as we have noted above, a somewhat higher incidence of interracial friendliness than do the whites. The most interesting difference between the race groups, however, appears in the children. Where the children of the whites usually follow their parents, the children in the Negro families follow less frequently. The children in the Negro families are friendly toward whites with but two exceptions (as compared with ten exceptions among parents). We found the Negro children in choosing-oriented families friendly too, irrespective of their parents' attitudes. So the Negroes tend to produce four-year-olds who are friendly, whether their parents *choose* or *avoid*, whether their parents are friendly or nonfriendly. The children of the avoidance-oriented whites are inclined to have learned racial avoidance along with general avoidance. It is in this group of children that we find most of the whites who are nonfriendly toward Negroes.

3. *The Accepting Orientation*

In families like Thomas' and Patsy G.'s there can be no question of much choosing, nor even of much avoiding. Getting along with people, and the getting of things, involves largely *accepting* whatever one can get. Where there are more possibilities than one, choice or avoidance can, of course, be exercised, but the possibilities are generally very limited.

Niceness emphases among these people tend to be matters of secondary concern. Adherence to simple and rather isolated principles—respect for other people's feelings, doing what is right, etc.—may be strong. But they lack an organized set of standards. Generally these people tend toward preoccupation with more immediate and pressing concerns than niceness in themselves or others.

In our eight accepting families who are white we are not unlikely to find acceptance of browns. Rejection is about as likely, however, and under some circumstances the rejection is strong. On the whole it is rather passive. The acceptance of Negroes tends to be passive too, but supported by such niceness principles (e.g., respect for the other fellow) as may have survived hard times and personal disorganizations.

All our Negro families of the accepting type show more or less fearful and defensive withdrawal, if not real antagonism, toward whites. They tend to have little to do with whites, and to regard whites as distinctly not-nice in the sense of being mean, powerful, dangerous, etc.

The children of both the whites and the browns tend to follow their parents closely in respect to feeble development of niceness standards. They just "like" or "don't like" the people they happen to meet, and matters of cleanliness and politeness are not very important. But prettiness is important, and the white children see prettiness as nearly inseparable from whiteness. It is very closely associated with whiteness or lightness in the minds of the Negro children too. For all that, these children, white and brown, are not given to across-the-line antagonism. A few show such orientation in a diffuse way or upon occasion, but there is no general trend toward interracial antagonisms among the children in either group.

Niceness and Race: Words and Values

It is difficult to demonstrate the importance of niceness standards in relation to race attitudes. Much of this relationship operates on a level which is beyond the conscious recognition of the people in whom it works. It has to be inferred by the Observer. A consideration of words which have both racial and niceness meanings, and of the values associated with them, will provide a basis for some logical inferences.

1. "Clean" and "Dirty"

There are words which Americans habitually use to describe properties or conditions which they usually like. There are others which they use just as habitually to describe properties or conditions which they usually do not like. The particular words and these habits of using them are, of course, matters of culture. The liking or not liking of certain properties or conditions is largely culturally determined, but not entirely so.

For example, American mothers are likely to use the word "clean" in respect to a condition which they like. The word might just as well be "glub." "Clean" is a wholly arbitrary designation which happens to have evolved among the other arbitrary sound combinations which we call the English language. This is the view of the objective observer, but it has nothing whatever to do with mother's view when she puts away the "nice, clean clothes," admires sister's "clean, shiny hair," or brother's for once "perfectly clean hands and face." She may rejoice in a "clean, new coat of paint on the kitchen walls," in a "clean, freshly scrubbed floor," in "clean, white shoes," or in any number of other clean things. In any case her basic views combine two ideas: (1) cleanliness is desirable in itself, (2) clean things are likely to have other desirable qualities—they are likely to be also nice, sweet-smelling, shiny, new, fresh, white, or to have any number of other pleasant attributes.

Cleanliness and the qualities associated with it are desirable to mother, and they quite soon begin to be desirable to her children, largely because they are culturally standardized desirables. These are among the "of course" values of American culture, and of some other cultures, too. But mother, like her Puritan cultural forebears, is likely to take a rather extreme view of the value of cleanliness, etc. The "cleanliness is next to Godliness" idea is more alive than many other traditional Americanisms, though today cleanliness is next to, and essential to, social success. But even apart from cultural traditions there are reasons for the high valuation of cleanliness. Once it has been experienced people are likely to begin to feel physically uncomfortable in close company with dirtiness. Furthermore, cleanliness quite naturally suggests whiteness, lightness, brightness, sunshine, fresh air, and some sensations of being in or around these conditions. It takes rather little, if any, cultural pressure to teach one to enjoy sunshine and fresh air. Probably, too, little if any is required to establish a chain of associations between cleanliness and pleasant sensations, or between dirtiness and unpleasant sensations. Our culture heavily reenforces such natural inclinations.

In American society one does not go far toward middle-class prestige or acceptance without being quite clean about one's home, belongings, and most especially about one's person. Personal cleanliness might help in almost any society, but in one so richly endowed with washing machines, bathtubs, and hot and cold running water it has become a prerequisite. One may *look* cleaner than he is, however, or one may actually *be* cleaner than he looks.

It is at this point that we come back to niceness words and race. The white man may look cleaner than he is and the colored man may actually be much cleaner than he looks.

The white man's cleanliness may be exaggerated because where there is lightness Americans are accustomed to see cleanliness. And where there is cleanliness they are accustomed to see the pleasant and desirable. Conversely, the colored man's cleanliness may be underestimated, or assumed to be absent, because where there is darkness Americans are accustomed to see dirtiness. Where they see dirtiness they are accustomed to see the unpleasant and undesirable.

Certainly our four-year-olds show strong inclinations toward exactly these associations. They chatter about their nice, clean hands, shoes, shirt, paper, bib, bed sheet, etc. The mention of cleanness is obviously by way of expressing pride or pleasure. It comes in the same breath with other words which also convey the idea of desirableness. Their almost equally numerous references to dirtiness just as clearly mean disapproval, displeasure, withdrawal, or rejection. Hence, when these same children say that a person looks dirty, we know he is not paying a compliment. He is expressing dislike of at least this aspect of the person.

We have noted before how frequently our children speak of Negroes as "dirty." They cannot possibly know, most of the time, whether the Negro actually is or is not dirty. They assume that he must be, because he is dark (or because he is not light). Color in the skin is seen as dark = dirty = unpleasant (not light, clean, pleasant, pretty, nice, perhaps even not-good.)

At least half of our children, of both races, have at one time or another remarked upon the "dirtiness" they thought they saw about people of color. A good many of them have done more than merely remark, in a casual way. "Dirty" is used as an epithet, or as a part of one. The casual remarks may be, and probably often are, the result of the child's own and independent observation. No one need have taught him to describe a Negro as "dirty," and he need have heard no one else do so. He may even have hit upon the use of "dirty" as an epithet quite by himself, though this is less likely.

The point is that a whole battery of unfavorable associations can arise around a Negro the moment the child sees him as "dirty." Most of our children are being exposed to a marked emphasis on cleanliness, and most especially on personal cleanliness. In view of this a child could conceivably wind up strongly inclined to reject Negroes, and having evolved the whole attitude by himself and starting from a strong negative attitude toward dirtiness.

He could, but he rarely if ever does. For along his path he meets, sooner or later, quite a large number of other words which tend to build unpleasant associations around Negroes.

2. "Black" and "White"

The child is likely, for instance, to hear the word "black" attached to Negroes. Since, in common usage, it has a meaning the very opposite of white, it carries with it the notion that people so labeled are the very opposite of white. Whatever ideas he may have or get about the desirability of whiteness (in people or things) can quite automatically lead to convictions concerning the undesirability of its opposite (in people or things). But the child does not even have to think of white and black as opposites in order to conclude that black people or things are undesirable. "Black" suggests dirt, darkness, death, and evil.

The oppositeness conveyed by "black" and "white" tends, as we have noted earlier, to underscore not only difference but also a wide separation. The fact that these terms are so commonly used as racial labels is an extremely important symptom *and* an important cause of the nature of American race relations. They suggest no in-between. They suggest that race is an either-or matter. Socially speaking it is. Biologically speaking, of course, it is not. But by the time the child is able to register this fact his thinking is likely to be well set in the either-or mold. Getting set in such a mold is almost inevitable in a culture which teaches many other either-or thought-ways (good-bad, right-wrong, etc.).

3. "Coarse" and "Fine"

Americans like "fine" things. The word has a wide range of applications to conditions and properties which are regarded favorably. The mothers of our four-year-olds speak often of "fine people." But their children hear the word in many other and in more specific usages. There are fine (and coarse) materials, fine houses, cars, books, movies—practically anything much liked may be described as "fine." So the general meaning of the word can hardly fail to be crystal clear to even a four-year-old.

When personal attributes are so described, the meaning is equally clear, and it is the attributes of whites which are "fine." They have fine (or smooth or silky) hair and Negroes have coarse (or kinky or rough) hair. Whites have "fine features," meaning small or delicate noses and mouths. Negroes have "coarse features," meaning broad noses and thick lips.

The child does not need to hear Negroes described in this fashion, or see Negroes who might reasonably be so described, in order to get the general idea that they *should* be so described. He has only to become accustomed to hearing "fine" and similar words attached to the attributes of whites. Then, as he gets the idea that Negroes are the opposite, he will think of and use words opposite to fine (etc.) in connection with Negroes. When he sees people whom he can identify as Negroes, he will mentally register any "coarse" features, physical or social, which they happen to have. He will be quite likely to fail to register any fine physical or social features they happen to have, since he is not prepared to expect them. The more learned he becomes in the ways of his culture the more he will see, and remember, what he expects to see.

It is highly probable that the learning of these and other value-laden words plays an important part in the making of race attitudes. These learnings, plus the influence of the parents' social orientations, are as important as specific exposures to the white-over-brown formula.

Chapter 8

"Friends and Relations—"

AS WE HAVE SEEN, our children are being exposed to family versions of major cultural patterns. Among these patterns are the culturally standardized ideas about race and race relations, and about niceness in things and in people. We have seen something of the recurrent types of family versions along both lines. We will now go on to an overview of these types, and to see how our parents do or do not instruct their children about race. Thereafter we will consider from what people, besides their parents, our four-year-olds have been getting their ideas about race.

Types of Race Views and of Social Orientations

Some of our children have parents whose view of race is primarily *rationalistic*. These people may or may not also feel friendly toward racially different people. They may or may not be satisfied with their own racial status. But in any event they have a way of looking at race which admits of the possibility of social arrangements different from those which now generally exist. They have also a sense of the value conflicts involved in the prevalent white-over-brown formula. Such parents give their children a picture of race relations as being complex and not entirely static.

Some of our children have parents who regard niceness in

people and things as very important, and who are in a position to choose the "nice." They may or may not be in the habit of seeing either niceness or the lack of it as existing in and around people of widely differing colors. If this is not their habit, they are inadvertently underscoring the ideas of racial separation and differential valuing. If it is their habit, they are contributing to the weakening of these ideas in the minds of their children. Some of our parents do contribute in this fashion and at the same time give a *rationalistic* view of race. The children in such families get a picture of people differing in niceness and differing in color as well, but no picture of "nice people" done in a monotone.

We have in our sample about eight each of white and of brown families in which there exists a combination of *rationalistic race view* and *choosing social orientation*. There are a few exceptions, but most of these parents, of both races, are basically friendly across the color line. This does not mean that the whites actively seek out and cultivate Negro friends, or even that they have no reservations about "social intimacy." It means for the whites a relative rather than an absolute emancipation from the white-over-brown formula, and it means much the same for the Negroes. The four-year-olds in these families fall largely in our medium-awareness category, and they are without exception primarily friendly in their across-the-line orientations.

We have other children, and many more of them, whose parents view race relations in a quite *conventional* manner. These people have a general resistance to departures from simple We-They thinking about race. Often they are also people inclined to emphasize niceness in a rather negative way. They are inclined to avoid what they regard as not-nice people and situations, and cross-racial contacts fall into this category rather often (rather more often for the whites than for the Negroes). Racial *conventionality* and habits of social *avoidance* may or may not go along with racial antagonisms in the parents, but the combination is frequently met. The four-year-olds in *conventional-avoiding* families are not given to cross-racial antagonisms if they are Negroes. If they are white, they are as likely to show antagonisms as anything else.

Still others of our children have parents whose views of race are of the *egocentric* sort. They see it almost entirely in relation to themselves and their immediate problems. These are often the people whose social orientation is largely of an *accepting* sort, with rather little emphasis put upon niceness. Among these people, parents and children, there are no marked trends in respect to race orientations save a strong tendency toward fearful and defensive attitudes among the Negro parents.

Parents and Other People

Parents *are* people, though their offspring, upon reaching an age of some independence, may be inclined to regard them as something else or something less. They are extremely important people, from the viewpoint of the four-year-old who has by no means reached such a state of independence. The objective observer will agree with the four-year-old, and recognize his parents as his most important source of ideas about his world. But he will also recognize some other important sources, and he will want to know how parents deal with matters of race where their offspring are involved.

Our parents tell us repeatedly that they hold other parents fully responsible for the ideas about race which turn up in children belonging to these other parents.

> "The child wouldn't say it if he didn't hear it in his home.—What else can you expect when the parents do it themselves.—It's the home—that's where they get it."

Comments like these we heard repeatedly. But these same people are shocked or at least surprised when informed that their very own little darling has been known to use some of the "vile language" or the racial epithets which other people's children must have learned at home. Theirs did not, of that they are usually very sure, and they are usually quite sincere about it.

However, the urgency with which parents disclaim their own responsibility tells an interesting story about their feelings. They unconsciously shift responsibility out of a sense of guilt. They very probably have race feelings which they would not care to advertise too widely. Hence they feel guilty whether they have or have not consciously aired these feelings before their children.

Policy vs. Practice

We conclude that very often parents are less responsible for the race attitudes of their children than they are generally believed to be. At the same time we are also impressed by the fact that parents are remarkably unconscious of the things they say in the hearing of their children—even of the things they do. We conclude too that they are uneasy with the subject of race, out of a sense of guilt, out of personal pain associated with race, or just out of a sense of incompetence in coping with matters of race.

Whatever the reasons, policy and practice often diverge sharply. Mrs. M., for example, seems quite unaware of the inconsistencies between what she "preaches" and what she "practices." Mrs. M. tells us that

> ". . . kids should not make any difference. That's why it is *not* a good idea for Carol to have a colored doll—just put ideas into her head and start her thinking. But I'll answer questions when she asks. Right now she thinks she's white—imagine—as dark as she is! So I tried to prove it to her. I held up the mirror to show her how she is—and darker than I am. When you (the Observer) were coming I asked her what kind of person you were, and if you were the same kind as her grandmother, or like the insurance man. She didn't seem to know."

Nadine's mother (N) has tried to discourage references to people in terms of race or color. This is a common policy (and a less common practice) among our parents both Negro and white. But like most other parents, Nadine's mother has not succeeded in preventing her children from "making a difference." Mrs. G. admits the fact, and in this respect she *is* unusual. She also admits her embarrassment when the issue is raised by her children, as well as her inability to cope with it. She believes she should answer questions frankly, but she admits that she lives in fear and anticipation of questions which she will be unable to answer satisfactorily.

Parental Unconsciousness

Parents tell us they will not let their children use racial epithets in the home. Then these parents proceed to use them, or they give us some good reasons for believing that they do so when they are not on their best behavior. Furthermore, the child does not need to hear racial epithets at home to be home-stimulated to use them. He can "get it at home," but "it" can be a general atmosphere of racial antagonism rather than the specific words with which to express the antagonism. He can "get" the atmosphere through a thousand big and little actions or inactions by his parents—things they do or fail to do, their gestures, facial expressions, tone of voice—in matters having to do with racially different people. He can "get" elsewhere the specific words in which to express antagonisms, or he can even invent them himself.

Our parents are generally quite unconscious of the importance of the general atmospheres they create, and even of the nature of these atmospheres. They are usually under the impression that they do not "teach" the child such prejudices as they may be able to admit that they themselves feel (and they are unlikely to admit to as much as they feel). It is true that they do not often consciously teach anything very significant about race. This being the case they can with a clear conscience state that since "we don't want our child to be prejudiced—we don't discuss race in front of him." The statement, however sincere, generally means that for one or several important reasons *in addition to* the one given, the parents feel more comfortable when they can avoid the topic.

Parental Avoidance

There is a prevalent feeling among our parents that race, like sex, is a rather hazardous topic and one best left alone, at least so far as the children are concerned. They feel so partly because both topics rouse their own emotions. They feel insecure in the company of both topics; they do not know how to treat them or what to say to their children about them. There are exceptions, of course. Our parents who take a *rationalistic view* of race are likely to be better able to cope with the subject, both because they can be less emotional about it and because they are better informed.

The white parents are likely to have the basically guilty emotions to which we have referred above. In some deep part of themselves there is a feeling that it is not right to hate or even generally reject Negroes *because* they are Negroes. In most of them there are some feelings about Negroes which can thus become a source of guilt. It is natural enough to avoid a topic about which one has guilty feelings, especially when it is so easy to convince oneself that no good can come of discussing it anyway. For example, "The child isn't old enough to understand," "Things (race relations) have been this way for generations and they're not going to be much different," or "There's nothing I (we) can do about it anyhow."

Our Negro parents have much deeper, stronger, and more personal emotions about race. It is a topic to which their attention is riveted, and at the same time the one topic above most others which they would like to forget. If they can forget it a little in their relations with their children, they hope to be so much the happier. And they, like the white parents, can so easily and similarly convince themselves that there's "no use talking about it" with the child anyway. Gail's mother will sometimes speak of a "colored" person, when Gail is around. Her father wishes she wouldn't, because "children will know these things soon enough. You can create things. . . . A young child doesn't understand and there's no use telling them a lot about colored and white and so on." Cynthia's mother tells us: "When it comes to the question of color I never say anything. They just have to meet problems and take care of themselves. We don't tell them anything about it, but still, *they know*."

In spite of their emotional involvements, both groups of parents could face racial discussions more easily if they knew what to say. They are not at all sure what one *ought* to think or feel about race, sometimes not sure what they *do* think or feel about it, and often quite sure that they ought not to tell their children what they think or feel about it. The more concerned they are with giving their children the "right" ideas, the more difficulty is created by their own uncertainties. In addition, they seldom have any adequate answers to questions like "why are Negroes black?" Not many of our parents have much more to offer in reply than "God made them that way." Even the parents have some sense of the inadequacy of such answers or of answers like the one Mrs. K. gave her Billy: "Why are they so dark? Why, because they sit in the sun."

The Negro parents tend to be particularly confused about what to say. Most of them wonder, in advance, what they will do when *the* subject comes up. Few of them make up their minds, and even fewer actually do it when the moment comes. Mrs. H., for example, tells us that

"I've said nothing to David except about things like his calling me 'boogy' because I'm darker than he is. I just said 'that's not nice. Take it outside.' . . . He hasn't mentioned it since. I don't say anything about his calling the dark children 'chocolate.' I have to laugh. . . . But when he's older—maybe five or six—he'll know the difference! There'll be nothing funny about that. When he asks questions—I don't know *what* I'll do. . . . I don't know what I'll say. . . . Thank God he hasn't asked any questions yet."

Mrs. H., like most of our Negro parents, will probably continue as she has begun. She will, that is, continue by largely avoiding the issue. She will deal piecemeal with the piecemeal evidences of David's growing awareness, without having ever made up her mind about what to do in a general way. She will dodge the tough ones—the "what am I" and "why are we" and "why are they" questions—as long as she can. She will answer them with few words and much embarrassment when she finds herself unable to dodge.

Mrs. H. is dodging now, by pretending to herself that David does not yet "know the difference." David is not entirely clear about the difference, it is true (he is one of our medium-awareness children). But the parents of children of high awareness "kid themselves" too—Colin's mother, for example. Colin is very much interested in the matter of race. He has a consistent sense of color kinds and a quite adequate racial vocabulary. He is even aware of family racial preoccupations. About the picture of a white man and woman, he said:

"Those are the people Mother and my grandmother are always talking about. Mother and Grandma would like them to come to visit us. Not the other ones (pictured Negro couple)—just the white."

But Colin's mother can tell herself that

". . . he knows no race difference now. Oh yes, he will describe people as 'white' or 'colored,' but I've told him he shouldn't comment on people's color, and his grandmother has told him never to call anybody 'black.' . . . He has never asked *why* they're different, but his grandmother did explain to him that God made the different shades and they're all alike. . . . She always answered all my questions —I think it's the parents' job—and I'm going to do the same. I'm going to tell Colin anything he wants to know, *when it's time*, and as much as he *should* know."

In spite of her convictions about her "job," Colin's mother is quite happy to see the job as something which she does not have to face *now*. Winona's parents were happy too at being able to put off Winona's puzzled questions. The questions followed upon a domestic scene raised by father after Winona had called someone a "nigger." "What does it mean?" Winona wanted to know. "Never mind," said her mother. "When you're older you'll know." Joyce's parents plan to "just sit down and talk to Joyce, *but not until the problem arises*. It's the parents' job—before she hears it the wrong way—or from white people."

Sometimes parents find a way out by telling themselves exactly the opposite, that is, by telling themselves that it is *not* their job, now or later. Joan M.'s mother deplores the fact that

". . . parents *tell* their children. If they would just leave them alone. . . . Oh I sometimes wonder what to do about it, but you can just ignore their questions."

Facing the Issue

A few of our Negro parents are able to face race discussions squarely if not entirely happily.

Gerard's mother, for example, undertook an explanation when Gerard's six-year-old brother came home with the news that "somebody is going to give away candy to the 'Brownies,' so I'll get some because I'm brown." Mrs. D. explained that

". . . they weren't talking about you honey, but you *are* brown. There are two colors of people—brown and white. They are two races. But even in each race there are different colors. Your grandma, for instance, is lighter than I am."

Alfred D.'s mother faces the matter realistically and firmly and crisply. A crucial exchange between herself and her son ran like this: Alfred: "What am I?" Mrs. D.: "You're colored." Alfred: "Why?" Mrs. D.: "Because your mommy and daddy are colored."

Our white parents do not have to cope with the "what am I" questions. They do not have to face the complexities of preparing their children for a status of extreme racial inferiority. They are not haunted by fears about whether their children will be able to "take it," or by painful personal memories of having taken it themselves. For these reasons, it is much easier for them to discuss race with their children. Yet few can do so as calmly as do Pamela's highly *rationalistic* parents.

Pamela's parents are informed, realistic, and sympathetic. They engage in lengthy intellectualizing about race, and

> "Pam gets it all if she's around. We don't try to keep her out of it. She knows a good deal about race and she's very much interested. When she asks questions we answer them as directly and as truthfully as we can."

Rosemarie's parents, though less well informed, are equally sympathetic toward Negroes and equally direct with their children. Mrs. F. reads her children

> ". . . little books about the different races. . . . I have told Rosemarie that God made the Negro children the way they are, but there really isn't much difference between them and her or her brother. . . . That was the only thing I could think of to say. . . . I don't want to give them just any kind of answer. I've tried to bring them up to feel no different."

Communication Problems

Communication between our parents and their children is often a devious process. We have just considered some of the reasons, but there are still others. The nature of both husband-wife and parent-child relations has its effects upon the parent-child lines of communication.

Among our families there is a high frequency of marital difficulties. About a fourth of our children see little or nothing of their fathers. The fathers of three are dead. A few fathers are in the armed services, the rest have left their wives or have been asked to leave, temporarily or permanently. There is one child whose mother has, in effect, deserted, and there are two who live with adoptive parents. In the families of ten more there is serious strife between husband and wife. That leaves about sixty percent of our four-year-olds living with their own fathers and mothers, and in homes which are reasonably free from discord.[1]

Mothers who have to carry the whole load of parental responsibility often have an unusually large number of pressing problems. So do mothers who are at war with their husbands. When one or the other of these conditions prevails the children are nearly always being exposed to an *egocentric* view of race or to an *accepting* social orientation, or both. These harassed mothers usually cannot give their children a very coherent picture of either race or the family's relation to the society around it. In spite of this, the children from broken or disturbed homes are as frequently highly aware of race as are the children from normal homes. Awareness can develop in the child whether he does or does not get coherence and consistency at home. There are other sources of ideas, in addition to the child's own ingenuity in putting together the scattered pieces he gets at home or elsewhere.

Relations between the child and one parent (or more rarely two) are tense in about a fifth of our families. In these cases the child is sometimes at war with one parent and in relative harmony with the other, or in harmony with a grandparent of whom he sees a great deal. But these embattled children too pick up and pull together enough pieces of the race relations picture to emerge aware of race. They do so just about as frequently as do the children who are on reasonably good terms with their parents.

In spite of communication problems our children generally show some of the distinctive marks of family race views or social orientations. With the exception of some fifteen children, we concluded that our four-year-olds had taken over significant parts of the thought and feeling systems of one or both parents. This does not mean that our children necessarily show a friendly orientation toward the other race when the parents' orientation is friendly, nor an antagonistic one when the parents' is antagonistic. Four-year-olds are more often friendly than are their parents, and quite often the friendly child comes from a home in which the general tone is not friendly. But it is true, nevertheless, that our children generally bear some marks left by the impress of parental influence.

Brothers and Sisters

The question concerning who is responsible for our four-year-old's notions about race is therefore not so easily answered. We cannot conclude, as our parents are likely to do, that "children get it at home," and assume that there is nothing more of any importance to be said.

It is quite true that the home remains the young child's primary source of contact with the bearers of American culture and its patterns, race-ways among them. It is truer for the four-year-old than for his older brothers and sisters. These older ones get out and about and see more of people outside the family. They then come back into it bearing whatever new notions they may have met outside. Parents may try to prevent them from airing the new words or the new ideas, but they are very likely to do so anyway. Our four-year-olds are also very likely to be all ears to the little gems handed out by big brother or sister, and almost half of our children have one or both for whom they can play the role of eager listener or copier.

Older siblings (big brothers or sisters) do account in part for the race ideas we have found in our four-year-olds. They are a source of ideas second in importance only to the parents themselves, and they are important for the same reasons. The young child spends more time in the company of his parents and siblings than with any other people (save in unusual cases), and hence has more opportunities to hear and observe their ways. Then, too, the small fry usually admire and want to be like their elders, and hence they soak up the ways of these elders without too much inclination to pick and choose. A favorite parent or sibling may exert an undue amount of influence, but our four-year-old will get something from everyone he sees very often (including, of course, grandparents, aunts, uncles, cousins, family friends, etc.).

"Come on In—"

Some of our children have siblings who make contributions to their range of social contacts as well as to their range of

ideas. There are big brothers and sisters, like those Elaine (w)
and Cynthia (N) have, who bring their friends home to play
with them. They are allowed to do so, whether or not the
friends happen to be of a different color. In crowded apartments little sisters are sure to be around and underfoot a
good part of the time, and likely to be interested in the affairs of
the "big kids." They are likely to be interested too in guests of a
color different than they are accustomed to see in their homes.
Not many of our children live in homes where racially different visitors are anything but a novelty.

Negroes are a novelty in Elaine's home, and one which
Elaine, like her mother, accepts without enthusiasm. Elaine
is very fond of her brother Bobby, who is three years her
senior. She trails along after him when she can, and her
mother is too busy or preoccupied with other worries to pay
very much attention. Negroes

> ". . . live right with us" (in the same building), says
> Mrs. D., "so the kids have always seen them. Elaine never
> used to bother with anyone who was colored—before she
> went to nursery school. She used to call them 'dirty.' But
> her brother brings the colored boys up to the house with
> him now and she plays with them and they get along. . . .
> It's funny—it don't seem to make any difference to her now.
> I can't get over the idea that she's used to them! When she
> was little she was kind of afraid of them, besides thinking
> they were dirty. Of course I explained that they weren't—
> just colored, and I explained again after she started school.
> And I've told all the kids—'if they're colored or white—
> you like them just the same.' "

In Cynthia's home, where three fairly dark brown children
live with parents of about the same hue, there have been a
good many visiting children of other colors. The M.'s live
in a large apartment building which is "all colored." But
Mrs. M. tells us that she doesn't have any trouble with the
people in neighboring buildings, many of whom are Irish.
She tells us too that Charlie (two years older than Cynthia)
has

> ". . . never picked his friends by race. He likes quiet
> children for friends—that's what he wants. His best pal
> now is a little white boy called Sonny. He lives across the

144 / **Race Awareness in Young Children**

street, and the boys are up here or over there all the time. Sonny's mother thinks Charlie is grand, and his father takes the two of them out riding sometimes. Joan (four years older than Cynthia) plays a lot with two little Irish girls. They come up here and have a dandy time, but the mother of one of them wouldn't let Joan in her house! Well it's wonderful the way the girls get along, and Cynthia with them when they'll have her. . . . Our kids have always played with white children at school and at Mason House (recreation center) and here at home. You have to be broadminded about these things. . . . I want them to play with all kinds."

"Stay Away—"

Mrs. M.'s sentiments are distinctly *not* shared by a great many of our parents. Those who take an opposite view are rarely of her color, however, and those who are most violently opposed are likely to live in Dover rather than in Harding (as Cynthia and Elaine do). It was from the parents living in Lower Dover that we heard the strongest sentiments against "mingling" or "mixing" among children. Frictions over housing have generated a great deal of steam and a considerable amount of heat in Lower Dover. Negro families have been squeezing into the widening cracks in the ranks of the Syrians, Italians, and other national minorities who have been accustomed to consider Lower Dover their territory. The big brothers and sisters in the families of our white four-year-olds have met the Negro children on the streets and in their schools. Usually they have met them with antagonism.

Six of our white children who have older siblings live in Lower Dover. In the family of each there is at least one older child who is strongly anti-Negro. More often than not sentiments are quite uniformly anti-Negro throughout the family.

Uniformity of sentiment within the family is not always the case, however. Older children may outdo their parents in antagonisms, as it happens in George L.'s family. The L.'s senior take a passive attitude toward the "race problems" which loom so large among the concerns of most of their neighbors. It is not that they feel any sympathy for "the darker brother," but rather that they are the accepting type, which we have met before. They are disinclined to dwell on the matter, and they do not allow their children to do so.

But their six- and eight-year-old boys, like most boys in the neighborhood, get caught up in the excitement of street fights with Negro boys, and go along with their white friends. They are followers rather than leaders in the fights and in the baiting of Negro children in their school. But like their friends they take a dim view of Negroes. Their little brother gets only the echoes of all this. George is small and frail. His parents protect him as much as they can from rough play and from the hazards of the crowded streets. He has no part in the fray, but he would like to be a big, bold fighter like his brothers.

In William K.'s family too there are differences of opinion about Negroes. William's parents are poor, harassed, and fearful. They have a notion that they are giving their children the "right" ideas by sending them to Sunday school now and then to "learn about morals," and by "not lettin' them call names." They have nothing more to offer but antagonisms. Mrs. K. admits, though reluctantly, to her own feelings about Negroes. "I'm afraid of 'em. They're different anyway. . . . I'm just afraid. They slashed a white woman around here." But her grown daughter offers a correction: "Ma, there are good and bad in every group," and the fourteen-year-old girl agrees. She belongs to a "mixed" club, and "pals around" with a brown-skinned girl of her own age. But these big sisters and their ideas are remote from William and his. William follows his eight-year-old brother in name-calling and in a feeble reflection of his antagonisms.

In Lorraine L.'s family there is a high degree of unanimity of opinion. The L.'s like to think themselves enlightened, tolerant people, and people who certainly don't encourage any other attitudes in their children. But the L.'s are also of the opinion that "it's going to take a long time before things are any different between the races. The way things are now you just better not mix with Negroes." They see to it that Lorraine and her older sister do not mix, save for their unavoidable contacts with Negro children in their schools. The L.'s are *conventionalists* about race and social *avoiders* in general, with antagonisms of a moderate order running through their *conventionalism* and *avoidance*. Lorraine and her sister are as like their parents in these respects as six- and four-year-olds can be.

In Sarah B.'s home live six children and their parents. The inevitable differences of opinion within this family come to an end at the color line. The children have heard enough from their parents about staying away from Negroes (and Chinese) to know very well where their parents stand, although they have also heard that they are not to call "dirty names" ("nigger" or "black"). From the eleven-year-old to the four-year-old they are intensely aware of race differences and antagonistic toward those who are different. The older children not only stay away from the Negro children in their school and at the other end of the street, but do so with a rock in hand.

Siblings of Different Colors

In the homes of our Negro children color sometimes plays a crucial part in the relations between the children. They love one another more or less because of color differences between them. They talk about these differences, and the little ones begin to understand how important it can be to have light skin and "nice hair."

In James M.'s family there are striking color differences. James' mother has long, dark hair and olive skin. She is a decided brunet, but racially speaking she is white. James' father is medium brown, and unmistakably of Negroid ancestry. The M.'s have two daughters who look like their father, while James "takes after" his mother. The girls, at the ages of ten and eleven, are intensely aware of the family differences. Isabel is proud of her long hair and pleased that she is lighter than Mildred. Isabel likes to say that "Mildred is colored and I'm white, and we have a pink brother," and she clearly prefers and tries to identify with whites. Whatever satisfaction Isabel feels in her relative lightness is matched by Mildred's discomfort. Mildred feels herself inferior, and suspects that when she is punished for some misdemeanor it is because she is colored that she gets the punishment and the parental disfavor. The importance of the differences between the two girls is underscored for them at school. There they meet many other Negro children to whom the degrees of color are of great personal importance.

But both the girls are proud of their "pink brother." They adore him, and he returns their affection. James knows about color differences, and knows quite exactly what James looks like. But these matters do not yet strike him as being very important. He loves all the members of his family. But he finds whites and whiteness prettier, and he knows there are people who don't like someone who is "black."

Explaining Things to Little Brother

The importance and desirability of lightness or whiteness have been emphasized in Donald K.'s home too. Donald has been exposed by his big brother to these values and to other notions about race. Donald's brother is two years his senior, and Mrs. K. tells us that

". . . as Donald gets older he copies Bill more. He does what Bill does and repeats what Bill says. . . . For example, Donald didn't want Hester and Wilfred to his birthday party after Bill popped right up and said he didn't want 'those old white kids' here. I said they were nice and were Donald's friends at nursery school and that it would be nice to have them. They came, but Donald didn't want Wilfred to have any of his toys or things.

"Bill started noticing color when he was first at nursery school. He wasn't more than three. The children were playing a circle game—he wouldn't take the hand of the little girl next to him because he thought her hand was dirty. She was darker than Bill. His teacher wanted to know why he'd say a thing like that. I told her we don't discuss color at home, but he's *so* fussy about dirt.

"I don't think Bill ever paid any other attention to color difference at nursery school, but there's been a great change in him since. Now he describes everyone by color. He says 'colored' or 'white'—I've never heard Bill say 'nigger'—but I've heard other colored children around here say it.

"Bill's mixed up about light people even now, when he's over seven. He speaks of them as 'white.' He thought a little girl he knows was white because she's fair and he could see the veins in her skin, and he said he couldn't see them in his. I try to explain to him that people are all different colors but we are all from the same race.

"Bill definitely prefers light people, especially girls. He seems to have the idea that if people are light they are pretty. He doesn't care for people with dark skin, although one of his best boy friends is dark. He likes him, but not the girls. He likes pretty and fair little girls with nice hair. He'll even comb it and put it in curls if he has a chance. . . . His father is dark, and of course he's noticed, but he's crazy about his daddy and wouldn't think of saying he was dark.

"Both the boys evidently feel it's nicer to be white. I don't know where Bill got it, but he got it so early. The children in the street probably say things—some of them may have had bad experiences with white children, but Bill hasn't. . . . Just the same, when he was about six and a half he said to his daddy—'are white people better than we are?' His father said 'all people are the same,' but for a while he seemed to have gotten the idea that *we're* better! Then one night when he wasn't yet seven he did a queer thing. After he'd had his bath he put powder all over himself—he loves to do that—and he came out of the bathroom with this white powder all over his face. I said to him 'you look awful—go wipe that stuff off your face.' He looked at himself in the mirror and said: 'No I don't mummy. I look just like a little white boy now.'

"His father was terribly upset, and terribly angry with him. He can see that Bill is getting that feeling already— the feeling that they are superior.

"Donald hasn't seemed to pay much attention yet. At one time he thought he was white—maybe it was because of nursery school. Anyway Donald was at school, and I think he was about three, when *Bill told him he was a little colored boy.*

"When Donald talks about the children at nursery school, he will just say: 'a boy at nursery school' did this or that. But Bill, if he's in on it, has to know right away: 'colored boy or white boy?' Then Donald will tell him. Bill always has to know which, and he cares. Donald can tell him, but he really doesn't care, yet anyway."

Big brothers and sisters make their contributions, directly or indirectly, deliberately or inadvertently, to the "education" of the younger family members. Their parents may encourage or discourage the process, like or not like what is being passed along, know or not know what is happening. But more or less of it does happen.

Playmates Around Home

We have seen that older siblings sometimes bring the four-year-old into contact with other children. But even lacking an older child to introduce him to children outside the family, and hence to new sources of ideas, our four-year-old moves in the society of children outside the immediate family. His playmates may be whomever he can find on the streets around his home. They may be children selected by his parents from among the neighbors' children or the children of family friends or relatives. He may have few playmates of either sort, but he nearly always has some contacts with children about his age, in addition to his nursery school contacts.

The parents of our children are of very different minds about playmates. There are those who turn their children loose in the neighborhood with a minimum of fuss about what they do or with whom they do it. At the opposite extreme are those who all but lock the doors to keep their offspring away from the physical or social hazards, real or imaginary, lurking on the streets or about the persons of the neighbors or their children.

Our Negro parents are just as likely to be fussy about the extracurricular activities of their four-year-olds as are the white parents. In about a third of the families of each kind there are strict rules and regulations about playing "outside." The restrictions amount, in most of these families, to keeping the child indoors with the mother, outdoors only under her escort, or outdoors only with certain carefully selected children. In families where one or more of these restrictions are practiced the child's play group is severely limited and he does not have much voice in deciding with whom he plays.

Among our Negro families the restrictions are rarely intended to keep the child away from white playmates. This is the intention only in the cases of Dianne, Alfred, and Herbert, all of whom have extremely race conscious and fearful mothers. Apart from these three our Negro parents are concerned with avoiding "bad influences" or with choosing good ones. When the parents believe no good ones are locally available they keep their children away from all local contacts and take them to visit friends or relatives whose children they approve.

Among our white families the restrictions are somewhat more often wholly or partly intended to keep the child away from racially different playmates. The wholly racial restrictions occur only in five white families living in Lower Dover. It is in this area, as we have seen before, that racial tensions are particularly high. Otherwise the white parents, like the

Negro parents, are concerned with protecting the child against the "bad" or with directing him toward the "good."

We have no families, Negro or white, more strongly directed toward careful choosing than that of James W. (N). It is James' mother, to be sure, who is largely responsible for this social policy. Mrs. W. belongs to a proud and conservative family which was established by James' great-grandmother. This matriarch was Irish, and in James' generation, like the intervening ones, there is strict adherence to the Roman Catholic faith. James' mother tells us that the matriarch was

". . . an aggressive and industrious woman who made her children proud and ambitious. . . . There were seven of them, and my mother was the only one who went over on the colored side. The reason the others didn't was that they wanted to get ahead. They knew they couldn't get what they wanted on the colored side. I have cousins who are holding important jobs in the big department stores and other places. Of course they can't afford to have their family background known, so I rarely see them. Most of them didn't even come to our wedding, but they sent gifts, and we're on very good terms.

"To me it doesn't seem worth all the strain they go through. I went through a long period of confusion myself, when I didn't know what I was. I think I was twenty-one before I got it straight in my mind and adjusted myself. I decided I was going to be colored, and stay in my own group, and never try to be anything else. We often darken as we grow older you know, and I just didn't want to fight it.

"White people, especially southerners, so often say there's nothing the Negro wants so much as to get into white society, and especially to marry a white person. Of course there are some who do. But we really don't need any other society. We have a perfectly lovely society of our own. There are groups like my club—we've been meeting regularly for a long time. The members are all well educated women and we have fine times together. I have a few white friends and I enjoy them too. . . .

"Of course there are many people, colored and white, with whom I wouldn't want to be seen on the street, and plenty of colored right here in the Project with whom I want nothing to do.

"I hope we won't have to live here very long. We want a nice home of our own near my mother and sisters in Upper Harding. While we're here I feel I have to be very strict with Jimmie. Maybe I'm too careful—I keep him very close. I used not to let him play outside at all, and now he plays here in the apartment most of the time. He has lots of toys, and we've tried to decorate and furnish his room so that he would enjoy it. . . .

"I won't have him running wild and playing with anybody and everybody. I keep an eye on him when he's out, and more often I take him to my mother's or to visit my friends and play with their children."

Whether or not parents are "strict" with their children, opportunities for interracial contact may be few or nonexistent. The four-year-old's limited ability to go any great distance from home, plus the tendency for his block to be "all white" or "all colored," accounts for the infrequency of mixed play groups of young children even in racially mixed areas of the city. But some two-fifths of our Negro children and half as many of our white ones do play in mixed groups. Their doing so may be encouraged by their parents or it may be merely tolerated.

On the whole the Negro parents are glad to see their children in mixed play groups. They reason that the child will grow up to a world dominated by whites. Hence, however little they like this prospect, the child must learn to "get along with them," and the sooner the better. They know all too well that getting along with whites requires some rather special skills, and they subscribe to the "learning by doing" theory of education in this matter.

They may do so with fears and misgivings, however, like Tony A.'s mother. She tells us quite proudly that there are

". . . lots of children on this street—white *and* colored, and they mingle all right. Tony plays with both, and he gets along fine. He just loves to be with other children. When he's home from school he's likely to have about fifteen of them on our porch. The children around here aren't rough. Their mothers are trying to get them to be well behaved."

Then Mrs. A.'s voice and expression take on the anxious quality which we have met many times before in our Negro parents, and she adds: "I don't hear anything *yet*, but I expect it in time."

What Mrs. A. expects to hear, in time, is that Tony is having racial trouble. Sam's mother is just as proud of her son's harmonious play with white children. But she too is anxious: "So far Sam gets along very good. He hasn't yet, as far as I know, been called out of his name."

There are others who *have* been "called out of their names," though not always by white children. Jimmy F. has heard himself called "black" by both a Negro child and a white one. Jimmy didn't quite understand why this particular "name" should be called at him, but he didn't like it. Jimmy's grandmother unhappily tried to explain to this medium brown child that he is not black really, and that he must never play with those children again. Jimmy didn't care to anyway, but since then he has heard other brown children called worse names.

Sometimes, however, there are friendly white children and dangerous Negro ones in the mixed play group. This has been Charles' experience. Charles "runs wild" on a street dense with children, most of them Negroes.

"There's nowhere else for him to play," his mother tells us, "but he sure hears all kinds of things and gets awful beat up by the big boys. He's got scars all over him. Just last week a brown boy about seven hit him in the head with a brick. We had to get it sewed up, it was so bad. . . . But there's a white family down the street that Charlie and his little sister just love to play with. Their kids act real nice to mine and so do their folks. They even take my kids in their house an' feed 'em."

There are other white children who "act real nice" with neighboring brown ones, and usually they have parents who very much want them to do so. Eddie R. does so, and his parents report that they "let Eddie out around the house so he can get to play with all kinds." They want Eddie to be "friendly and sociable with everybody, because one person's as good as another."

There are just four other white families who take this view, and who actively seek cross-racial contacts for their children.

Only one, besides Eddie R.'s family, lives in a neighborhood so mixed that the seeking bears much fruit. Vesta M.'s family does, and makes the most of what Vesta's parents regard as a "wonderful opportunity to break down the barriers and get to know one another when we're living as neighbors." The M.'s have Negro friends whom they invite to their house and in whose houses they visit in turn. They worry about the prejudices of their white neighbors and about the name-calling Vesta hears among the children, but rejoice in her reactions:

> "We've watched Vesta pretty close to see how she'd take these things, but we've never been able to see that she feels any difference between the colored and the white. She never repeats any of the things she must hear the older children say. She's crazy about having playmates, and it doesn't make any difference what color."

The M.'s, unlike so many of our parents, evaluate the reactions of their offspring quite correctly. Vesta is but moderately aware of race and quite without racial antipathies.

A vivid sense of race is not necessarily fostered by the play group, mixed or otherwise. But it sometimes is. Candy's parents know this, for they too watch their only one with sharp and discerning eyes. Candy plays with white and brown, but it is from the latter that she has heard some things which made her wonder and ask.

A five-year-old made it his business one day to "explain" to Candy about her family. "You and your father are white," he volunteered, "but your mother's not." This was utterly confusing to Candy, in view of the actual close similarity between her parents and between them and herself. All three are light, and all three are Negroid. The lightness has brought other comments less explanatory and more resentful. Candy has heard it said bitterly that "you think you're better than anyone else 'cause you're light (or white)!" She protests that she doesn't think she is better, and goes home to try to get another perplexity cleared up. It dawns upon her that, whatever this is all about, one's color is an important matter.

Chapter 9

More Friends

WHEN WE were talking about parents and their points of view (in Chapter 8) we noted that they incline to some very definite ideas about where children learn about race. As many of our parents see the matter, other people's children get ideas about race at home. Their own children, however, get them elsewhere, and very often at school. This reasoning comes into operation most particularly when the racial ideas in question are matters of name-calling or other behavior for which parents do not care to be held responsible.

All of our children go to nursery school. Hence the parents of all of them have this institution to blame when it may be convenient, or perhaps even justified. Some racial name-calling and other overt recognitions of race do in fact occur there, as we shall see. Such incidents are rather rare. Nevertheless, our parents are quite correct in seeing in the nursery school a new and important source of ideas.

The nursery school, with its teachers and children gathered in it, provides the four-year-old with yet another social world. It provides him with new and different contacts and experiences. Just as his contacts and experiences at home and in his neighborhood give him opportunities for learning about race, so does his nursery school. The general atmosphere at home and in the neighborhood can teach him as much as can the open racial incidents he observes or participates in there. So, too, he can learn from the general atmosphere as well as from the open incidents at school. Our parents overlook the importance of this general atmosphere. We shall try to assess its nature and importance, and we shall see what kinds of open incidents occur at school.

The Three Schools

Our four-year-olds function in one of three nursery school societies. Nineteen of them go to the Lower Dover Nursery School. There they move in a society made up largely of white people. They see one Negro teacher, and a very few Negro children. At the Coleman House Nursery School, to which twenty-one of our children go, they frequently see teachers who are white. Apart from these contacts they operate in the society of people who are more or less brown. At the Rodney Nursery School the remaining sixty-three of our children meet a truly biracial society. The teachers they see are more often white than brown, but the children with whom they play and eat and nap are a little more often brown than white.

Getting Admitted—How and Why

Our children get into nursery school for a variety of reasons. Obviously they have parents who are not opposed to nursery schools in principle, religious affiliations notwithstanding (thirty-four families, thirteen of them colored, are at least nominally Roman Catholic or Greek Orthodox).[1] Our parents not only are not opposed to nursery schools—one or both are actively interested. If this were not the case their children would never have appeared on the rolls, for all three of the schools have waiting lists and parents often register their children well in advance of the age at which they become eligible. (They are usually eligible at two and a half years.)

These schools are attractive to parents for a number of reasons. Harassed mothers living in cramped quarters and usually lacking adjacent play space have obvious problems. These are importantly relieved by getting the four-year-old into school five days a week from nine until three or thereabouts. But these are *not* child care centers designed to release working mothers, or even primarily for the relief of harassed mothers. Most of the mothers do not work, and the school authorities tend to discourage their doing so. These schools are designed for the education of the child. They are educational institutions rather than "dumping grounds," and this fact is made very clear to all comers. The parents are not always so preoccupied with the educational aspects of the situation. But a third or more of them are at least as interested in the educational function as they are in gaining some peace for themselves and playfellows and safe play space for their children.

All three schools are long-established institutions which enjoy considerable prestige in the Harding and Dover areas. Most people there have heard of them, and have heard that they are highly regarded by educators, as they indeed are and deserve to be. Added to all these advantages is the fact that fees are adjusted to income and are low in any case, since the institutions are subsidized from the Community Fund of the city.

The schools admit on the basis of several considerations. The child must live within a fairly well-defined area around the school. (See map, Chapter 1.) He must be of an appropriate age, reasonably sound physically and psychically, and have priority (by virtue of date of registration) over other equally qualified candidates.

Race, religion, or national background are not disqualifying factors, and the schools pride themselves on diversities of these sorts. The school at Coleman House remains racially uniform primarily as a result of the concentration of Negroes in the area upon which it draws. Another factor is the firm conviction of the people in the area that Coleman House belongs to Negroes, since it was established for them and has never developed a biracial tradition. The Lower Dover school has been traditionally associated with whites in the same fashion, but it is losing its homogeneity as Negroes find housing in the area. At the Rodney School biracialism has become a cherished tradition. This has occurred over a generation which has seen the Lower Harding area itself transformed from all-white to biracial.

A few white parents, and more Negro parents, particularly favor the Rodney School *because* of its racially mixed group. Very few Negro parents and a good many white parents like Rodney for other reasons, and *in spite of* its biracial character. We cannot assume, as the casual observer does, that racially prejudiced people will not send their children to a racially mixed school of their own choosing. In Harding and in Dover they do just that, and not infrequently. Ian's parents, whom we met a while ago (Chapter 6), are a case in point.

New Faces—Strange Faces

We do not know in how many parental conferences the child may have heard the pros and cons of the mixed school discussed. But the white parents sometimes tell us that they "prepared" the child for this facet of his nursery school experience. They did not want him to "say something" embarrassing upon encountering brown schoolmates or teachers.

Discussions of this sort may have provided the background for Vivien's reluctance about coming to Rodney. Vivien's parents make a rare admission about what is probably a rather rare occurrence. They tell us that Vivien

". . . resented coming to Rodney because of the colored children. . . . There are several colored in our neighborhood and she must have had some trouble with them. Now she just loves school. She says the colored children are 'all right,' but she only talks at home about little Peter, who is white. Personally, it seems to us that the colored children are very nice."

It is usually the white children, and not the brown ones, who have "reactions" to the mixed nursery school. It is they, at any rate, whose reactions show and are talked about by their parents. Burton's mother, for example, tells us that

". . . going to Rodney was certainly an experience for both of us. Burton had seen Negroes on the street—it's quite mixed around where we live—and he had even played some with Negro children, but he just never paid any attention. Well—when he first went to school he did! He came home and told me 'my teacher is black—and George and another little boy and a little girl at school are black.' And he wanted to know 'why is her hand black'—about one of them. . . . I just ignored the question. After a while he got over it and now he doesn't say anything."

Initial reactions are not always forthcoming, but reactions at one time or another usually are. A month or more after entering school, Eddie R. asked his parents the "why" question so common to white children: "Why are they black?" Mr. R. explained: "God made them that way." He added, with conspicuous haste and emphasis, "they are just as nice as the others." Eddie's mother remembered to add: "You shouldn't say 'black.' Say 'colored.'" But Eddie wanted them to know that "black" wasn't his idea. "One of the kids at school said our teacher is black and we are white." "It doesn't matter," Eddie's father insisted. "God made all nationalities. The important thing is whether they're good people."

Among our Negro children reactions to the racial aspects of nursery school appear most frequently at the Coleman School, and it is understandable that they should. Rather few (about one-fourth) of our Coleman House Negro children have previously had sustained contacts with whites. They meet at school an all-Negro group of playfellows but they are in close association with teachers, some of whom are white. Their whiteness is conspicuous in this group, and particularly so to children unaccustomed to being socially close to whites.

More than half of the children at Coleman House have reacted, in one way or another, to this unfamiliar situation. They show that they notice the racial distinctiveness of the whites, but it is significant that they do not ask the kinds of questions white children ask under similar circumstances. They do not ask "why are they white?" as white children ask "why are they black?" Only one question, "what color are you?" (addressed to the white Observer), even approximates the nature of the inquiries white children make. The Negro children are not even given to questioning, but rather to making comparisons and commenting upon their conclusions. They remark upon "the white teacher with long hair," upon "the small mouth and nose" of a white teacher, upon "white faces," and upon "brown and white" teachers.

"—Speak no Evil—"

It must be stressed at once that the schools actively do *nothing* with the intention of stimulating race awareness in the children. That the children usually get some such stimulation at school is largely a function of their own powers of observation, association, memory, etc. These are brought to bear upon a new social situation in which both races are represented. The newness of the situation is in itself a stimulus to seeing and actually *registering* what may have been seen before and *not registered*. Furthermore, the registering process in one child can be a stimulus to others, especially if the first one talks. But the school staffs very consciously avoid drawing attention to race. They deal with children, parents, and one another upon a basis of the usual considerations of the well-trained professional in teacher-pupil, teacher-parent, and teacher-teacher relationships. Inevitably factors having to do with personal compatibilities enter as they must in any human relationship, however professionalized.

There is a general feeling among the nursery school teachers and directors that it is rather shocking to mention race publicly, just as one does not talk openly about sex (in these or other schools with "nice" teachers who are creating a "nice" middle-class atmosphere). Racial identity is deliberately and consistently ignored; racial differences are dealt with by behaving as though they did not exist. This is the official policy, and departures from it are rare, private (as in conversation between teachers), or instigated by the parents or the children themselves.

It is the children who are most likely to break the silence that hovers over the race issue in these schools. Even they do it rather seldom. Perhaps they would do it more often if they were not susceptible to the general atmosphere of polite hush. But occasionally they comment on physical differences or they hurl epithets. The teacher's reactions will be well concealed behind a practiced facade of professional imperturbability. She will be quite as surprised or mildly shocked, however, when her four-year-olds indicate race interest and a race vocabulary as when they indicate sex interest and a sex vocabulary. But great store is set upon the maintaining of that professional aplomb. This is best ensured by behaving as though nothing had happened—nothing been said—the taboo around race (or sex) talk never broken. Furthermore, it is believed to be sound pedagogy to ignore sex talk, "cuss words," and other four-year-old provocations, so why not race talk too. The theory is that if the child gets no "rise" out of anyone he gets no satisfaction, loses interest, and stops doing what his "nice" teachers feel "nice" children should not do.

It is this policy which accounts for the fact that teachers

do not put a stop to the occasional name-calling or race talk which does occur. A while back (in Chapter 7) we met Tony R.'s mother and found her upset about an incident at Tony's school. The hated word "nigger" had been freely bandied about in a nursery school group and the teacher had let the episode run its natural course. She was adhering admirably to nursery school policy, but Mrs. R. neither understood the policy nor would have approved had she understood. She is one of those relatively "old-fashioned" mothers who believes in immediate and direct action. Almost all our Negro parents, and most of the white ones, would agree with her that in such cases pedagogical theory might better be thrown out the window in favor of the "feelings" of the Negro children and their parents.

So the racial hush-hush hovering over the nursery school works both to create a repressive atmosphere and to allow the prolongation of incidents which might otherwise be "nipped in the bud." The repressive atmosphere reduces the possibilities for racial learning at school while the other half of the policy works to increase the possibilities.

Friends and Favorites

We watched our children closely as they moved through the life of the nursery school. We watched for any signs of race awareness or race orientation. We saw rather few signs, as compared with the many which emerged in our private sessions with the children. Yet there were some.

We watched very carefully the development of friendships and personal attachments. Would this development be affected by race? We concluded that in general it is not, but that some children, some of the time, are influenced by racial considerations.

We observed, recorded, and analyzed the interactions between the children for signs of racial influences. At the Rodney School, where the races are about evenly represented, we made an intensive study of the interactions in a group of twenty-six four-year-olds.[2]

Our detailed observations brought to light some strong friendships and personal attachments, as well as the over-all picture of interpersonal contacts. Some strong interracial friendships developed in this group of children. One of the most conspicuous was the devotion between Ian (w) and Ned (N). This relationship is the more interesting since Ian's parents are, by their own admission, prejudiced against Negroes and unenthusiastic about the racial mixture at Ian's nursery school. It it interesting too that Ian did not talk at home about his friend Ned. His parents were surprised, and perhaps a little shocked, when they eventually heard about this friendship. Furthermore, Ian and Ned knew what they were doing, racially speaking. Both are moderately aware of race and have developed a medium degree of feeling about it. Their personal congeniality simply and completely took precedence over any other considerations.

In general, and in all three schools, the pattern of friendships and affections is dictated by personal congeniality factors. When friendships and favoritisms cross the race line we can assume that personal congeniality is more important to the principals than any cross-racial reluctance which may exist in their minds. We can assume this to have been the case for Ian and for the five other white children (among our total of forty-six white children) who established particularly strong friendships with Negroes. And we can assume that race differences were not sufficiently important to prevent the rest of our white children from interacting with Negroes in a quite "natural" fashion most of the time.

Where we find whites favoring whites and Negroes favoring Negroes we cannot be so sure what is involved. We do know that at least a dozen of our children formed attachments with others on their own side of the line. This happened with white children more often than with Negroes.

It is among our Negro children that we get indications that race differences are important bases for admiration and favoring. In these children the admiration, and the favoring, run much more *across* than *along* the race line. We find almost a third of our Negro children favoring a white (child or teacher), and nearly as many making it very clear that the whiteness is importantly involved. Sometimes they are devoted to a white teacher, like Barbara at Coleman House. Barbara calls the object of her affections "blond hair." David H. likes his white teacher partly, at least, because he admires her hair. Malcolm thinks his white teacher quite wonderful. "I want to be like you," he says.

The admiration Negro children show for whiteness, and

their interest in it, often takes the form of a preoccupation with the *hair* of whites. We have seen this interest appearing in what the children say and do in private, but when they are alone with us they indicate an even greater interest in over-all color than in hair. In public their expressions of interest are more likely to have to do with hair. Often they stroke, fondle, ruffle, or just lightly touch the hair of white children.[3] White children, significantly enough, very rarely make the same gesture.

Race Talk

We have said that overt comments about race are not common in the public exchanges among our nursery school children. We have seen that teachers provide an example of public reticence about race, and we have noted that some children have been warned by their parents concerning public comment or the use of epithets. In spite of example or warning the topic occasionally breaks into the open, sometimes matter-of-factly, but more often in moments of stress.

The matter-of-fact comments are likely to be of the sort the Observer hears often in his private sessions with the children. The comments are brief and incidental. They can easily be missed by teachers busy in another part of the room or with other children. The following episodes contain examples of the matter-of-fact comment:

1. Sam (N) playing "fireman" with Ian (w) and Nathan (w). Sam observes casually, "there are two white firemen." Nothing more is said. They continue their game.

2. John (N, and quite dark) asserts: "I'm the white boy," upon hearing another child murmur something about a "black girl."

James (N, and quite light) corrects John: "No—you're a dark boy." No reply from John.

3. William (N), looking at a book with John (N), points to a pictured white child and says: "That's me." John corrects: "No, that's not you, that's a little white boy."

William runs to his teacher with the book, asking: "Isn't this me?" She replies: "I think it's a little boy, but I don't think it's you." Nothing more from William.

4. Norman starts a discussion of color by asking his teacher (N, medium) "What color are you?" She evades the

question. Sam continues the topic, labeling her and others "brown" or "white."

James (N), who has been a listener to this point, says: "I'm white." Sam, after a moment's hesitation, replies: "No, you're colored." James is silent.

5. Thomas (N) is drawing with crayons. His teacher comes by and asks what he has drawn. He replies: "A little white girl." No comment from the teacher.

6. Thomas (N) remarks to another Negro child (after the departure of a Negro visitor): "I was talkin' to that colored lady."

7. Vesta (w) chants the traditional "counting out" rhyme: "Eeny, meeny, miny, mo—catch a nigger by the toe—."

Norman (N) gives an immediate rebuke. "You mustn't say that. 'Nigger' is a bad word. You must say 'tiger' instead."

Vesta amiably repeats the rhyme, making the substitution exactly as instructed.

8. Ian appears at school wearing a black Hallowe'en mask. Nathan catches sight of him and shouts gleefully: "Ian is a nigger."

Nathan's mother, greatly embarrassed, hisses in his ear, "no, he *isn't!*"

Nathan, quite unperturbed, insists, "Well, he looks like one!" (End of episode—*until* Nathan's mother "got him home.")

9. Brenda (N, quite light) gives Mrs. H. (w student) a characteristically critical head-to-toe appraisal on a warm summer day. Then she remarks: "You got a pretty dress, and you got no stockings on. Why you got no stockings on? I know why. You want your legs to get brown. I don't want my legs to get brown. You know why? Because they look funny. My mother's got brown legs, and they look funny."

Mrs. H. murmurs disagreement. Brenda insists: "Oh yes they do!"

When race becomes an issue in moments of stress there is likely to be name-calling involved. It may be done in a merely peevish fashion or it may carry a heavy load of anger or frustration. The following episodes suggest the kinds of outbursts to which about a dozen of our children were liable upon occasion.

1. Ian (w) playing soldier with his good friend Sam (N).

Both are armed with "pretend" guns. Something Sam says annoys Ian. He retorts: "Shut up you little darkie you—you son of a bitch. I won't play with you!"

Sam observes quietly: "The little darkie has a gun too." They go on playing together, and quite happily thereafter.

2. Quentin (N, quite light) is much given to the use of the word "nigger" when he is angry or even merely annoyed.

"Go 'way you niggers," he loftily orders a mixed group of younger children.

"You little nigger!" he yells at Roland (w) when the latter displeases him.

"Shut up you niggers—black girls!" he screams in a rage over some real or fancied provocation from Nan (N) and Brenda (N). Nan picks up a familiar challenge and hurls back a familiar retort: "Shut up yourself you stinkin' nigger." Several children of both races have been standing by fascinated with this exchange. Only Ian adds his voice, chiming in now on Quentin's side: "Shut up nigger yourself!"

These examples drawn from a mixed group can be paralleled by incidents in the racially uniform group at Coleman House. Interpersonal bickerings there were occasionally accompanied by name-calling of the same sorts with only minor variations. There is no need to illustrate this aspect of nursery school life further. But it is an aspect of that life, though a minor one from the standpoint of frequency. It is a spectacular one, from the standpoint of the children, but rather less so to those who are already familiar with racial epithets. To those who are not, the name-callers offer an introduction to another bit of the realities of life. Even here, in these cloisters for the very young, the racial realities sometimes intrude.

Outside the Cloister

In the nursery schools earnest, hard-working, and devoted people do their best to create little oases of racial democracy. The Negro parents generally know it and treasure this experience for their children, and so do a few of the white parents. It is for this reason that we often hear regret and anxiety in the voices of the Negro parents, and sometimes in the voices of the white ones, as they tell us: "If *only* our youngster could go on in schools like the nursery school! But next year he will have to go to public school. Things will be very different there."

Things *are* very different there, and very much more as they are in the neighborhood and in the community generally. Few of our children have met racial democracy outside their nursery schools. It is likely that few will meet it elsewhere, unless they build their own.

Chapter 10

The Personal Equation

IN PRECEDING CHAPTERS we have seen something of American race-ways and related social-ways as practiced by the parents of our children. We have met some friends and relations, and kinds of situations, which are significant in bringing the ways of the community within the grasp of our children. We know that these four-year-olds have more or less familiarity with race and its social meanings. But we have seen little of the personalities of our children, or of the fashion in which all these cultural and social factors integrate in their individual lives.

The various factors which have significance for race awareness and the making of race attitudes can be called the *terms* in the *personal equation*. By examining representative equations we can arrive at generalizations about the relative significance of different terms. With this as our final goal we go now to the personal equations in the lives of eight children, four of them white, and four of them brown.

Part I

EQUATIONS WITH A WHITE TERM

Paul C.—No comment

Paul is "all boy," even to a precocious fondness for fair-haired girls. He has two favorites at the Dover School with whom he can be very tender. Generally speaking, tenderness is not in his line. He goes in for boxing—an exercise quite congenial to a big, rough, sturdy boy, and an interest fostered by the ex-boxer who fathered him. Paul likes active, aggressive play anyway, and he plays hard. He is stubbornly inclined to make things go his way in the play, too. For all his manliness he can throw a fine infantile tantrum or retreat into a thumb-sucking sulk if they don't. Still, Paul is a good mixer who makes himself attractive to his playfellows most of the time. He cares about doing so. Grown-ups, unless they can box, are rather uninteresting.

He finds his father very interesting indeed. Paul's mother did too until father lost his temper more completely than usual and fancied her his opponent in the ring. Mrs. C. regarded this attack on an unprepared amateur as something less than sporting, and withdrew to the shelter of her mother's wing, taking Paul with her. But father cooled off and repented, mother relented, and domestic harmony was restored. Paul went on with his boxing lessons and grew more manly and rough and stubborn as he grew in devotion to his devoted father.

The C.'s settled themselves more comfortably in their apartment, repapered the walls, modernized the kitchen, and bought two more radios. With one for each member of the family there can at least be no trouble over the radio. Mrs. C. keeps the apartment immaculate, Paul goes to school impeccably turned out and polished. No one can say that the C.'s are not doing well, even if they do live in a very shabby building in the "booze and bum" area of Lower Dover. They work hard at "doing well" too, Mr. C. at his routine factory job, Mrs. C. in her glamorous position behind the glass window through which the movie house patrons thrust their money.

It takes some thought and effort to keep up appearances and keep clear of the "bad" influences in the C.'s neighborhood. Grammar school education and a lack of any special abilities notwithstanding, they stay well ahead of most of the people around them. There are other American-born Italians in the vicinity, and there are Irish too, but none of them better Catholics or more responsible parents.

As for the Negro families in the neighborhood, the C.'s distinguish between the good ones and the bad ones. They happen never to have had any Negro friends, though from a distance Mr. C. admired the heroic exploits of a fellow soldier who was brown. Then, too, the C.'s have had quite pleasant dealings with Negroes on various jobs. All in all, they find themselves broadminded on the race question. They don't at all mind having Negroes living somewhere about. If it were a matter of their living in the same house it would be different. But the way things are it isn't bad. As Mrs. C. says, "Some of the Negroes are all right. You never see them. They're very nice."

The C.'s really aren't very much interested in the matter one way or another. They are busy people, they have their own friends and their own interests. So long as no one gets in their way they are quite indifferent. "Social problems" and "matters of principle" are not the kinds of things about which the C.'s get excited.

Paul knows nothing about race, his parents tell us, and they don't propose to call the matter to his attention. They do try to watch his choice of playmates around home, but without interfering very much. He has to be kept away from a bad gang of Negroes who roam the streets, but apart from that he plays at liberty with boys of his age. There are Italian, Irish, and Negro children among them. Paul gets along with all of them.

The C.'s only child in fact leads a quite comfortable life. He is in the happy position of having no great problems. Father lays a rough hand on him now and then, but mother only shuts him in his room when he misbehaves. Paul understands father's way better and snaps to attention when father speaks to him. Mother is a frail creature, nice enough, but quite overshadowed by father. There is fun at home, fun outside, and fun at school. The world is a pretty good place and a safe one. There is nothing to worry about.

Paul's parents are almost correct in their assumption that he knows nothing about race. Paul is not much interested. Colors, textures, details about things or about people are lost in a blur. He sees size, strength, movement—especially big movement.

He has some hazy notions about people being different. The word "Indian" comes into his mind when he sees a picture of some people who look different. So does the word "red." "Brown" he also supposes may have something to do with people—the matter is unimportant so he carelessly applies it to the people in the picture, though they happen to be white.

There, in another picture, is a boy whose hair is certainly

not like his, however. And if you insist, why yes, Paul looks like those boys right *there*—and he points to the white ones. He begins to warm to this game a little, and to insist with some vigor upon his points. The white boy—"him!"—could be Paul's brother—certainly "not them" (the brown boys). He makes the same points in the same fashion when asked which children he would like to play with (w—not N). He points to the whites when asked which is nicer, prettier, good, a suitable friend, etc. He observes the two brown dolls and concludes that they belong together. "That's her mother," he volunteers. Having reached this new high of verbosity Paul subsides into silence and gestures again. There is some eloquence, however, in the way he makes faces at the brown dolls.

Paul thus turns out to be one of our low-awareness, weak-orientation children. He has essentially no race vocabulary, his perceptions are feeble and spotty, and his interest low. He senses his resemblance to other boys whom grown-ups call white and he is inclined to prefer this kind—his kind. He has a notion that browns go together and a vague feeling of distaste for them, and that is all.

THE TERMS

1. *Paul has limited powers of observation and generalization* (as compared with others of our four-year-olds). He is a child of just average mental capacity (I.Q. 100). But this is not the crucial fact about his mental operations. The crucial facts are rather that he has not developed a *habit* of concentrating his attention upon personal traits or features, and that he has not developed a habit of classifying or generalizing about these or other items. He is content with taking passing note of this, that, or the other item and flitting mentally to something unrelated. He is not interested in pulling the items together into some kind of order.

He is generally inclined to exercise his body rather than his mind. He throws his energies into physical activities. His mental operations follow as an adjunct. Hence he is not motivated to develop observational and generalizing powers to the degree that he might.

2. *Paul is interested chiefly in gross muscular activity.* When his attention centers upon people it is upon what they are actively *doing,* or what they can actively do, rather than upon what they *are.* It is the attributes of people-in-action and

not of people-as-such which catch his eye and stimulate his interest.

3. *Paul identifies strongly with his father.* If Paul's father were inclined to mental gymnastics, to an interest in people as such, *or* to strong feelings about race, Paul would very likely reflect these inclinations. He in fact reflects his father's lack of such inclinations, for Paul aspires more or less unconsciously to be exactly like father. The son is becoming a mirror personality.

4. *Paul comes close to fitting the textbook outline of the "well-adjusted child."* This fact by itself is not necessarily significant. The happy, secure, outgoing, getting-along-fine kind of child can be highly active mentally. He can throw into the process of exploring and ordering the social world all the energy which the unhappy, insecure, introspective child throws into morbid thrashing and lashing. Or the well-adjusted child can, like Paul, throw his energies into hard play, boxing, or other activities which deflect his attention from other matters.

Neither type is likely to be driven to find somebody upon whom to work off gripes. The well-adjusted child has relatively few and feeble gripes. So Paul has no great need for a victim.

Hester N.—"The chocolate ones—"

Hester is a bland child. The word describes her personality and even her looks. Her coloring is medium and not eye-catching. Her facial expression is composed, almost blank. She is big for her age, sturdy, and slow moving. She is withdrawn and shy, especially with other children. But watching her with them, one concludes that passivity plays a part in her tendency to wander idly around the fringes of a group in which others are throwing themselves vigorously into singing, a game, or outdoor play. Hester moves with such deliberateness that she finds the tempo of the group alarming, and she is not inclined to fit her tempo to the others.

There are no marked limitations to Hester's abilities. She can do the things four-year-olds are expected to do in the way of dressing, toilet routine, painting, pasting, swinging, and so on. She goes through the motions at the proper time, but without verve. She works steadily at the project in hand, but without evidence of unnecessary activity either physical or mental. She can speak in fluent sentences but she seldom does so. She seldom cries, gets angry, or shows any other strong emotions.

Hester is at home in a very shabby third-floor tenement apartment located in an "all-white" area. The shabbiness of the building is matched by the apartment interior, which suggests both poverty and neglect. Yet Hester comes to school looking neat enough, and she is always clean. It is simply that Hester's mother too has an easy pace. She doesn't "get around to" her housekeeping, which is much less important to her than a number of other things.

This indifference in Mrs. N. is not at all in accord with the middle-class atmosphere in which she grew up. But Mrs. N. is no stickler for "nice" middle-class ways as such. Some of them, like keeping a clean and orderly house, are just not worth the trouble. She would rather invest her time and her moderate energies elsewhere. Not that she carefully plans the disposition of either—rather she drifts *into* pleasant eddies or *with* the currents which she does not care to fight. She is individualistic, but certainly not rugged.

Mrs. N.'s few strong motivations are toward art and music and the people she likes. She sees to it that the children hear a concert now and then, but she does not worry about their street play. She devotes considerable energy to getting them baptized against father's wishes, but little or none to dealing with father's alcoholism or his proclivities for violence toward the family when he is drunk.

Hester's mother is a gentle, kindly woman who is revolted by open meanness and harshness. Her sympathies go out to Negroes, Jews, and other people about whose special problems she has some first-hand knowledge. She can, in fact, work up more indignation over their problems than over her own. She has had close friendships with Negroes and she continues to have them. She was one of the very few white mothers at Rodney School who struck up a genuine friendship with a Negro mother. On Mrs. N.'s part this friendship was primarily an unself-conscious response to a person whom she liked, rather than a humanitarian gesture. Hester's father joined willingly enough in this friendship when an evening party involving husbands was arranged. Hester and her brother went happily to a children's party at which they were the only white guests.

So the N.'s follow mother's lead in respect to interracial attitudes and associations, as well as in religion and "culture."

In her quiet way Mrs. N. does exert some pressure upon the rest of the family, and about some few matters she cares enough to do so.

It was she who taught her daughter to see "chocolate" skin where Hester had spontaneously seen "dirty" skin. The idea stayed with her, and Hester's unusually positive orientation toward Negroes has that pleasant association at its root. Hester quite characteristically gave no indications of favoritism among the children at Rodney School, but at home she waxed to what was, for her, a high level of enthusiasm about one of her schoolmates. Her favorite was Norman, a handsome little boy of a milk-chocolate hue. Norman paid no attention to Hester, and he was often raucous and disturbing —not at all the kind of child she might have been expected to admire. But admire him she did, and without wavering.

Hester broke her public silence with the Observer. She indicated a quite typical medium level of awareness, and chatted almost vivaciously about "white" or "light," "brown" or "chocolate" people. She knew herself to be among the white ones, and inclined to think them prettier, but she had no other reservations about "the chocolate ones." She spoke of them in a tone and manner conveying sensuous delight with the notion, a friendly orientation, and no sense of distance or separation.

THE TERMS

1. *Hester is deliberate.* In her slow, calm way, Hester thinks things over. She will not be hurried, but she gets around to thinking about the things that catch her fancy. Her mental capacities are quite average (her measured I.Q. of 90 is probably somewhat low due to her reticence in the testing situation). But, like her mother, she can give sustained attention to a few matters which she finds of interest. She was intrigued by the "chocolate" idea, and she has given "the chocolate ones" some thought and scrutiny.

2. *Hester is mild and kindly.* Like her mother, she is not given to strong emotions or to conspicuous action. But she is friendly and sympathetic, and inclined to stay with an idea she likes.

3. *Hester is no conformist.* She is like her mother in this too. There is nothing assertive about the nonconformity of either mother or child. They simply refuse to be stampeded. The refusal is made up of an almost stubborn passivity and,

in respect to Negroes, simple kindliness. Both of them respond to a few people whom they happen to like. If these people also happen to be brown, it is either unimportant or it becomes an added point of interest.

4. *Hester is her mother's child.* The similarities between them are, as has already been suggested, quite striking. Hester is so like her mother, and so much with her, that intergroup attitudes pass easily from one to the other. Mrs. N. does not protest about her attitudes, she quietly goes into action. Hester has seen and been drawn into her mother's friendship with brown people. As usual, Hester follows her mother. She does so out of inclination and habit, and because she too feels quite comfortable among "the chocolate ones."

Deborah G.—"A white with a white and a brown with a brown—"

Debbie "has what it takes." She has, both in and around herself, about everything it presumably takes to build a healthy, happy childhood.

She is, first of all, a most attractive little girl. She has a pert little face set with merry hazel eyes, and above the face a soft tangle of light brown curls. From this small, lively person there emanates a spontaneous, unself-conscious friendliness. Debbie is eager, chatty, and quick on the conversational "pick-up." She is also quick on the emotional trigger, and a little inclined to flashes of jealousy, anxiety, or excitement. A brief flood of tears, a spell of worry, a few minutes of shrill yelps and giggles will occasionally break her generally even and sunny course.

Debbie has a twin, a little boy who is quite like her and very much loved by her. Danny is a little more steady, a little more sober, and a bit less quick. He is something of an anchor upon which Debbie depends, but she has other reliable anchors. She has two big sisters, and the bigger of the two plays a motherly role toward her. The other provides more competition and rivalry, but there is deep affection among all four of the children in this family.

The pattern in close familial bonds is set by Debbie's parents, whose mutual respect and affection is conspicuously strong. The G.'s are intelligent people, professionally trained to deal with problems in human relations. They carry their professional know-how into the daily routines of family living, and with it goes unusual warmth and spontaneity.

The G.'s do not pamper their children. They lack the resources for pampering via any great quantity of material comforts or luxuries, but these are rather unimportant in their scheme of things anyway. Their home is too small, too crowded, and too cluttered. They would like to have a bigger and better one, but they are much more concerned with the kind of living that goes on in it. Mrs. G. is casual about clothes and matters of personal grooming, but not in the least casual about matters of physical or psychological health. She and her husband keep a sharp eye on matters like these. They are never too busy to visit at the schools to which their children go, or too assured to listen to what their children's teachers have to say.

This tells a good deal about the G.'s, because they are very busy people. In addition to their respective jobs as bread-winner and homekeeper they find an endless number of other chores to do. Their interests, and their abilities, lead them inevitably into presidencies, chairmanships, and committees. They become involved in parent groups, civic groups, and re-ligious groups. They arrange programs, circulate petitions, and help to raise money for one or another group or cause. Their interests are liberal, humanitarian, and deeply religious.

The G.'s send their older children to a Hebrew parochial school. They do so, they tell us, reluctantly and in protest against the greatly inferior public school in their vicinity. All of their children have been to the Rodney Nursery School, an experience which the G.'s value highly. They would like to have them continue at school with children of varied racial and religious backgrounds, as they would tend to do in the public schools. But sound education ranks even higher among the things they want for their children. This they will not sacrifice in favor of social heterogeneity, and so their older children go to school with other Jewish children, and choose their neighborhood friends from the children of Jewish families.

Debbie's parents have misgivings about this situation. De-voted as they are to their own faith, and eager to see this devo-tion repeated in their children, they "don't want their children to be prejudiced." They were delighted when the daughter of the sole Catholic family in the neighborhood be-came the good friend of their eldest. They could then use this family as an example to prove that "not all Christians are mean and cruel," an opinion to which they find the second eldest rapidly inclining.

Ruth has some reason for her unfavorable opinion of Christians. Like her mother, who also grew up in the Upper Harding border area, Ruth has been called "dirty Jew" and spat upon by Christian children whom she meets on the way to school. Mr. and Mrs. G., for all their highly *rationalistic* approach to intergroup problems, are at a loss with a personal problem like this.

"We can't tell her to say she isn't Jewish, and she wouldn't lie anyway. If she weren't so sensitive, it wouldn't be quite so bad, but she takes it very hard. . . . She's scared to death and beginning to hate Christians and other people who persecute Jews. She even talks about the English —because of the Palestine business—as being as bad as the Germans. She's gotten that from listening to the radio I guess—I don't think she gets it from us. . . . Sometimes, though, I wonder how much we do have to do with it.

"Anyway, even Debbie is getting it. . . . We don't know what to do about it. We've tried to explain to the children about differences in religion and differences in race. We've told them that people have different ideas about religion and that we should respect other people's ideas, but we don't necessarily take theirs over. We've said that we don't want them to be exclusive—we want them to play with all kinds of children whenever they can. About race I've tried to explain that there are just natural differences in color of skin, and hair, and eyes, and pointed out the differences right in the family. I did that with Debbie when she first started to nursery school. We saw a Negro on the street car and she said 'look—that man didn't wash his face.'

"Debbie hasn't had anything more to say since about Negroes, but she thinks the English are 'terrible' and she divides the world into Jewish and Catholic."

Debbie is, in fact, intensely aware of being Jewish. At school one day she looked critically at the meat she had left on her luncheon plate, and explained: "I can't eat the meat at school because I'm Jewish, and my Mommie's Jewish, and my Daddy's Jewish. I'm not supposed to eat the meat at school." The comment brought no response of any kind (and Debbie ate the meat). To the Observer Debbie talked about her twin, and found in a picture a white boy who "looks like Danny." Why? "Because he's the *color* of Danny." And what color is Danny? "White of course," snaps Debbie impatiently, "Do you think he's not Jewish?"

Debbie is highly aware of color differences, and of very subtle differences in color and in other physical attributes. These matters are so obvious to her that she plays with them and turns her lively humor loose with them. She tells the Observer, with a mischievous grin, "That's you!" pointing to the Negro woman in the picture. "And that is Miss ———," she adds, identifying her brown teacher with the white woman. She makes other perverse identifications, thoroughly enjoying what she senses to be a fine joke on the Observer.

When she gets down to business, however, she makes it clear that she not only knows just what color people really are, what kind of hair they have, etc., but also that she has definite preferences. She states them politely and even a little reluctantly. Nevertheless the "colored" or "brown" or "black" people are "funny" or "not sweet," and she states flatly: "I don't like the brown ones." The "white" or "lighter" people are prettier, nicer, and "the sweetest."

Debbie has a sense of social distance too. At school she never rejects the brown children, but her favorites are white, with one exception. The exception is a little girl quite like Debbie in interests and personality, and very light. With the Observer, Debbie spontaneously groups the brown dolls and separates them from the white ones, saying, "Brown—and brown—and black hair. I put these together. They're not the sweetest. I put the sweetest with the sweetest. A white with a white and a brown with a brown."

THE TERMS

1. *Debbie is quick.* Her mental activity is of an exceptional order, and so are her mental capacities (I.Q. 138). Her active mind plays over and feeds upon every aspect of the people and things around her. She notes details and classifies like and unlike people and things. She notes racial details and makes racial groupings exactly as she notes and generalizes about family groups, religious groups, and other phenomena.

2. *Debbie has important models.* In the four older members of her family, Debbie has examples in mental alertness and

in a thoughtful approach to social phenomena. The fact that the members of the family are emotionally close to one another facilitates the transfer of ideas.

The *nature* of her parents' ideas gives Debbie a starting point for her thinking. They set an example in being strongly *for* the in-group. This is quite different from setting an example in being *against* the out-group. Yet, as Debbie's parents are aware, in-group preference and constant association are very likely to leave the out-group (or groups) looking strange and distant at best.

3. *Debbie has a very strong sense of "We."* The Jewish in-group is her reference point. She has a sense of its unity, its differentness, and of her place in it. She values the We and measures others against it. If the others are unlike it they are automatically somewhat less attractive.

4. *Debbie is reasonable and moderate.* She is never harsh, rough, or violent. Her native gentleness is supported by a habit of *thinking* about questions rather than leaping to sudden and unqualified conclusions. The vehement and rash are not congenial to her, and her orientations toward race are lacking in these qualities. She has perhaps never heard racial epithets, but it is doubtful whether she would use them if she had. She states her white preferences and brown rejections with a mildness quite in keeping with her own personality and her parents' values.

That she departs from her parents' equalitarian ideals is a consequence of her own observations concerning physical differences, a tendency to associate color with dirtiness (and perhaps of other unfavorable spontaneous associations), and a preference for her family and the people most like its members. This last is an unavoidable consequence of close family ties and of her parents' strong in-group adherence.

Elaine D.—"I don't like colored kids—"

Elaine looks like a frail reed. She is small for her age, delicately built, and delicately blond. If it were not for the corrective glasses she wears, she would be quite a pretty child. Glasses and all, she would look much prettier if her clothes were better. They are never unclean, nor is Elaine herself. But her clothes are old, faded, mismatched, and often lacking buttons.

So Elaine looks like a frail and self-respecting waif. One would expect to find her shy, sweet, and gentle. She is, in fact, sweet upon occasion. Her demonstrations of affection are sometimes cloyingly sweet, but they suggest bids for affection as much as expressions of that feeling. Shy or gentle Elaine distinctly is not. She is bossy and domineering, and highly vocal about it. She will "take over" the controls from adults quite as readily (if she can) as from other children. She knows what she wants *and* what they should want, or even feel. She can sometimes convince them that she knows better than they do. The children around her must be strong characters themselves if they are not to become cowed and dependent.

This willful little creature is a bundle of strong emotions. At school she is often very gay when her craving for close human ties finds satisfaction. When things are going well she is imaginative in her play and quite cooperative. When they are not going well she may resort to very babyish fits of tears and sulks or sly evasions of authority. She is very sensitive to the reactions of others, and rather easily becomes angry or jealous. She often needs to be comforted—to be reassured that she is loved, but reminded that attention and leadership have to be shared.

Elaine's sensitivities extend to her physical as well as her social environment. She appreciates the beauties of nature and the beauties created by man. Cleanliness and neatness are extremely important to her. She makes a great fuss over clean or new bibs, sheets, doll clothes, and so on, and is a keen observer of the condition of the things among which she moves. She is full of questions, partly because she does want to know more about her world and partly because questions swing attention her way. Whether questioning or not she is inclined to be a chatterbox whose conversation flits about erratically.

At school Elaine meets adults who treat her quite differently than she is treated at home. She knows the steady hand of adult guidance at school rather than at home, and inclines to respond to it with trust and a greater sense of comfort. She learned to do so after a period of uncertainty about the newness of the nursery school—a period during which she wailed and had tantrums upon her mother's departure. She has learned to take mother's comings and goings with indifference, but her conversation at school suggests that she feels warm affection for the members of her family, particularly for the brother two years older than she.

Elaine's mother is what the Rodney School staff calls "high-strung." Mrs. D. is sensitive and emotional like her daughter. She is sometimes harsh with the children when she is angry, though she loves them and looks after their essential needs. She manages to keep the two older boys and Elaine's little sister clean and clothed, fed, and medically attended. But Mrs. D. lacks the energy, or the knowledge, to do much more.

Neither she nor Elaine's father, who does hard manual labor all day long, have much to give their children in the way of intellectual stimulation or skillful handling. Their undistinguished natural endowments have had little development through either formal education or breadth of experience. They do the best they can for their children within these limits and the limits set by their inadequate income. The public agencies come to their rescue occasionally when the going gets extremely rough. They turn to the parish priest for counsel about child guidance or other domestic problems. This is natural enough to people in the first generation removed from the Irish parish of the old sod.

Elaine's parents have had ample interracial exposure, but it has meant little to them. Their views of race are largely of the *egocentric* sort. They tolerate the Negroes who are their close neighbors, and Mrs. D. tolerates the mixed play groups in which her children move. She gives the whole matter rather little attention, but there is neither friendliness nor sympathy in her attitude. She inclines to vague fears about Negroes—they are alien creatures. They are as far outside the range of her understanding as they are close within the range of her contacts. Mrs. D.'s incidental neighborhood contacts have been supplemented by those she has had at Rodney School. Elaine's favorite brother preceded Elaine there, and Mrs. D. has had ample opportunity to meet and learn to know both Negro teachers and Negro parents. She has met them, and nothing more.

Mrs. D. instructs her children to "like them just the same" whether their teachers and playmates happen to be colored or white. This is the best way to avoid trouble in cases of unavoidable contact. Furthermore, Elaine knows, presumably because her mother has instructed her, that " 'nigger' is something you don't say seriously." Elaine has not been known to say it at school, seriously or otherwise, but her mother knows her to have said it at home. Mrs. D. holds that "she learned it in nursery." She indicates her surprise that Elaine now accepts Negro playmates whereas she "used to call them 'dirty'" and "never used to bother with anyone who was colored." This too is something Elaine has picked up at nursery, and something about which Mrs. D. is by no means enthusiastic.

Elaine's mother need have no concern lest her third child and older daughter become too friendly across the line. In her public behavior at school Elaine shows a slight tendency to favor white children. In her private behavior (with the Observer) she shows a strong tendency to favor whites and to reject Negroes. Her awareness of race is high and her feelings about it quite clear-cut. She states them in no uncertain terms, and not once but repeatedly: "I don't like black ones—I like white ones." "One's good (w woman) and one's naughty (N woman)." "I don't like this father (N)—I like this one (w)." "I like all these (w dolls)—and I don't like anybody else." "I like white girls. Black girls hit me." And, Elaine assures us, she would not invite the pictured brown boy to her house to play "'cause *I don't like colored kids.*"

This deceptively mild-looking little girl carries her emotionality and her strong convictions into her feeling and thinking about race. She has a firm sense of affinity with whites and an equally firm preference for them. She feels superior to Negroes and either indifferent or antagonistic toward them. Negroes are for her sharply and consistently set apart, and she likes herself and her own kind the better for being so different from the other kind. She bolsters her doubts about her own attractiveness by seeing people so unlike herself as very unattractive.

THE TERMS

1. *Elaine is sharp-eyed and curious.* She sees details about people, partly because she is interested in people, partly because she is generally interested in details. Her intellectual powers are of an ordinary sort (I.Q. 95), but they are fully focused upon the getting of affectionate response and a dominant position in relation to other people.

2. *Elaine is discriminating.* She has strong likes and dislikes, a strong tendency to categorize good and naughty, clean and dirty, black and white. She takes satisfaction in making unqualified judgments and in stating them firmly. She enjoys saying: "I like—" or "I don't like—." Doing so enhances her

feeling of being superior, sure, and in command. It is a feeling which needs enhancing.

3. *Elaine is unsure of herself.* She is a moderately insecure child. Her assertive and aggressive ways are in part expressions of this insecurity. She is testing herself against other people, measuring her strength and charms against theirs, in the need and hope of finding reassurance about herself. She is an inherently strong-willed and emotional child who has not been helped to direct her strength and her emotionality effectively. She has not been provided with the self-controls or the social techniques she needs to achieve the effective use of her potentials and the appreciation she craves.

4. *Elaine has been inadequately guided.* Her parents influence rather than guide her. She copies them and reacts to their personalities, but they do not exercise either strong or consistent controls. She is more comfortable where there are controls. The lack of them enhances her insecurity.

In matters of race she has absorbed the general atmosphere of her home—basic antagonism combined with lethargic acceptance, adding to it something of her general emotionality and assertiveness. There are no home controls in this respect either. She rejects Negroes if she feels like doing so and accepts them if she wishes. Her mother observes either reaction with mild interest and quite sympathizes with the rejection. Meanwhile she feebly opposes it with a principle of social equality which has little or no personal meaning for her.

5. *Elaine needs a target.* She is well along toward finding one. "Black ones" are a conspicuous target upon which she can release her domineering and judgmental tendencies, her emotional excesses, and the angers arising from her personal discontents. There is little to prevent her doing so. Preventive controls, either outside or inside herself, are few and feeble.

Part II

Equations with a Brown Term

James F.—"What does it mean?"

Jimmy is sociable. He is something of a favorite with the children at Coleman House, and the teachers, too, find him attractive and appealing. He is attentive and responsive to them, as he is to his fellows. He is ready to carry on a fluent conversation with anyone at any time, he plies people with questions, cajoles, bargains, smooths over differences. The more children involved in his play, the better he likes it. The more close, numerous, and lasting his friendships, the happier he is. Jimmy is affectionate and sympathetic, but also sensitive and jealous, especially where the attentions of adults are involved.

At home Jimmy is accustomed to receive the alert attention of his parents, most particularly his mother. He has been her "baby" for four years, but there will soon be another to take his place. So we meet Jimmy at a moment when he is not quite at his best. He has been very happy playing the baby role, and he is not yet ready to give it over to another. Moreover he is somewhat involved just now in an investigation of sex, which he gathers to be somehow related to the loss he is about to suffer. His mother has "explained" about babies and their origins in the best rational-scientific manner. Still Jimmy remains confused and preoccupied about grownups and what happens between them.

Jimmy's mother is not worried about him. But this is not to say that she is indifferent. Mrs. F. is indifferent to nothing which involves the happiness and welfare of her children. It is rather that she understands exactly the "phase" he is going through and has not the slightest doubt about the outcome. Jimmy will get over his temporary disturbance, everybody will be happy about the new baby, everything will work out quite satisfactorily. She will see that it does.

Mrs. F. is a determined and confident woman. She knows what she wants and she has no real doubts about her ability to get it.

"I made up my mind a long time ago," she says, "that I would prove I could do just a little better than other people. I decided that success and achievement are what count. It takes brains, independence, and ambition. Well— I have plenty of independence and ambition at least. Sometimes I think one of my sisters got all the brains in our family. She's really dark—quite a bit darker than I am—but that girl is getting places. She's topnotch.

"I should have gone to college, but I was having babies when other girls my age were still getting the education I wish I had. Thank goodness I managed to get through secretarial school— that's come in handy. My working for a while now and then has helped a lot. My husband's 'maintenance' job doesn't pay very well. He picks up a little extra on the things he makes in his spare time, but all of what we both bring in has to be stretched to the limit. . . . We've managed, and we always will."

Jimmy's mother also decided a long time ago that she wanted four children. The fourth will soon be lying in the neatly decorated bassinet beside her bed. She has no doubt that her husband will get over his resentments and his reluctance toward the new member of the family. The three of them will manage in the big bedroom, Jimmy's big sister will have the little one, the two boys will share the third. The apartment is big enough for them all. It is comfortable and attractively furnished too—Mrs. F. has seen to that—she sees to everything. As she says,

"You have to *plan* for things. . . . I plan my life. I'm on my own—working for me. My husband has only lately seen the value of what I want to achieve. He hasn't my ambition. He's easy-going—he likes to play.

"So do I, but the job comes first. Nothing gets in the way of my giving the children the best of me—the best of everything I can give them. I do a lot of club work and committee work—all kinds of things. Sometimes I have a job downtown too. But the children don't pay for it. My mother helps me out. She's a good woman, and good with the kids. They've been with her quite a lot. But when I'm not working I'm home at noon to see that they have a hot meal, no matter what else I have to do. I'm never too busy to see that they get to the clinic for their shots, to get their teeth cleaned, or whatever they need. And I see that their clothes are in good condition and that they look right when they go out of the house. I like nice clothes myself. I want my children to like them—to take an interest in their appearance, and to be immaculate about themselves.

"They do pretty well. I'm proud of them, I might as well admit. I've tried to train them by the best methods, but I don't spoil them. I insist on politeness and obedience and cleanliness—things like that—but I give them lots of love and I reward them when they come through. They know I will—when I make them a promise I keep it. I try to understand their little quirks and handle them accordingly.

. . . We talk things over—I'm honest with them—I tell them exactly what I think so they'll know where they stand. . . . I think we get along mighty well—and the kids with each other too.

"Naturally, I have ambitions for them. I want them all to go to college. They're getting a good start—the older ones go to a parochial school you know, and I'm going to send Jimmy too. We're Catholic and my religion is important to me. I want the kids to have religious education. Besides, they mix with all kinds at the parochial school and I like that. I'm all for mixing.

"I know the problems all right. Susan is one of three colored girls in her school—that first week of school she had a hard time of it, but I let her fight it out. She's made her way—now she has a girl friend who is white and the two of them will talk on the phone by the hour if I don't put a stop to it. They seem to be crazy about each other. Susan's going to have her friend over some day—she hasn't been able to come yet—they live so far away. . . . Susan gets along fine.

"I keep an eye on the children but there has been no real race problem with the older ones—they seem to accept it. Jimmy pays very little attention. He did once say a woman who had her picture in *Ebony* looked like his teacher, but that's about all. . . . I will tell him when the problem comes up. Now I just see that he doesn't have books like *Little Black Sambo*. . . . We're not 'black'—we're *brown*. I detest that book and I detest the word. Jimmy was called 'black' once—when he was out at his grandmother's. He went and asked her 'what does it mean?' . . . So was Susan, 'black nigger' to be exact—and right here in the Project where there are nothing but colored children! . . . Jimmy knew about that too.

"Those are the things that happen sometimes. . . . Of course being colored means problems, but as I see it everybody has problems. The thing is to get in and lick them. . . . I'm not going to let anybody run our people down—I'm proud of the things we've accomplished, but I'm not going to go around with a great big chip on my shoulder. My husband's the same way. He won't take abuse, but he's not one to go borrowing trouble. The men he works with like him a lot and he likes them—but he'll stop them from telling jokes and things like that.

"We have friends from school that we still see—one of them drops in here every once in a while like a bad penny. We go out with some people in mixed groups sometimes— once we were the only colored at a party, and we had a good time. . . . I had a white boss one time who was a peach—he didn't care the least thing about color. And I've worked with all kinds—on my last job two Jewish girls, two Irish, and I was the one colored. Believe me, I heard all sides! . . . I think there's more trouble between the Jews and the Irish, and I must say the Irish have my sympathy.

"I've hit some lemons of course. I was turned down when I tried to get a job at one of the biggest stores downtown. There are bound to be things like that though. We have to overlook a lot and rise above it."

Jimmy's mother does "rise above it," just as she actually does nearly everything else she intends to do and reports having done. Moreover she is inclined to see things for just about what they are. Her estimate concerning Jimmy's inattention to race is no exception.

Jimmy's race awareness *is* low. In school he gives no sign of noticing or caring about color differences between the children. His friendship-seeking is quite unrestricted. But to the Observer he shows an occasional flash of awareness and of feeling. He does not notice color, hair, and such very often. He has a quite adequate color vocabulary, though he uses it rather seldom. He knows that "black" is not a complimentary term and that it applies to himself and other brown people. He knows his own color identity but he is not entirely happy about it, since he is developing a liking for whites and whiteness as he becomes more aware of differences.

Jimmy is beginning to feel that there is something wrong— something other than the new baby. It has to do with his color, which can be called "black" although it isn't black. His mother says it isn't, and she *knows*, and he can see for himself anyway. "Black" is not a good word—his mother hates it and his grandmother told him never again to play with the little boy who called him "black." Susan was mad when somebody called her "black nigger." That is a *very* bad thing to say to anybody.

Jimmy wonders about these things sometimes, and feels a little uneasy. But there are other things which take his attention, and he forgets. He does not find it easy to keep his attention for long on any one matter, and he very soon tires of the effort involved in trying to piece together some little things about color in a way that makes any sense. He turns back to what is fun, much easier, and much more important to him—winning friends and influencing people. This is a highly satisfying business. With lots of children playing with him and grown-ups paying him attention, and all of them liking him, he can feel safe and successful. Anyone likes to feel safe. Jimmy likes especially to feel successful—successful with people.

THE TERMS

1. *Jimmy is not a thinker.* He finds it hard to keep his mind on a problem, to observe closely, to sort out little things seen or heard, and to arrange them in a meaningful order. His mental powers are quite average (I.Q. 102). Certainly he could make more use of them than he does, but he can always go to mother for the "answers." He much prefers to do so, and for at least two reasons. First, mother knows everything. In addition, Jimmy has not learned to enjoy being independent.

2. *Jimmy is young for his age.* That is, he has not outgrown habits of infantile dependency to the degree common among his age-mates. He likes being mother's baby and getting her attention or that of some other grown-up if she is not around. Having these habits of infantile dependency, he is not moved to think for himself unless something he values highly is at stake.

3. *Jimmy values social success.* He has a strong need to surround himself with people who love and appreciate him— a need which is itself an expression of dependency. The need is strong enough to occupy the best of his attention and to stimulate him to think for himself, to take initiative, to do relatively independently things which he has learned will make him popular.

The pursuit of popularity absorbs him and rewards him. He has begun to be concerned about race largely because he senses that his popularity is threatened by his color. This is the entering wedge. Jimmy will be driven to do some observing and thinking about race to the degree that he sees it threatening his popularity.

4. *Jimmy's mother molds her children.* She is the dominant influence in Jimmy's life, and she is highly *rationalistic* about race. She has thought it through, she understands her position and is able to feel almost comfortable in it. This sense of comfortable assurance is in Jimmy, and it promotes a casual acceptance of such racial items as have penetrated his consciousness.

Furthermore, Mrs. F. has many interests. She stimulates her children to think about and want the many things she thinks about and wants. Her interests and wants tend to be not so much *across* race lines as *above* them. This race-free *choosing-orientation,* too, is in her children.

Paul B.—*"I don't like that black one—"*

Paul stands alone. There are limits to the aloneness which a four-year-old can achieve, but Paul makes the most of the possibilities. He can be physically adjacent and emotionally removed. It is through this kind of control that he achieves his isolation. He cuts himself off from people, and he appears to have done it quite consistently.

He has learned to pull the shades—to close his face to cover his feelings. His expression is watchful or suspicious, but a sheepish grin may play around his mouth when he is saying what he knows to be untrue. He has a well-structured face, very dark and distinctively Negroid, borne on a well-built and well-coordinated body. He is strong and skillful with his hands whether he is painting or fighting. He does either with a certain detachment, as though he were enjoying the exercise and his own skill without caring very much about the outcome.

Paul can be loud, aggressive, and fast moving. If he chooses he can enter into the group play with other children and get along with them, contributing ideas which are accepted. He prefers boys and boyish play, and he is liked chiefly by boys whose interests he occasionally shares. He has no general popularity, nor does he seem to care. He can intimidate other children physically and hold his own with them generally. He knows it and does not push, though he will sometimes compete physically or verbally to be first or to get what he happens to want at the moment.

In relations with his teachers at Coleman House, Paul is rather less withdrawn than with his age-mates. The attention and affection of his teachers is more important to him. He likes their encouragement and wants their approval. In relation to them he is more the little boy and not so self-assured after all. He tends to like his teachers. He shows them affection and tries to win their favor and avoid their disfavor, by deceit if necessary.

Paul's teachers find him a challenge as well as a provocation. They know that much emotion is controlled and restrained behind that mask he wears, and that his psychological health is not what it might be. They know some of the reasons.

Paul's mother is perhaps the major reason behind his problems. Mrs. B. is a large and gaudy woman, self-engrossed and extravagantly ambitious. She fancies herself becoming a singing star of the network or the stage, and imagines herself presently cutting a quite glamorous swathe to that goal. It would be a far cry from the domestic service in which she and Paul's father worked at the time of their marriage. Mrs. B.'s vanity is inadequately fed on such dreams, but it would perhaps be inadequately satisfied in any case. She improves upon the realities in talking about them, and sets Paul a pattern in deceit, perhaps even in self-deceit.

Mrs. B. is the mother of two more children older than Paul. She is, by her own evaluation, a self-sacrificing mother and a devoted wife. She talks, without encouragement, about how much she loves her children and their father, and of her concern for their best interests. But Paul arrives at school in clothing which is dirty, worn, and torn, he is sometimes forgotten and left there, or he may reach home under a neighbor's guidance to find the door locked and his mother's whereabouts unknown. Paul roams entirely at liberty among the Project children whether his mother is at home or not. Her protestations to the contrary, the evidence suggests that Mrs. B.'s interest in her four-year-old is of an incidental sort.

Paul's father appears to function as no marked antidote to his mother's influence. Mr. B. has two major preoccupations which absorb whatever energy survives a laborer's day. Both his preoccupations came with him years ago when he ran away from a home in the deep south. Religion is one of them —race is the other.

Mr. B. is a Baptist of the deadly serious sort. He pores over his Bible in all spare moments, and anticipates a glamorous future of his own. He aspires to become a minister, or a deacon at the very least. To this goal he is as dedicated as is his wife to hers. Paul and the other children again play a distinctly subsidiary role, though father practices his future career upon them. They are read to from the Bible, they are prayed with and prayed about, and they receive sermons of great moral worth.

Paul is responsive to neither of his parents. He does not obey his mother, and he rarely shows affection for her. He observes thoughtfully that "My mother screams and laughs. Makes my ears hurt. I jump into bed." He is aggressive toward his father, but some of father's exhortations have taken at least temporary root. At school Paul refuses to dance, because father says dancing is sinful. And Paul has developed a sincere respect for the power of the Almighty. "I bet," he says, "I just bet you can't beat God."

In terms of color Paul is considered the ugly duckling of his family. He is darker than his siblings, and conspicuously darker than either parent. Mrs. B. takes particular pride in her own light and also powder-lightened skin, but she is darker than Paul's father. Mr. B. has suffered for his lightness, and continues to do so. His preoccupation with race stems from a childhood made miserable by an older sister who taunted him with being white. Years later Mr. B.'s mother confessed what the older sister guessed—that Mr. B.'s father was a white man. Mr. B. winces at the frequent questions raised concerning his ancestry, and addresses himself furiously to the expunging of sin from the world.

The B.'s are quite unable to cope with race in any consistent or rational fashion. Their view is of the sort which we have called the *egocentric* type. Mrs. B. professes a sophistication in cross-racial contact which is belied by her behavior, and talks about principles which she does not understand. Her husband grasps little beyond his own racial problems. Both are largely untutored people floundering between the southern folk-ways of their childhoods and the northern folk-ways of their adulthood. The result is confusion. Scraps of superstition, half-truths, and grandiose principles lie in undigested masses in their minds. They think that race and color ought not to be talked about, "because we are all human beings," and several presumably relevant quotations from the Bible are advanced to support this point. They think Negroes and whites ought to get along together, but when their big boy brings home a white playmate they tell the child to go home. The south is fine—"they discriminated but they treated us nice.

They have just as nice things for colored down south as they do for white up here,"—but they would not think of going south again.

Mrs. B.'s most consistent attitude is compounded of racial inferiority and pride in her relative lightness. She wants, above all, personal fame and the money which she regards as inseparable from it. She envies whites for their advantages in respect to these goals. Beyond this highly personalized aspect of it she cares rather little about the problem of race. She has nothing to give her children in the way of racial guidance, and they do not come to her with questions.

Paul's race awareness is of a medium order, but his feelings are strong. He is not clear about kinds of people, though he has a notion that there is a "black" kind, and another kind which he only occasionally labels "white." He sometimes calls the black kind "Black Sambo" (his mother has read the book to him). Paul probably sees himself as being actually very dark, and he clearly prefers not to do so. He always finds white figures prettier and nicer, and he rejects "black." He tell us: "I don't like that father, he's got a black head," and "I want to tell you which one I like; I like that one (w), *I don't like that black one.*"

THE TERMS

1. *Paul is shrewd.* He has the shrewdness of a child who has learned to rely upon himself. He is not an inherently gifted child, if his I.Q. of 107 be taken as the measure. But the score represents a performance in which two intellectual capacities (or habits) are high. Paul shows perceptual acuity (particularly with respect to the human figure) of a high order, and he demonstrates a long attention span.

Paul is a keen observer who can keep his eye on whatever ball is of importance to him, and these capacities have been enhanced by circumstances. He has lived nearly five years with parents who pay him little attention and whom he has found untrustworthy. The experience has taught him to find his own way, and to size up other people with care. In the process of doing so he takes note of the marks of race, along with other attributes.

2. *Paul is a bystander.* He has found, again by experience, that there is safety in staying clear of the fray, at least until he can see how to move in without getting stepped on. The bystander is likely to get a clearer view of the active partici-

pants than they get of themselves. Paul has not been too busy to see what the active participants look like, or too busy to think about what he looks like.

3. *Paul keeps his opinions and feelings to himself.* There is safety in this, too, when rewards and punishments are so erratically administered at home. He cannot be sure when he can safely say what he thinks. Hence he says little, or says what he does *not* think or what he knows to be untrue. Deceit as a weapon of self-defense has been demonstrated for him by his mother. It works for him too.

Mother and father do not like talk about color (from their children, at least), and they do not say anything about it which Paul can understand. So Paul does not talk about color either, and he gets no help in understanding it. A confusing matter becomes the more confusing because observations and questions cannot be brought out and talked about.

4. *Paul is looking for something.* He does not know what it is, but he has a feeling of need. He needs affection and reassurance, particularly from grown-ups, because he gets so little at home. He looks for the nice and the attractive grown-ups, and follows cues picked up from his mother's high valuation of lightness. At school he finds grown-ups who are nice and attractive, and he observes that they are often light. So Paul is finding what he needs tied up with the attributes most unlike his own. In this there is cold comfort, and the seeds of new troubles.

Sam S.—"And now I'm brown."

Sam is a charmer. Everybody loves him. Big and little, white and brown fall for his wide grin, his lively humor, his bright and imaginative ways, his vigor and joy in living. As his mother says, he "just walks right up to people and makes friends everywhere he goes." He likes people, and he is not afraid of them. He knows how to make friends and he wants friends.

At nursery school Sam is a leader and an organizer. He contributes ideas, gets the others interested in them, and keeps things moving. He is quite unself-conscious about all this, and quite confident. He rarely "shows off" or shows jealousy or envy of another child's similar abilities.

He has a wide range of interests and appreciations. He is alert to the details of things, and appreciative of colors, textures, cleanliness, and prettiness.

Sam is not a handsome child, but his face is eager and open and happy. He is a good strong brown, and even if he were not, no one would guess wrongly about his largely Negro ancestry. He is about the same color as his mother, but his father is markedly lighter. Sam's mother says that

". . . as a baby he was light. He was just about a year old when he began to darken up. Sometimes he will say to me 'why can't I get like so and so?'—meaning somebody who's lighter than he is. I don't say anything more than that people are different and they can't change. I don't know if he thinks it's nicer to be light, or what."

Sam *does* think it's nicer to be light, and he knows that he was once lighter than he now is. Looking at dolls with the Observer he points to the white one and says: "I *was* white, like this, and now I'm brown." In spite of this candid admission concerning his present color, Sam is reluctant to identify himself with brown dolls or with the Negroes in pictures. He thinks the white dolls are prettier and he greatly admires and loves a very blond little girl with whom he goes to school, and a blond teacher. He toys with their hair and gently touches their skin.

Sam's mother is a steady, hard-working, sensible person. She needs all her strength and ability, because she has to look after Sam and herself single-handed. She divorced Sam's father two years ago because he behaved like an irresponsible child. He still comes around to see "the boy" once in a while, and the boy loves seeing him, but gets along quite nicely when he doesn't. Sam has a devoted uncle who partly takes his father's place, and he has two devoted grandmothers whom he often sees. His mother's best "girl friend" gives him a great deal of attention, and so do the neighbors and the grown-ups at Sunday school and nursery school. He does not lack for attention and affection from adults, father or no father.

Mrs. S. and her son live in the only home Sam has ever known. It is a nice home too, for Lower Harding—a two-bedroom apartment in a substantial and well-kept building not far from the Rodney School. The apartment is shiningly clean and in almost rigid order. Spotless white slip covers protect the upholstered living-room furniture, the family photographs are precisely placed on either side of the table lamp, and Sam's things are in the places provided for them. His mother shows us around, starting with

> ". . . the little table in the living room for his books—he knows those are his to read any time he likes, but he mustn't touch anything else. All his loose toys go into a big box here in the corner of the kitchen, right beside his little table and chairs. . . . He knows how to keep his room neat and clean —his shoes and rubbers there—his snowsuit goes there— and his stuffed animals lined up beside his bed."

Sam and his mother are themselves as clean and tidy as their home. Neither in their apartment or about themselves is there any luxury, any emphasis on style or even on beauty. Things are sturdy, sensible, and above all, *clean.*

Mrs. S. keeps a firm hand on the rein, so far as Sam is concerned. She is proud of her son's winning ways, his brightness, and his many little social triumphs. But she is quite convinced that her training has had as much to do with Sam's successes as have his native talents. Certainly Sam wins people partly because he is automatically polite and considerate, and (for a four-year-old) unselfish and interested in the other fellow. His mother's training may have much to do with these talents, but he is equipped with native intelligence of an order well above average, and with real talents for dramatics and mimicry.

Moving in racially mixed groups, as Sam does, is nothing particularly new in his family. His mother still has Syrian and Italian "girl friends" with whom she went to high school or to the trade school where she learned dressmaking. Mrs. S. has her own skills in getting along with people, and she tells us that she

> ". . . never had any trouble at any time with any white person or any of them calling me out of my name, and Sam hasn't either so far as I know.
>
> "Sam plays with white children around here, and at school I think he has mixed with more of the white ones than colored. He did at summer camp too.
>
> "I've been waiting for it—but nothing has happened. One day he did hear somebody say 'nigger' and he came home and used it. I told him that it means 'not pertaining to any particular race—just a low mean person.' I said

'that's the right meaning of it, so don't use it.' He didn't believe me so he went and asked my mother, and she said I was right."

Mrs. S. is rather *conventional* in her views about race. She welcomes the friendships of whites for herself and for her son, but she has no real expectation of more than an occasional friendship and an absence of "trouble." She avoids "lower class" elements, white or colored, and likes and hopes to "stay in with nice, respectable people."

Sam is keenly aware of color and he has rather strong feelings about it. He has been known to talk about it at school, and he talks about it at home. He began to do so when he was just about four.

"He's started to distinguish," his mother says. "That is, he'll tell about the children, and then to make sure I know which one it is, he'll say 'the brown one' or 'the white one.' He's done that a lot lately, and he never used to. I suppose he heard the children talking—I think they have a lot to say about it sometimes."

When Sam was four and a half his mother had forgotten his early use of color terms.

"Just about two months ago he began to talk about the children as being 'white' or 'brown' or 'colored,'" she tells us. "He never says 'Negro.' Now whenever he tells me anything about the children or other people he describes them that way. I don't know why he started doing that all of a sudden, but now he does it all the time."

Again when her son was five, Mrs. S. said:

"Now he talks about people being 'colored' or 'white.' That's just recently he's talked about 'colored,' and probably from hearing the other children. He knows what it means, but everybody is the same to him."

Apparently Mrs. S. did not know that the word "black" had also appeared in Sam's racial vocabulary by the time he was a little over four. At that age he repeatedly described dolls as "black," and often coupled the word with "ol' lady" or "ol' girl," while he coupled "white" with "lady."

He gave to the Observer other evidences of awareness and some feeling. He was less than four and a half when he carefully segregated the brown and white families in the picture puzzle and identified his own color, past and present. He also indicated a feeling for the superior power of whites. He said the white boy would get the lollipop, if there were only one. Why? "Because he wanted it." The white boy would get the swing, too, if there were only one and both he and the brown boy wanted it. Why? Because the white boy "ran and jumped on it."

Sam's sense of himself in relation to other people is one of almost solid satisfaction. There is really nothing very wrong in his world, except for the fact that he is not the right color. Like his mother he "has no trouble" and people "don't make any difference," but he knows that "the difference" is there and that it is important. It is a hard fact which politeness, cleanliness, talent, industry, and the exercise of the utmost charm do not erase. It is puzzling, too, since one can change from light to dark but not go back again.

THE TERMS

1. *Sam is bright.* His brightness is more than a matter of an I.Q. of 114, however. It is a matter of being a keen observer, and of being "sharp" at drawing logical inferences. He "puts two and two together" fast, and gets the answer. This ability suggests some imagination too, and Sam has plenty of it. All these traits are useful tools for putting together a picture of the social world and one's own place in it. Furthermore, Sam tends toward critical habits of thought. He did not believe his mother's definition of "nigger," probably for the very good reason that it did not square with the way in which he had heard the word used.

2. *Sam is a secure and highly sociable child.* He likes people and very much wants to be liked by them. He wants to be a leader among his peers. He is keenly aware of other people too. He easily loses self-awareness in his absorption in others. This implies a particularly strong and secure sense of self. The insecure self-doubter who lacks an organized picture of the self and its relation to others is not likely to be able to give attention to those others as Sam does.

Giving one's attention to others promotes the process of seeing what these others are like, racially and otherwise. Wanting to be liked by them, and even to lead them, promotes the polishing of social skills and the assessing of one's social assets and liabilities. This is *not* to suggest that the four-year-old sits down and "figures the angles." Rather, it implies that a child having Sam's social motivations, and his general alertness, will unconsciously "figure" and will develop a *feeling* for his social assets and liabilities.

Sam knows what color he is, and he has a feeling that he is not the right color. He also has an idea that people who are white get what they want just by the taking of it or because they want it. With these two notions rattling around in the busy brain of a child who knows what *he* wants, the amount of charm and energy Sam "turns on" in social relations looks to be *in part* an effort at compensation for being the wrong color.

3. *Sam has standards.* He is acutely aware of cleanliness and order, as he could hardly fail to be in a home like his. He likes the cleanliness at least, and associates it with pleasant and attractive people and things.

He likes lightly pigmented people too. Whether he does so partly because they suggest cleanliness, we cannot be sure, but it is possible. It is highly probable that he likes them because other people he knows do so. He did not, for instance, get out of thin air the idea that he was once lighter than he is now. It is a fact about which his mother has talked, just as she did to the Observer. Sometimes Sam has been within earshot, as he was not when the Observer was his mother's audience. His father is lighter than Sam—this, too, is a point of family interest which has undoubtedly been repeatedly discussed. Knowing the importance attached by Negroes to such matters one must suppose that Sam has heard other references to color differences. The feeling tones—admiration, pride, or envy— in word or voice or gesture would be sensed by most children, and especially so by one attuned to other people.

Sam's mother gives him, though largely unconsciously, a quite *conventional* view of race and an *avoidance* orientation toward "lower class" people. His responsiveness toward her and his sensitivity to social cues help him to catch these feelings and to sort people into color and niceness categories.

4. *Sam has had a social life.* He has had an unusually wide range of contacts and social experiences, in spite of the lack of a father or of other children in his home. He sees and goes places with relatives and his mother's friends. He goes to

Sunday school, nursery school, camp, and dancing class, and he plays and visits about in the neighborhood with both whites and Negroes. His mother says she doesn't know where he learns all the things he brings home. The answer undoubtedly lies in these varied contacts and in his alertness and social sensitivity.

Joan M.—"I'd like to be white."

Joan is one of those "little ladies" of whom people say "isn't she a lovely child!" She is pretty and graceful, she has "nice" manners and an easy, friendly way. She is affectionate and gregarious—usually an amiable follower in her group at nursery school. Her teachers at Coleman House agree that she never does anything wrong. She is that joy of the nursery school teacher—the "well-adjusted child." She is, moreover, almost exactly what her mother wants her to be.

Mrs. M. delights in Joan. But this is not to say that she is any more fond of her daughter than of the two older boys. She is devoted to all of them, but she always wanted a girl, and she loves to make pretty clothes for Joan and dress her up. Mrs. M. loves to dress up herself, and to go out looking very smart and doing justice to her own prettiness.

Joan was sent to nursery school because her parents wanted her to have playmates. They will not let her play on the streets alone nor will they let her play with just anyone. But Mrs. M. decided after a while that even nursery school was a bad influence. Joan had begun to behave rather less like a lady—to yell and fight with her brothers, to disobey, and to use unbecoming language. Her mother was sure that the rough children at nursery school were the cause of it all. Joan went to nursery no more.

The M.'s want their children to be "good." The older ones are forbidden to play with "bad boys," and their parents will let them know when their language or their friends are not approved. White children are almost automatically in the approved category, for the M.'s respect white people. They are proud and pleased when Joan and her brothers can play with the children of Mrs. M.'s white employer, or the few other white children they encounter.

The M.'s were born and raised in the south, and their ties with "home" are not yet broken. Their children spend whole summers there. The M.'s discuss the "race problem," comparing the south with New Dublin. They agree that there should be equal rights for the races, but not social equality if the whites don't want it. Mr. M., who works with white men, is inclined to "take" whatever they choose to "dish out." His wife is deferential and equally humble, but rather more inclined to "take offense." She is deeply conscious of her racial inferiority, and very eager for marks of acceptance and approval from the whites, of whose superiority she is equally conscious. Mrs. M. is sympathetic toward Jews. " 'Own-kind' hatred—it's so much worse than white-Negro hatred," she observes. "Anyway, they've been very nice to me."

All of these views and feelings the M.'s try hard to keep from their children. Mrs. M. can discuss sex with her sons more comfortably than she can face the matter of race. Race words in their vocabulary are forbidden, their questions go unanswered, their comments are ignored. Mrs. M. thinks it curious that the children almost never mention color. She is, in fact, greatly relieved that they do not.

Mrs. M. is a very intelligent and a very strong-minded woman. Her daughter, with whom she has firm bonds of sympathy and affection, is very like her in these ways as well as in others. Joan, too, feels strongly about what is good or bad, right or wrong, pretty or ugly. She has learned, however, to keep some of her opinions to herself—since mother does not like to hear them—just as she has learned that mother does not like and will not tolerate emotional fireworks. But Joan is quite able, given time and encouragement, to pull out those hidden opinions and suppressed emotions when encouraged by the Observer to do so.

Joan's mother says of her child's race awareness: "She *knows*—but she hugs and kisses 'em all." Mrs. M. may believe, or want to believe, that there is nothing more to be said. Joan herself has little more to say in public. She comments with interest and admiration upon "the white teachers with long hair," and that is all.

Alone with the Observer Joan's reticence on matters of race wears away. So does her public poise and composure. Her attention is being brought to bear upon something which touches her deeply and personally. She becomes vehement, emotional, and aggressive. The Observer, whom she likes, becomes an enemy who has trapped her into betraying her public self, and Joan takes her revenge. She says that the Observer looks like a Negro. Why? "Because I *want* it to be like you."

Joan, like the rest of the family, is medium brown, and she knows it. She can admit her own resemblance to a brown doll which has long, silky hair which she admires. But on the whole she pretends that she looks like the white dolls and the white girls in the pictures. "White" and "pretty" are almost synonymous for Joan. White is also "good" and "bestest." But "black" is "bad" or "too funny." "No black ones," she says. "I hate 'em. I wouldn't like to be black ones like them. *I'd like to be white.*"

Upon a basis of this evidence, and more, the Observer concludes that Joan is highly aware and that she conceives of two kinds of people. There are "black" and "white," or as she sometimes puts it, "black-faced" and "white-faced." She has strong orientations too; a strong out-group affinity, an out-group preference, a sense of the superiority of the out-group, antagonism toward the in-group, and friendliness toward the out-group.

THE TERMS

1. *Joan is sharp-eyed and logical.* Her I.Q. test yielded a score of 130. The Observer notes concerning her test performance: ". . . her comprehension is at the seven-year level. Her ability to draw logical inferences is very high. She is perceptually very acute, and she remembers her observations. She has good powers of discrimination."

Children equipped with abilities like these do not turn them off when they meet the marks of race. They do not even do so when race is a tabooed subject, any more than the children of middle-class Puritans turn off their natural interest in sex. Both do what Joan has done—they go on observing, thinking, and feeling, but they stop talking.

2. *Joan has strong likes and dislikes.* She is her mother's child in this. She knows exactly what is good and what is bad, what is pretty and what is not pretty. Her exclusive use of the racial labels "black" and "white" is characteristic of her either-or view of things. Her vehement expressions of preference and rejection are equally characteristic. Her values are clear-cut and strongly held.

3. *Joan is greatly interested in "looks."* In this, too, she is like her mother, whose emphasis upon the importance of personal appearance has been transferred. Moreover Joan is pretty. She has found her looks a source of satisfaction. But that source is threatened by the value conflict in herself. She

now feels that white = pretty. She is not white, therefore she perhaps is not pretty after all. It is a conflict which arouses uncomfortable anxieties and doubts.

4. *Joan is a conformist.* She is a "little lady" and she tries to be everything that conformity to conventional standards of niceness demands. Her conformity to her mother's will and expectations is promoted by the similarity and affection between them. The fact that her mother is a highly *conventional* person (racially and otherwise) and given to vigorous *avoidance* of the socially not-nice provides Joan with a congenial model. She conforms quite comfortably.

Discomforts come from the dilemma in which conventionalists like Joan and her mother find themselves. They accept the conventional belief that with whiteness goes superiority, prettiness, niceness. All of these are extremely important to them—again conformity to conventional values. But they are brown. Conformity seems to promise security, but for the people who are brown, it is a trap.

Part III

THE SIGNIFICANT TERMS

There is no *single* key to the how and why of race awareness and race orientation in our children. There are at least six major *kinds* of keys, each of which has its own varieties.

We have reviewed eight cases, in each of which we have seen a distinctive *combination* of certain of these factors. If we were to review all the rest of our 103 cases, one by one, we would find in each a distinctive combination of causal factors, a distinctive *personal equation* made up of certain ones among the total of possible significant terms. We would also find in each case, as we have in the ones we have reviewed, an interplay—an interdependence—between the several terms in each individual equation.

RECURRENT TERMS AND COMBINATIONS

Upon consideration of our entire sample we arrive at some generalizations concerning terms which recur, combinations in which they are likely to appear, and the relation between these and race awareness and feeling. We conclude that certain terms and combinations promote high awareness and strong feeling, and that cross-racial antagonisms appear in certain types of equations.

Table 3 presents a summary of the factors which can play a significant part in determining awareness and orientation. The remainder of this chapter is devoted to a review of these factors and to the high awareness-strong feeling and the cross-racial antagonism types of equations.

Table 3

SIGNIFICANT TERMS—SUMMARY

1. *Individual Attributes*
   a. Personal appearance; coloring and features, structure and use of body
   b. Sex and age

2. *Individual Situation*
   a. Past and present interracial contacts
      (1) Frequency
      (2) Type (pleasant-unpleasant; with equals, superiors, inferiors)
   b. Unusual circumstances (long illness, loss of parents, residence in different sections of the country, etc.)

3. *Models* (for total personality, as well as race-ways and social-ways)
   a. Persons (father, mother, siblings, juvenile or adult friends)
   b. Dominance
      (1) Degree
      (2) Type (conscious, deliberate; unconscious, result of close relationship)
   c. Communication
      (1) Easy, spontaneous, informal, unrestricted
      (2) Self-conscious, formal, taboos and prohibitions
   d. Race-views, social-orientations, race attitudes
      (1) Rationalistic, conventional, egocentric
      (2) Choosing, avoiding, accepting
      (3) Affinity, preference, superiority-inferiority, friendliness-antagonism (in-group, out-group)

4. *Needs and Interests* (healthy or unhealthy)
   - a. Physical activity
   - b. Mental activity (rate, constancy)
   - c. Social activity
     - (1) Goal: relatedness; involves awareness of and concern for others, self-assessment, etc.
     - (2) Goal: "success," popularity, dominance, affection, attention, reassurance
   - d. Conformity: nonconformity
     - (1) Nonconformity:
       - (a) Indifferent, bland, unconcerned, nonassertive, retreatist
       - (b) Assertive, self-conscious, aggressive
     - (2) Conformity:
       - (a) Average degree, unself-conscious
       - (b) Extreme, compulsive, righteous
   - e. Controls, definitions, limits, boundaries
   - f. Dependence-independence
   - g. Target

5. *Values*
   - a. Form
     - (1) Strength of adherence
     - (2) Degree categorical (either-or); attitude toward deviation, difference, etc.
   - b. Content
     - (1) Degree emphasis upon clean, white, light, etc., and obverse
     - (2) Degree emphasis upon "niceness" (good-bad, right-wrong, etc.)
     - (3) Degree emphasis upon "looks," personal appearance, personal esthetics

6. *Characteristic Ways*
   - a. Action-ways
     - (1) Tempo
     - (2) Vigor
     - (3) Range (of movement)
   - b. Feeling-ways
     - (1) Emotional tone (characteristically mild or strong, steady or fluctuating, etc.)
     - (2) Emotional quality (outgoing-responsive, etc., *vs.* withdrawn-unresponsive, etc.)

c. Thought-ways
   (1) Observational and perceptual habits and capac-
       ities (especially for personal appearance and
       behavior)
   (2) Generalizing and synthesizing habits and capac-
       ities (classifying, ordering, inferring, discrim-
       inating between like and unlike features,
       behavior, etc.)
   (3) Attention-paying and concentrating habits and
       capacities (deliberation, speculation, etc.)

1. *Individual Attributes*

a. Personal appearance

The social definition of the child's racial identity is
more important than his *actual* color or other racial features.

We have in our sample "white" Syrian children, and
other "whites," who are darker than some of our "colored"
children. The darkness of these "whites" is an insignificant
factor for two reasons: (1) it is not combined with other
Negroid features (hair, lips, nose forms) as it sometimes
is in the "colored" children, and (2) the dark whites are
known to belong to families in which there are *no* members
showing Negroid features, and to families having *no* suspi-
ciously close ties with people who show Negroid features.
Therefore, it is not color as such which is significant, but
color *combined* with other Negroid features or with social
bonds involving Negroes.

For our children who are socially defined as "white,"
personal appearance factors function very differently than
they do for the so-called "Negroes." To bear the marks of the
white race is to be indelibly stamped "socially acceptable on
grounds of race." Conversely, to bear the marks of Negroid
ancestry, be they ever so faint, is to be equally indelibly
stamped "socially rejected, or at least questionable, on grounds
of race."

As the child becomes aware of his own markings,
which he does in the process of becoming aware of his total
individuality, he is likely to begin to grasp the social meanings of his markings. Personal appearance is heavily emphasized by Americans generally, and it is heavily emphasized
in at least half of our families. Hence the significance of the
personal appearance factor is bound up with the child's sense

of individuality, with his perceptual keenness, and with community and family emphasis upon the importance of personal appearance.

For all our children there are, of course, some social advantages in being what Americans regard as pretty or handsome, well built, graceful or well coordinated, and without physical defects. But whether they do or do not possess some or all of these advantages our children can be affected in one of two ways by their physical attributes. (1) They can be relatively unaware of them and depend upon them relatively little for social success, or (2) they can be quite aware of them and learn to depend upon and exploit their advantages or smart under their disadvantages. If they are affected in the first way they are less likely to take note of race than if they are affected in the second way. This follows because the child whose own physical attributes are important to him develops the habit of focusing on the attributes of others and making comparisons.

Differences in personal appearances are significant for the Negro child when he is among other Negroes as well as when he faces whites. In either case his appearance is judged partly, and importantly, in terms of white standards of attractiveness. The more nearly he approaches white standards the more he will be admired by the members of both groups, and the more he will be envied by less white-appearing Negroes. Whether he is the recipient of admiration and envy or of commiseration and pity, Negroes will soon teach him how important his degree of Negroidism is. His mother is particularly likely to dwell upon the topic with respect to himself at various ages, with respect to his siblings or other children, and with respect to her friends. He can hear the topic discussed by almost anyone else who knows, as all Negroes know, how important are shades of color, kinky versus "nice" or "good" hair, "fine" features versus "coarse" ones, etc.

Our dark Negro children tend to a higher level of awareness than do our light ones, but the emphasis upon racial elements in personal appearance is important for all our Negro children. A greater proportion of our Negro than of our white children show high awareness, and the emphasis upon racial appearance seems surely one of the most important reasons for the difference.

b. Sex and age

Among Americans personal appearance is more stressed for girls than for boys. We find in our sample that girls appear among the high-awareness children more often than do boys. The connection between learning that personal appearance is important and taking note of racial appearance is demonstrated in this difference between girls and boys as well as in the difference between Negroes and whites.

Race awareness is, of course, partly a function of age. Other studies have shown it in older children.[1] In this study we have discovered that children between four and five can vary from almost no awareness to a quite sophisticated awareness. Eight of our children were less than four years and two months old when the study ended. None of the eight showed high awareness, but five of them showed medium awareness. Six of our children were more than five years and two months old when the study ended, and of these only one was highly aware, the rest mediumly aware. High awareness appears in children of four-three and low awareness does not appear in children over four-eleven. Hence we conclude that even within the narrow range represented in our sample, age is a significant factor, but that it is by no means a crucial factor.

2. *Individual Situation*

a. Interracial contacts

Children who live in areas where they frequently see (and perhaps even come to know) racially different individuals are presented with direct perceptual stimuli to awareness. They are also presented with indirect stimuli since, in these areas, race is an immediate issue and often talked about. For these reasons awareness may dawn somewhat earlier in our children than in others who live in racially homogeneous areas. We cannot know, on a basis of this study.

We do know that there is great variation among our own children in respect to frequency of interracial contact of more than a passing sort. We know that a third or more of our high-awareness children have had few sustained contacts across the line. Hence many sustained contacts are not essential for high awareness. The difference between few and many may be less crucial than the difference between few and none, however.

We find that high awareness is a little more frequent

among the Coleman House children than among the children at the Dover and Rodney schools. But this fact does not reflect more interracial contact for the Coleman House children. On the contrary, it is they who have often had rather little of it outside nursery school. In the new situation they see a few white faces. The newness of the total situation and the newness of sustained contacts with white people may make them a little more sensitive to racial differences, just as the white children who come with little interracial experience often "react" to the mixed groups.

Sustained contact probably promotes awareness most effectively if initiated suddenly and as a feature in a wholly new and generally stimulating situation.

In respect to racial orientations, *frequency* of interracial contact is probably of less significance than is *type* of contact. Contacts incidental to a generally pleasant situation, like the nursery school, are certainly conducive to friendly acceptance across the color line. But this favorable association can easily be cancelled out by street play conflict (first-hand experience or vicarious), parental cautioning against Negroes, or any one of a large number of other factors. Certainly, for a majority of our children, the nursery school is the most important stimulus toward equalitarian and friendly cross-racial orientations. But it can by no means ensure their appearance.

b. Unusual circumstances

Hospitalization has proved a racially significant experience for half a dozen of our Negro children.

Loss of a parent, with a subsequent shift in residence, sometimes brings about in the child a new sensitivity to surroundings which are themselves new.

Residential shifts and visits to different parts of the country, or even of the city, are likely to have an alerting effect.

3. *Models*

The importance of the child's models, the people whom he sees often and from whom he is disposed to learn, has been repeatedly indicated.

The child's models provide him with more than their own views of race and their orientations toward society. They give him the pushes or pulls which most importantly affect his total personality. His reactions to race depend upon and are fitted into this personality. Hence the personality-shaping function of his models is quite as important as their specific influences in respect to race.

Furthermore, we have seen that the child can, and often does, learn as much from the general atmosphere generated by the people around him as from their specifically pointed comments and actions bearing upon race.

From the people who are the dominant figures in his world the child learns most, and most especially when the lines of communication between child and dominant figure are open. He soaks up not only what they give him but also what they themselves *are,* and frequently he absorbs the conflicting views—the inconsistencies—they harbor.

If their awareness is high and their feeling strong, the child's awareness is likely to be enhanced. If they let him question, and if they have something coherent to say in reply, his ideas will be clarified, and erroneous notions which he has built more or less independently can be corrected. Taboos on racial discussion do not prevent the development of awareness or feeling, but they do allow for the persistence of confusion, conflict, and inaccuracies.

4. *Needs and Interests*

The child may be deflected from an awareness of race by preoccupations of one or another kind. The preoccupations may be the expression of healthy and more or less inherent inclinations to enjoy physical activity, to conform to the play interests of other children, and to depend upon them or upon older people for cues as to what is and is not important. Psychologically healthy children who are preoccupied with average four-year-old concerns are unlikely to become keenly aware of race unless their attention is drawn to it by striking incidents or by their models (intentionally or inadvertently), *or* unless these same children have an excess of the thought ways which are conducive to awareness (observational and logical keenness, habits of concentration on people and the details of their looks and behavior).

Deflective preoccupations can also appear in the insecure—the psychologically ailing—child. He may develop such needs for personal reassurance and relief from anxieties that he is almost incapable of registering anything beyond his momentary urges to beat somebody up, to cling to the teacher, to knock down another child's carefully built block-pile—anything to let off steam or get attention. This kind of child is like the grown-up whose view of race is of the *egocentric* sort. He is preoccupied with his personal trees, and the forest hardly exists for him.

But the insecure child, in his random thrashing about, may also hit upon a ready-made target in the racially different person, and a fine mode of expressing his own frustrations in racial name-calling. If he finds release and at least temporary satisfaction in expressions of racial antagonism he is likely to persist in such expressions.

Racial name-calling, like other provocative behavior, can serve still another function, and one which is especially important for the insecure child. His trouble is in part that his world is shifting sand—impermanent, unstructured, and lacking in boundaries. He tosses out provocations in an unconscious quest for boundaries, and someone to set them for him. When he meets controls and limitations he gets with them a reassuring sense that there is some structure and order around him, and someone who cares to help him find it.

At the opposite extreme is the child whose security lies in close conformity to the lines laid down for him. If the color line is one of the boundary lines discovered or pointed out to him, he is likely to accept that one along with the others.

The child who conforms in a healthier, less compulsive way is freer to explore and examine. He may arrive at high awareness in the process, but he is less likely to automatically assume the race orientation of his models. So, too, the child who is not overly dependent upon adults for security, or compulsively tied to a central source of satisfaction (such as social success or dominance).

Our children who are nonconformist are not all of the insecure and aggressive kind. They sometimes are retreating for safety rather than lashing out blindly after it. Or they may simply be indifferent and blandly unconcerned with some of the things other people regard as important. In either case their detachment gives them a certain advantage in getting an unobstructed view of race, and perhaps a fairly calm view of it as well.

5. *Values*

Children who are inclined to strong likes and dislikes, and to either-or (black-white) thinking, are very likely to carry these habits over into their responses to race.

Those who have learned to value highly the clean, white, nice, pretty, etc., and to take note of the conditions, tend to build unfavorable associations around Negroes.[2] The tendency operates in Negro children about as frequently as it does in whites.

6. *Characteristic Ways*

a. Action-ways

A fast tempo and extreme vigor in physical activity are not conducive to race awareness, but they do not prohibit its development. In a few of our high-awareness children these traits appear, associated with extreme insecurity. A wide but not frantic range of movement—getting about, seeing new people and situations—can contribute to awareness.

b. Feeling-ways

Both the mild, steady child and the excitable, violent one appear among our high-awareness four-year-olds. These extremes tend to fall into combination with detached observation on the one hand and target-hunting nonconformity on the other. Either can be conducive to awareness, but the second is more conducive to strong feeling about race.

c. Thought-ways

High I.Q. does not of itself bring high awareness. The I.Q. range in our total sample is large (80 to 145), and this range is almost completely represented among high-awareness children (whose I.Q.'s range from 93 to 138). The I.Q. range and average for our Negro children are almost identical with those for our white ones (Ns 80 to 137, average 108; ws 84 to 145, average 111), yet we have more Negroes than whites in the high-awareness category. The excess is not accounted for by a concentration of high I.Q. Negro children in this category. The high-awareness Negroes differ greatly in I.Q., and average about the same as the Negro group as a whole. It is true, however, that of twenty-six children whose I.Q. is 115 or above, only *one* is low in awareness (ten are high and fifteen medium), while *six* of the twenty-four children of I.Q. 100 or below are in the low-awareness category (four are high and fourteen medium). It is also true that we find in the low category but one child of I.Q. above 109, while the medium- and high-awareness children cover the entire range.

I.Q. is, therefore, significant only in a general way, but it does become somewhat more significant as the extremes of our range are approached.

Particular mental capacities, and habits of using them, are very much more significant. Perceptual keenness, tendencies toward logical classifying and generalizing, habits of paying thoughtful attention to people and to details of their appearance and behavior—where these terms are found in the *personal equation*, we are not likely to find low awareness.

We conclude that:

A. There is never a *single* cause, a single term in the *personal equation* (or a single event in the personal history), which *alone* determines the young child's interest in and knowledge of race and race differences, or his feelings about his own or another racial group.

B. There are at least six major kinds of determining factors, and a number of related and subsidiary kinds within each major kind.

C. Each *personal equation* contains a number of major and minor terms. A dozen or more quite distinct factors are likely to be directly or indirectly involved in "causing" a child's particular brand of awareness and feeling, or the near absence of either or both.

D. Each *personal equation* represents a unique *combination* of terms. The uniqueness of the combinations, of course, produces a kind of awareness and a combination of feelings which are unique.

E. The terms in a given *personal equation* are interrelated; they function in interdependence.

F. In spite of the uniqueness of causes and of results in given cases, some generalizations can be made.

For example, high awareness and strong feeling will result from a combination of a majority of the following factors:

*. *Individual Attributes*
    a. Child strongly Negroid (color, hair, nose, lips) and/or
      highly conscious of own attributes, and given to comparing self with others, and
      has siblings and/or parents quite different in appearance, and
      has parents and/or siblings given to commenting upon or differentiating in terms of attribute differences.
    b. Child female and/or 4 years and 3 months of age, or above.

2. *Individual Situation*
    a. Child has sustained contacts with racially different people, and
      these were initiated suddenly and coincidentally with a new experience, and
      these contacts occur in, or are themselves part of, an emotionally charged situation involving conflict, anxiety, tension, sense of inferiority or of superiority.
    b. Child experiences wide variety of new situations involving need for major readjustments, such as hospitalization, travel (especially in southern U.S.), new home, temporary or permanent loss of parent or parents, much visiting about, etc.

3. *Models*
    a. Child strongly identified with parent (or parents), older sibling (or siblings), other juveniles or adults, who are
      inclined to strong emotions, "black-white" value judgments, awareness of and interest in race, "race talk" and/or discriminating behavior, involved (personally or vicariously) in expression of interpersonal or intergroup antagonisms where racial difference is (or is believed to be) a provoking element.

    b. Child generally dominated by his model or
       models, either
          because they try to dominate, mold,
          etc., or because child copies model.

    c. Child gets personality tone, general
       and/or specific race orientations from
       model due to
          constant association, identification, and/or
          unrestricted flow of ideas between
          them.

    d. Child gets from model
          conventional race view,
          avoiding social orientation,
          in-group affinity, preference,
          superiority or inferiority,
          in-group friendliness,
          out-group antagonism.

4. *Needs and Interests*
    a. Child not unusually absorbed in physical
       activity, and
    b. Unusually given to high and sustained
       rate of mental activity, and
    c. Unusually given to social activity either
       out of healthy desire for social
       relatedness,
          and involving habits of social
          interest and awareness and critical
          self-assessment, or
       out of less healthy preoccupation with
       achieving popularity, dominance,
       attention, etc.
    d. Child either
          blandly nonconformist, detached ob-
          server, or aggressive nonconformist,
          target-seeking, or
    e. Compulsive conformist, liking social lines
       and boundaries (as color line), and
    f. Highly dependent on model to define situ-
       ations, draw lines, etc.
    g. Child welcomes target (victim) for personal
       emotional outlet, and discovers it in the
       racially different, via models, incidents,

accident (e.g., random name-calling gets response).

5. *Values*
   a. Child given to strong likes and dislikes and not given to seeing in-betweens, degrees, complexities, and given to suspicion toward or offhand rejection of the new, different, unfamiliar, and
   b. Highly conscious of cleanliness, "niceness" (the "good," "right," etc.), personal appearance ("looks," "prettiness," etc.).

6. *Characteristic Ways*
   a. Child given to either
      very fast tempo, high degree of vigor, and wide range of movement, or
      very slow tempo, low degree of vigor, and limited range of movement, and
   b. Child given to strong and/or fluctuating emotions, and to either
      free expression of them, or
      strong inhibition of expression.
   c. Child has I.Q. of 115 or above, and/or is given to habits of
      noting details of personal appearance and behavior, and to
      generalizing, classifying, discriminating about and between people, and to
      concentrating, speculating, paying attention to details of appearance and behavior.

G. High awareness does not necessarily bring with it either strong feelings or feelings of antagonism (toward either own kind or other kind). Neither do feelings of antagonism depend upon prior attainment of high awareness.

H. *Antagonisms are likely to result from a combination of several of the following factors, especially if these are combined with other factors conducive to strong feeling (those noted under Point F):*

1. *Individual Attributes*
  a. Child greatly *likes* own looks and general
     physical type, and dislikes looks and
     general type of others to degree that
     they are different. (Leads to out-group
     antagonism; fairly frequent in white
     children, rare in Negro children.)
  b. Child *dislikes* own looks and general
     physical type, and likes looks and
     general type of others to degree that
     they are different. (Leads to in-group
     antagonism; unknown in white children,
     fairly frequent in Negro children.)

2. *Individual Situation*
  Cross-racial contacts (personal or vicarious)
     frequent, recurrent, and associated in child's
     mind with conflict, tension, anxiety, sense
     of inferiority or of superiority (ego-threat,
     threat to self-esteem; ego-enhancement, boost-
     ing of self-esteem).

3. *Models*
  Child identifies with, communicates with,
     and/or is psychologically dependent upon indi-
     viduals who
       incline to strong likes and dislikes,
          preferences and rejections,
       adhere to and voice either-or, black-
          white value judgments,
       value highly the familiar (as such),
          dislike the different and unfamiliar
          (as such),
       value highly cleanness, lightness, fine-
          ness, niceness, prettiness, etc. (as
          such),
       associate these valued aspects with own-
          kind people, tend to be unaware of or
          to reject possibility of association
          of valued aspects with other-kind people,
       incline to strong sense of in-group identity,
          and

incline to value in-group membership and
continuity, or
incline to rejection of in-group membership
and continuity, and
behave very differently with and toward
people seen as good-bad, right-wrong,
nice-not nice, pretty-ugly, own kind-
other kind.

4. *Needs and Interests*

Child has little faith in himself or others,
he is suspicious, assertive, aggressive,
he is seeking dominance, attention, adula-
tion,
he is a conventional-conformist,
he is most comfortable in sharply defined social situations.

5. *Value*

Child given to strong likes and dislikes, and
not given to seeing degrees, in-betweens,
complexities, and
suspicious and rejecting toward the
strange, different, unfamiliar (as
such), and
he has an extreme concern for and satisfaction with things and people clean,
light, nice, pretty, good, etc.

6. *Ways*

Child given to fast and vigorous activity, and
to
strong, and/or fluctuating emotions, and
to
discriminating between like and unlike
things and people.

Chapter 11

"America for Everybody"

"THIS IS SUPPOSED to be America for everybody, and everybody is supposed to have a chance to give it what he can, but —you know how it is."

Yes, we do know how it is, Mrs. K., and so does any reasonably intelligent, honest, and interested observer of the American scene.

Such observers are given to worrying about how it is, wondering what can be done about it, sometimes doing something about it. A great many important and effective kinds of things are being done. But the job is big and slow.

One of the reasons for its being so big and slow lies in the childhoods of Americans. They grow up more or less as our children are growing up in New Dublin, learning to think of Negroes and whites as very different kinds of people, widely separated, inferior and superior.

There is no inevitability about such learnings. A very few American children grow up without them, and a great many people in other parts of the world do so. Most Americans could.

We can have "America for everybody" a little faster if we do something about those childhoods. There is a little hope for our grownups, but in our children lies the big hope. While they are very young and suggestible, before their thinking jells and their feelings curdle, we can give them some tools for building "America for everybody."

The tools they need are neither few nor simple, however.

We Americans, with our naive habit of assuming that there is always a simple answer, will have to stop making that assumption. The word "prejudice" appears rarely in this book about the beginnings of race attitudes, not because our young children are failing to show the beginnings of prejudice, but because "prejudice" suggests something too simple. It suggests that "prejudice" is something one has or does not have, gets or does not get, like the measles or the mumps. It suggests a unit of personality, and that in turn suggests that "it" could be prevented by dealing with that particular unit.

The preceding chapters have surely demonstrated that there is no "it"—no prejudice unit-of-personality—in our children. It is true that the personality of the young child is less well integrated than that of the adult, and that the child's race orientations are relatively piecemeal and diffuse. If it were not so there would be less basis for the generally accepted idea that early childhood is a stage of comparative susceptibility to influence. There would be less basis for our concern here with influencing young children in respect to race. Still, prejudice is no simple unit-of-personality in adults either, and talking as though it were only confuses the issue.

What we have to deal with is not a simple matter. It is a complex set of causes lying behind a complex set of ideas, habits, and feelings. So, if grown-ups are to give children tools for building racial democracy, they must cope with complex causes and complex results. They must remove or alleviate the conditions which directly or indirectly promote the growth of antagonistic cross-racial orientations in children. They must also strengthen and support the conditions which directly or indirectly promote cross-racial friendliness or, better still, which promote a race-free view of society.

Before we talk about ways and means of accomplishing these ends, we must acknowledge the fact that a great many earnest and informed people throughout the United States are working to accomplish them. *Our major point here, and the major practical implication of this study, is that too few of these people are working with young children.*

We who observed the New Dublin four-year-olds believe that training for racial democracy should begin very early, that four-year-olds are none too young. This study will have served a practical purpose if it demonstrates to people who deal with young children and who care how those children feel about race, that they *can* do something about race feelings.

If the adults surrounding young children are unaware that they can do something, they are unlikely to be motivated to try. If they try, they are very likely to accomplish something, whether or not they have any special training in educational techniques. One need not be an expert. The crucial step is to become convinced that something important can be done to guide the young child away from racial antagonisms and toward healthier, more socially constructive feelings. Once this step is taken, the intelligent adult of good will can accomplish wonders.

Techniques are important and useful, but good will is indispensable. We have seen that the general atmosphere in which the child moves at home and elsewhere is highly significant. We have seen too that grown-ups tend to be unconscious of its significance and unconscious of the kind of atmosphere they are creating. So the second crucial step is to examine the atmosphere.

In the atmosphere of good will, the child meets *people*—individuals—each of whom is seen to have a particular combination of more or less interesting and attractive characteristics. The more interesting and attractive people are of assorted racial, national, and religious identities. So are the less interesting and attractive ones. Minority group identity is seen as incidental to the individual's qualities as a person. The person is dealt with on a basis of his individual qualities. His racial, national, or religious identity is an interesting item of quite secondary concern.

Into an atmosphere in which group identity is of primary concern out-groupers (*They*) do not often penetrate. *They* even less often get into it alive and looking reasonably human. This is to say that the child is introduced to a stereotype of the out-grouper, rather than to a real person or a realistic portrait.

The real person means more to the child, but there are some inevitable limits to the number and variety of real people whom he can meet and get to know. The limits, however, are less narrow than they are often said or believed to be. Opportunities for bringing into the child's orbit real people of varied race, national background, or religious affiliation can usually be created without too much effort. It may take a little more effort to make the meeting a constructive learning experience for the child. We cannot assume that it will automatically become such, but making it one can be a source of great satisfaction to the adult of good will.

When real people in all their rich and interesting variety cannot be brought into the child's range of contacts, portraits will have to do. They can do very well indeed, if they are honest portraits. Stereotypes are more or less dishonest; the degree of unnecessary warmth with which they are defended is a pretty good measure of the degree to which they are felt to be dishonest. Honest portraits of racially or otherwise distinctive types of people are not difficult to come by these days, though they are not often drawn in terms understandable to the young child. There are still very few books for young children in which lifelike portraits appear, but there are some (and *Little Black Sambo* is not one of them). For five to seven-year-olds there is, for example, *In Henry's Backyard* (Ruth Benedict and Gene Weltfish).

However, ready-made portraits are convenient and helpful but not necessary. The grown-up who has honest pictures in his own mind will find ways of sketching them in simple outline for the young child. He will sketch them informally and spontaneously, at a time when he has the child's attention and interest. And he can tailor his efforts to the child's personality and experience.

There will be, in the natural course of events, a great many such times. It may not always seem convenient to stop for a discussion at the very moment when Johnny asks "Why are they black?" or Mary observes thoughtfully that "some people are brown and some are white." If it *is* convenient, there is no better time. If it seems not to be convenient, the grown-up may well ask himself whether he is dodging the issue, as our New Dublin grown-ups so often do. If he is not dodging, he will come back to the issue at a more convenient moment, and he will find one soon. Johnny or Mary will probably still be interested, and the grown-up will have had a little time in which to plan his approach and decide how he can most effectively provide guidance for this white child.

The grown-up might deal with Johnny's question in some such fashion as this:

"Why are they black? Do you know anyone who is really black? Take another good look, or another good think. Do you still say they are really black, like Daddy's best shoes, or the squares in the linoleum? No, of course not. Then let's get it straight—that's the way to *start* answering any question.

"Now, the people you were talking about are what color? Yes, brown, of course. Sometimes people are brown like that chocolate candy you see in the glass case at the store, or like Daddy's coffee when he puts just a very little cream in it, or like Mummy's when she puts in quite a lot of cream. If Mummy kept putting in more cream, until there was almost no coffee look left, and maybe some red candy instead of sugar, her coffee would get to be about the color of some other people you know. Yes, you, for example, and Mummy and Daddy. But look—you and Mummy and Daddy aren't exactly the same color. See the differences? People just naturally grow in different shades from lots of brown to very little brown, sometimes with some pink mixed in.

"The coffee gets lighter as you put more cream in it. People are lighter because they have less brown stuff growing right in their skin. You know that it can grow there, because you know what happens to you in the summertime. You get tanned while you play in the sun—the sun makes more brown stuff grow in your skin. The name of the stuff is *melanin,* if you'd like to know another new word.

"Melanin can grow in your skin, and make it look brown, because the sun has been shining on you. You have only a little of it in your skin without the help of the sun. But some people—like those people you were talking about— don't need the help of the sun. Their melanin just grows in their skin naturally.

"People grow in different shades of brown—sometimes almost no brown and some pink—and the trees and bushes grow in different shades of green. Wouldn't it be funny if the trees were shades of brown and pink and we were shades of green! But once we got used to seeing green people, we would think that of course people *should* be green, and then we would start noticing different shades of green. Of course the shade of green wouldn't be any more important if people were green than it is in the trees and bushes. When you go to the park in the summer, you see a lot of different shades of green—look for them next time you go. And the differences make the park prettier and more interesting than it would be if everything were exactly the same.

"It's that way with people too—the different shades of brown and pink aren't really very important—they just make people prettier and more interesting than they would be if they were all exactly the same."

This kind of discussion could be done with a whole group of nursery school or kindergarten Johnnys and Marys, taking off from a comment by one of them. It could be embellished with a little fantasy in which all the people are turned into shades of green. They remark upon one another's differences, and otherwise they go right on behaving just the way they did before their color changed.

The discussion or some little fantasy could lead into color play. Provided with a pot of coffee (brown poster paint), a pitcher of cream (yellowed white poster paint), and a little red paint, the children could play at mixing them, and putting sample strokes of different mixtures on the big paper on their easels. More and different "games" could be played along these lines. The imagination of the children and their grown-ups would readily enough invent them.

With or without further embellishment, if Johnny gets a sketch done more or less in this style, he is getting some quite fundamental ideas built into it. They are ideas which can be restated in other contexts later on, and which will need to be.

Johnny is getting here the idea that color is something which *can* be talked about, and talked about openly and rationally. It is of the utmost importance that he get the idea that color can be dealt with *rationally*, and to set him an example is to help him get it. He will not contribute much to tomorrow's world unless he does get it, and eventually practice it.

The kind of reaction Johnny gets when he mentions color tells him a lot about the way his models view it. To Johnny color is one of the things about people which he sees and quite naturally wonders about. He is likely to ask about a good many other things having nothing to do with race, and get an open, fairly rational answer. If he gets the same kind of answer when he asks a question which does have to do with race, then he is being told—in terms of general atmosphere—that racial features are just one among the many interesting things about people. This is a constructive and rational view. If he gets no answer, or an evasive or emotional one when he asks about color, then the atmosphere tells him that this is something special and especially important.

In the present adult world, it *is* something especially important. In the future adult world, it need not be. We are helping Johnny get ready to make that world a reality when we start him thinking of racial features as items of interest and quite worthy of investigation, and not much more.

It would be neither honest nor accurate to pretend to Johnny that race is an unimportant item in the present adult world. A little later he will see for himself that it is important. He will hear racial name-calling; he will catch the tones along with an overheard scrap of conversation about "Negroes moving in—neighborhood going down," or "dancing together—now that's carrying equality pretty far," or "would you want your sister—." Johnny's grown-ups had better not attempt to kid him (or themselves) about the present racial realities. When Johnny comes up with a question about those realities, he must have a straightforward answer, but it can also be made clear that today's realities belong to today's grown-ups, while tomorrow's realities belong to him, and he can make them different. His grown-ups can tell him:

"Yes, there *are* people who call names, who have objections to living in a mixed neighborhood, and so on and so on. They are people who for one reason or a good many reasons have not been able to get away from some ideas that have been floating around in this country for a long time, and causing a great deal of trouble. It's a sad thing that unnecessary and trouble-causing ideas should live so long, and make so many people very unhappy, but ideas like that often do live on and on. They do because it's so hard for people to get rid of notions they've grown up with.

"You're lucky, Johnny. You won't have to carry around a useless load of trouble-causing ideas that you don't know how to dump—don't even know you're carrying, for that matter. You won't have them because you're lucky enough to be getting straightened out on this business of color and what it's all about.

"Color differences *are* important now to a lot of people in this country, but they won't be when a lot of children like you grow up. They don't *have* to be important. It's habit in the thinking of people in the United States that makes them seem so important. In some other countries—like Brazil and

Hawaii, the people don't think color is very important. They don't have our habit."

An allusion to the habits of these other people leads easily into an investigation of the way these people live. Johnny and Mary will enjoy pictures and stories about life in Brazil or Hawaii, and they can learn from them a great deal more than that race is treated differently in those countries. Some simple concepts of distance, of geography, of plant and animal life, and of how these people use the resources in their worlds for food, and clothes, and houses—these will come along with the original focus on race, and provide education along several lines while relieving race of undue emphasis.

When his grown-ups help Johnny to see racial reality in a broad social context, and without accepting it as a necessarily final or desirable product, they are making a major contribution. Seeing racial reality, and seeing it fairly whole and as a man-made yet still malleable thing, is a very sophisticated view. It is also a rational and accurate one. Accuracy is inseparably linked with racial sophistication and sanity.

When Johnny's grown-up answered his "Why are they black" question, he insisted upon accuracy. The people in question are in fact brown, so he helped the child to check his observation, and to correct his description of what had been observed. He then pointed out that this is the way to start answering *any* question. It is, and the habits of accurate observation and reporting are extremely sound ones in general, while being indispensable tools in the minds of our builders of the better racial world.

Johnny's grown-up made two useful points with his references to candy and to coffee, and his drawing Johnny and Johnny's parents into the sketch. He tied color differences up with pleasant and familiar things and people, hence strengthening pleasant associations around the topic of color. And he created a concept of human color as varying along a scale. There is no suggestion here of either-or thinking, or of either figurative or literal black-white categories. All the emphasis is placed upon the fact that there are degrees of difference, and that these *unite people on the same scale* rather than dividing them into two sharply separated kinds.

The word "black" had to be eliminated from Johnny's thinking for three reasons: (1) as we have already said, it is inaccurate and inaccuracies are not to be encouraged, (2) it is an impolite racial epithet, and hence had well be removed from Johnny's racial vocabulary before he uses it intentionally or accidentally and hurts someone's feelings, (3) it suggests its categorical opposite "white," and a whole train of categorical opposites can follow in quite automatic association with black-white usage (dirty-clean, etc.).

It will be noticed that the word "white" was never offered to Johnny. He will, of course, discover it and use it eventually, but it is an unfortunate term and not to be underscored. It is just as inaccurate as "black," and it has just as much categorical and associational meaning. There really is no good and currently used substitute for it, since the technically more respectable word "Caucasoid" is pretty cumbersome. "Brown" or "browned" and "bleached" would, however, be a delightful and accurate pair of terms to substitute for "black" and "white" or "colored" and "white."

Later on Johnny might be given "browned" and "bleached" along with a little sketch of the history of the human family. He would then be introduced to the fact that of the three great branches of the present human family, the Mongoloid division is probably closest to mankind's original color, while the Negroid and Caucasoid divisions represent the end results of browning and bleaching, respectively, over the centuries.

While Johnny is very young his grown-ups probably do well to stay clear of race-group labels, of whatever variety. No matter what the nature of the labels, they imply sharply separated categories or kinds of people. Unfortunately, our present society *is* broken into sharply divided categories, but these do not mirror biological realities (as we have noted before in this book). Johnny will do well to concentrate at first upon learning something about the biological realities. They are precisely of the sort conveyed by the image of coffee with more and more cream added to it.

The biological differentness of the "white" and "Negro" groups in the United States is a social myth. What we actually have here is a brownness continuum which proceeds without a break from dark brown to the extreme bleach of the extreme blond. If Johnny gets this picture firmly fixed in his mind *before* he gets used to race-group labels, he will be able to use them later without being misled by them. He will know that they represent shorthand designations for socially defined race groups made up of people whose color actually varies over a wide range. We hope he will also know that their other characteristics vary widely too.

Teaching Johnny early to think of color on a continuum can help him to learn to think of other characteristics as varying in the same fashion. For instance, people vary widely in respect to "niceness" and "not-niceness," (however Johnny's grown-ups choose to define these terms). "Nice" and "not-nice" are at the opposite ends of a scale, rather than standing for mutually exclusive categories.

Johnny needs to develop two very important habits: (1) the habit of thinking in terms of continua along which people vary in respect to almost any characteristic he can think of, and (2) the habit of placing people on *one* continuum without leaping to the conclusion that they thereby automatically fall into the same place on others.

For example: Johnny sees Mr. K., who is dark brown. Mr. K. falls close to that end of the color continuum which is farthest removed from Johnny's own place on the scale. Assuming that Johnny regards himself as nice, good, attractive, etc., he may be tempted to leap to the conclusion that Mr. K. is far removed in these qualities because he is far removed in respect to color. The temptation arises out of either a spurious logic or some knowledge of how grown-ups incline to rate Mr. K.'s niceness, goodness, etc., or out of both logic and learning. In any case Johnny needs help in developing the habits of making ratings on *one* scale at a time.

The sketch Johnny was given made still another point which will bear repeating later. It was suggested that color differences in people have just about the same significance that they have elsewhere in the natural world. That is, that they are not important, except as they lend the interest of variety to the view. The idea that human variety can be a source of esthetic interest and satisfaction can do Johnny no harm. And it is important for Johnny to think of *variety* as attractive, because it makes *all* the shades essential, and equally essential, to the total attractiveness. It will take much more than this to keep him equally appreciative of the looks of Negroes and of whites, but every little helps.

It will take, before too long, the meeting of other questions or comments having to do with racial features. There may be more about color, and some about other features. Our New Dublin children commented upon color and color differences more frequently than upon hair, or noses, or mouths. Yet the more highly aware among them were often taking note of the whole cluster of physical attributes and reacting to the cluster. Sometimes the reaction is in the nature of a general rejection.

Let us suppose that Mary one day comes up with such a general rejection. She says firmly: "I don't like colored kids." Mary's grown-up wants to know why. Mary knows why, or at least she is ready with her reasons. She doesn't like them "because they look funny. They have funny faces—big noses and big mouths, and funny hair."

What can the grown-up do with that one? Surely not ignore it. Silence could be taken to mean agreement, or at least no disagreement. Mary's grown-up does not agree, and she follows the course usual to her when she regards Mary's opinions as biased, unkind, or otherwise inconsistent with a fair and sympathetic view of other people. Mary's grown-up helps Mary to reconsider. She might do it rather like this:

"So you 'don't like colored kids.' You sound very *sure* when you say it like that. You sound as though you knew a lot of them, and that you didn't like a single one. I wonder if that's true. I wonder if you're really so sure, and I wonder how you *can* be so sure. You know, people need to have a lot of very good reasons before they get so sure about anything.

"Yesterday I was sure when I said I knew where I had put the doll you couldn't find. You looked where I said it was, but no doll. Then you said I was a 'silly' to tell you something that wasn't true. I *was* a 'silly'—I was a 'silly' to be so *sure*. I didn't have very good reasons for being sure. I just had an idea—it was a 'maybe' kind of thing. So, I should have said 'maybe I know where the doll is.' And you should have said 'maybe' I don't like colored kids—unless you had a lot of *very* good reasons for being sure.

"Now when I asked you why you don't like them you gave me some reasons. You said it was because '*they* look funny, *they* have funny faces,' and so on. Those aren't good reasons until we know who 'they' are. Then we can look at them carefully and decide if something's funny about them.

"Who *are* these 'colored' kids you don't like to play with? Jane, and Susan, and George and Harry at nursery school, and that's all. So you don't know very many 'colored kids' after all. And you can only like or not-like the ones you know. The ones you don't know you couldn't have any good reason for not liking, could you? How could you not like them if you don't know anything about them?

"Now let's see just what we can remember about each one of these children you *do* know, and you can look next time you see them to make sure that we remember how they *really* are.

"Yes, you remember that Jane is light brown, like that Easter coat you like so much. No, nothing very funny about that is there? And Jane has a little face—a cute little face. What about her nose and mouth? You don't remember. Then there's nothing so funny about them. And she wears her hair in little short braids—they're cute. So when we think about it carefully, there's nothing at all funny about Jane after all.

"When you and Jane play together, what do you do? Play house, go on the seesaw, look at books—yes, and those are the kinds of things you play with other little girls, aren't they? And does Jane know how to do these things? So she does. Do you like to play house with Jane? Yes, and to seesaw with her? Yes, and to look at books with her. Now what is there you *don't* like to do with her? If you can't think of anything you *don't* like to do with her, and if you like to play house and so on with her, then I guess you *like* to play with Jane. Yes—and so, that means you *like* Jane, doesn't it? Of course, there aren't any good reasons why you shouldn't.

"You see we've found out already, because we stopped to think it over, that you were much too sure. You were a 'silly.' Here's Jane—she doesn't look funny, she's a little girl you like and like to play with. Jane is nice to play with.

"What about Susan? She grabs your blocks and sometimes she pulls your hair. She's not nice to play with. You don't like Susan. Now are there any other children who do things like that? Yes, there are quite a few, and you don't like them either—and they don't look like Susan. Do the children you *don't* like to play with look alike? No, of course not. Each one has his own special looks. And the ones you *do* like to play with—Jane, and Nancy, and Richard and the others—do they look alike? No, they don't look alike either, so it seems that there are children you do like to play with and others you don't like to play with, and that their looks have nothing to do with it.

"Now what about George and Harry—we were going to remember everything we could about them too. Are George and Harry fun to play with? Yes, and George is dark, velvety brown like those big chocolate candies you like. Harry is a nice medium brown, like our chocolate pudding, and both of them have hair that grows in crisp little curls. But do they have noses and mouths just alike? No, George's nose is different from Harry's, or Susan's, or Jane's, or yours—so is his mouth. They're all different.

"Do you think your nose is funny—or your mouth? No, you don't, but maybe that's because they're yours. You're used to looking at your own nose and mouth, you know, and people often like what they're used to. They like it just because they are used to it. That's not a very *good* reason, because they could just as well get used to something else. Of course, George doesn't think his nose is funny, or his mouth, any more than you think yours are. He's used to looking at his.

"One thing we *can* be sure about, and that is that people have different color, different noses, different mouths, different hair. We can't be sure that any *one* color, or nose, or whatever, is funny. Different things look funny to different people.

"I think we've found out what you can be sure about, and what it is you don't like. What you don't like is something about the way some kids play with you, a way that makes playing with them no fun at all. But the way they play doesn't seem to have anything to do with the way they look.

"What you can say, and be very sure about, is that there is *something,* about some kids, *that you don't like, something about their way of playing,* and not about their looks."

Mary's grown-up had to deal in particular cases and personalities to get her general points across, to make her sketch meaningful in terms of Mary's experience. Another grown-up, dealing with another Mary, would have to do the same, and be grateful if Mary knew enough particular people to illustrate the general points. These points could be made in a variety of ways, however, so long as they are made slowly, patiently, and in such a fashion that Mary can follow each step, and follow it with her feelings as well as with her mind.

The first step, in this case, was to suggest to the child that unqualified generalizations of the "I don't like" order do not make sense *unless* the maker bases them on something substantial. An intimate knowledge of a large number of cases would be substantial, especially if the cases showed a high degree of uniformity. Mary's grown-up makes it pretty clear to the child that she does not have this range of knowledge, and that the cases she does know show few or none of the uniformities Mary was asserting for them. Mary's grown-up is saying, in effect, that easy generalizations about the racial groups (even easy generalizations as such), are likely to be found unjustified when you get down to cases. She is teaching a habit of *cautious generalization*. It is a habit indispensable in our builders of the better world.

She is also teaching the habit and techniques of *systematic problem-solving*. Mary's grown-up turns their conversation into a problem-solving inquiry, a careful investigation complete with systematic observation and ordering of the facts bearing upon the problem. She then helps Mary to draw the conclusions justified by the evidence at hand. It is a rational, friendly discussion in which Mary is drawn along as an active cooperator. Had it become a debate, with Mary's grown-up opposing Mary, we can quite safely assume that Mary's devotion to her original opinion would only have been strengthened in the process of defending it against attack.

Mary's grown-up makes it a point to help Mary see that *she* is not under attack. The tone of the discussion conveys this, but it is especially reassuring to Mary to have the grown-up acknowledge a piece of her own "silliness." The grown-up is very wise to do so when she honestly knows herself to be guilty. She provides the child with a wholesome example in rational self-criticism. She establishes herself, by the nature of the whole discussion, as a model who practices rational and rationally critical thought-ways, but she does not put herself in the dangerous position of the self-styled (even implicitly self-styled) paragon. She knows, and makes it clear that she knows, that she is no paragon. She gives Mary no cause for subsequent disillusionment and the inclination to reject the whole model because she one day finds a flaw in it.

Mary used the word "colored." We assume that she is a high-awareness four-year-old who has a quite clear notion of "colored" as a kind of people. Her grown-up wasted no time on a direct attempt to persuade Mary not to use race-group labels. The whole discussion was an implicit persuasion away from *thinking,* much less talking, in terms of color groups.

The grown-up used Mary's own term only as a point of departure. She used it no more than she needed to, and she used no other race-group labels whatever. She even avoided talking about "kinds" of noses, mouths, or general physical types. She did so, of course, to keep Mary's focus on *degrees* of difference, on a continuum of physical traits, rather than upon categories.

Mary's model is teaching the habits of rating people on a basis of *one* characteristic at a time, and keeping ratings on physical attributes separate from ratings on social ones. The idea of the continuum—of *degrees* of difference in both social and physical attributes—is implicit in the way she helps Mary to see her friends. But she suggests that the really important continuum is the social attribute one.

By the end of the discussion, it is social rather than physical attributes which have become the central issue. "Looks" have faded in importance. They have taken their proper place in the total perspective. They have become interesting incidentals about the people Mary knows. They are placed in perspective as matters of secondary importance, about which people have different opinions. The opinions are seen to be the result of familiarity, of what one is "used to," rather than being views which are inherently right or wrong.

Mary is being helped to see that tastes in looks are not absolutes, and that her kind of looks can as well be rejected as can somebody else's kind. Rejection is a good antidote to the egocentric tendency to feel that one's own looks, or general type of looks, set a standard which other people can be expected to accept. The white child can get a dangerously large dose of ego-inflation out of a conviction that his is the only desirable kind of looks. It is a conviction difficult to shake, because his natural inclination to use himself as a standard is repeatedly nourished by evidence that grown-ups accept the "white" kind of looks as a standard.

Mary will soon discover this, if she does not have a sense of it already. But if she is meanwhile being helped to see attractive features combined with a more or less brown skin, she need not be overwhelmed by the consensus which fails to do so.

Mary's grown-up referred to Jane's face and to her braids as "cute." She referred to Jane's color in terms of Mary's prized Easter coat, to George's color as "velvety" brown, to Harry's color as a "nice medium brown." She referred to the boys' hair in terms of "crisp little curls," and she brought in the pleasant associations with rather special foods. All of this will help Mary to see these attributes for what they in fact are—interesting and attractive. She will see cute little braids and crisp curls where others may see short kinky hair. She will see a nice, luscious, or velvety brown where others may see black, dark, or dirtiness. And she will be less apt than the others to get carried away with the idea that prettiness = whiteness, or its near equivalents.

Later on Mary's appreciation for the beauty and charm of non-white attributes can be (as it needs to be) further strengthened. Mary's grown-ups can find many ways to introduce her to people, real or pictured, whose beauty meets race-free and rather universally accepted standards. Art galleries, occasional "spreads" in picture magazines, and an occasional movie will help her to see beauty in people of widely varied physical types. She, and perhaps her class or play group, might collect pictures for a "people of the world" exhibit or scrapbook. The object would be to see how many different countries or types of people they could represent by pictures of attractive people.

The picture collection could become a starting point for the collection of information about one or several of the countries or types of people. The possibilities of this are endless, and any of them would serve to increase both knowledge and appreciation of the culturally and racially different and exotic peoples. Whatever strengthens Mary's understanding and appreciation of people culturally or physically unlike herself makes its contribution to her tools for the building of racial democracy.

It is very probable, however, that young children will sometimes come up with still other ideas or behavior quite out of line with that future racial democracy. Or they may be the victims of such ideas or behavior. There may be name-calling, for example.

Suppose that Billy goes in for name-calling, as we have seen that the nursery school children sometimes do. One day in a fit of temper Billy yells at his brown friend Harry: "You dirty black nigger." Do we ignore the episode, and Harry's obviously hurt feelings?

There will be differences of opinion, and there is no necessarily "right" way. Neither is the handling or mishandling of an occasional incident going to determine Billy's future attitudes, or Harry's. Their attitudes will be built by a great many incidents and influences. Still, we had better make up our minds what we are going to do about name-calling. Earlier in this book (Chapter 9), we noted some of the advantages and disadvantages of ignoring it. Let's try another tack.

Anyone who manages to get along at all peaceably with young children, and to give them a sense of security, has to set up some limits for their behavior and make those limits effective. It is reasonable to expect Billy not to seriously damage the furniture, the cat, or other people's feelings. Other people may give him more provocation than does the furniture or the cat, but he has a right to expect them to consider his feelings and he has an obligation to consider theirs. So he is expected to learn to take turns and share his toys. He can equally well be expected not to throw things, whether the things be sharp-edged toys or equally sharp-edged words. He can be expected to learn some rules of the game, and to play fair in terms thereof.

When Billy fails to meet any of these reasonable expectations, it is time for a penalty. The penalty will, of course, have to be tailored to the nature of the particular failure, to Billy's nature, and to the circumstances. But Billy should be helped to understand that there *are* limits, and he can be helped to understand that throwing sharp-edged words, racial epithets among them, is outside the limits. The penalty should be accompanied by the explanation that such words *can* seriously damage other people, and that the offense *is* in the same class with throwing other damaging things.

There is an obvious objection to dealing with Billy's name-calling in this fashion. We are telling him unmistakably something that he may not have fully realized before. We are telling him that the racial epithet is an effective weapon. If he very much wants and needs weapons, whether or not there are penalties associated with their use, he will be glad to know that he has one and eager to use it again. But there are two answers to this objection. The first answer is that Billy either already had or soon would have had a full realization of the weapon value of the racial epithet. Our New Dublin four-year-olds generally had a very good notion what they were doing when they used them. The popular belief that "of course he doesn't know what he's saying" is a piece of adult naiveté or wishful thinking. It is tied up with the adult wish to believe young children racially innocent and uninterested.

The second answer is that if Billy very much wants and needs weapons, he has some *big* problems which had better be looked into. We are only treating the symptoms of a state of psychological ill-health, and not getting to the causes of the difficulty, whatever we do or don't do about his name-calling. If Billy does not have big problems, his name-calling is only an expression of temporary anger or mischievous experimentation. In any case, we can do him no harm by discouraging his expression. But we can invite harm to someone else by the tacit encouragement which our silence with Billy might lend.

If Billy is penalized for calling racial names and told that they can hurt, he is going to want and deserve an explanation. So his grown-up is inviting a job for herself when she administers the penalty. The job had better be done later, after both of them have cooled off and recovered from their irritation over the name-calling and its sequel. Then Billy's grown-up might proceed more or less in this fashion:

"Do you know that words are *things?* Another time I told you that words can hurt people as much as hitting with heavy blocks or with sharp-edged toys like your steam shovel. Words *can* hurt because words are things too. Not things you can see and touch, but just as real as if they were. They can be heavy like blocks, or sharp like the corners on your steam shovel. They can hit people and leave bruises and cuts. Not bruises and cuts that you can see and touch, but just as real as if you could.

"Do you remember when Joey called you a 'big dope'? You got mad at Joey, didn't you? You thought he was mean to say that. It hurt your feelings. Maybe he was right just then. Maybe right then you were acting like a 'big dope.' But you didn't stop because Joey said that. You got mad and threw your crayon at Joey, and kicked the table. Joey didn't help you stop being a dope. Because he hurt your feelings, he made you act more dopey than ever.

"That's what people usually do when they get hurt by words. Their hurts don't show in bruises or cuts, but they show some way. Maybe they cry, or maybe they just sit very still and don't say a word or make a move. Some people are noisy about their hurts and some are quiet about them. But getting hurt makes them unhappy. Often it makes them act dopier than ever too. It isn't any fun to see people unhappy, especially if we've done something to make them unhappy. And it doesn't help anything to make people act dopey.

"So you see what Joey did when he called you a dope and what you did when you called Harry a name. Joey hurt somebody's feelings, and so did you. You were unhappy when Joey hurt your feelings, and you didn't have any fun when you made Harry unhappy.

"The name Joey called you, and the name you called Harry, are hurting things. The reason they can hurt is that these word things have something inside them. Inside them there is something which is called a *meaning. Meaning,* that's a new word for you to have—a word that you can use a lot and have fun with. Now the *meanings* inside the hurting words get put into them by people. Every time someone uses one of these hurting words in a hurting way, he puts just a little bit more meaning inside it. It is the meaning that makes the word heavy and sharp.

"So every time you use a hurting word you make somebody else unhappy, you have no fun, *and* you make the hurting word heavier and sharper. Then it can go on making more people unhappy. It doesn't sound like much fun for anybody, does it? It *isn't.* It never is any fun for anybody.

"The words you used have had a lot of meaning put into them. Each one of them has been used so many times, by so many angry and unkind people, that they are full of angry and unkind meanings. They started being used by angry and unkind people because they already *had* some hurting meaning. You know what the meaning is when someone says 'Billy is very dirty.' It means there's something about you right then that they don't like. That's the way with the other hurting words you used. They had a 'don't-like' meaning a long time ago, and so angry and unkind people picked them up and threw them when they wanted to say 'don't like.' And the more the hurting words were thrown, the more 'don't-like' meaning was put inside them. By now they're *very* heavy and sharp because of all that.

"So the meaning of the words you threw at Harry was: 'don't like—don't like—don't like!' Maybe you really didn't like what Harry was *doing* right that minute. But you didn't say so. You *said* you didn't like *Harry.* Maybe you had a good reason for not liking what Harry was doing at that minute. If you did have a good reason you should have told Harry your reason. If you had told him you might have helped Harry stop whatever he was doing.

"So you made a mistake. You said a hurting thing instead of nothing, or a helping thing. Saying nothing can't hurt anybody and helping things can be said quietly without hurting anybody's feelings. It's fun to think of ways to say helping things."

Billy's grown-up tried to accomplish these things:

(1) She tried to help Billy achieve some understanding of the power that lies in the meanings of words, and of how they get that power. She was, in effect, saying that the use of powerful words requires the same care and sense of responsibility that Billy knows is required in the use of dangerous implements.

She tried to make word-hurting meaningful to a four-year-old by suggesting that words are *things* which can produce real hurts. Billy has some experience of real hurts produced by tangible things. Some fairly unfamiliar ideas were being approached in terms of familiar experiences.

(2) Starting with an emphasis on the negative and destructive power of words (their hurting potentialities), she moved to an emphasis upon their positive and constructive powers (their helping potentialities). Thus she was not focusing Billy's attention entirely upon a type of verbal behavior she wants to discourage. She was swinging his attention toward a type which she wants to encourage. She encouraged by building an association between hurting words, unhappiness, and no fun, and between helping words, happiness, and fun.

(3) She tried to help Billy understand the feelings of his victim by reminding him of his own experience as a victim. Billy's imagination may not be equal to the task of putting himself in Harry's shoes, but his memory of his own experience may make Harry's real for him. Reminding Billy of his own experience serves the further purpose of suggesting these things can work both ways—that what he *gives* he can also *get*, and not like getting.

(4) She avoided suggesting to Billy that the particular epithets he had used have a particular racial meaning. She

even avoided repeating his words and thus re-emphasizing them, save for the first one (dirty). This one she recalled because she could suggest that "dirty" could be used against himself.

There was no need to tell Billy, in effect, "you can hurt Negroes *especially* by using these particular words." To tell him this would be to implicitly teach racial differentness and to suggest a race group as a target. If Billy's grown-up can teach him to throw epithets toward *no one,* she will have taught him a fundamental lesson which will discourage his throwing them at Negroes. She will have put racial epithets in the general context in which she suggested that all epithets belong—that is, among the kinds of verbal behavior which are characteristic of angry and unkind people. Presumably Billy does not and will not care to mark himself as one of these.

(5) Billy's grown-up did not attack or blame him, nor did she moralize. But she made it very clear that he had made a mistake, and a kind of mistake which is outside the reasonable limits of free choice. She pointed to the essence of his mistake—to the facts that he had said what he actually did not mean, and that he had hurt and not helped.

She was again shifting Billy's attention—this time away from the *person* of his victim (a Negro child) and toward a specific bit of that child's *behavior.* She was in fact saying: "you are perfectly justified in rejecting a certain bit of behavior if you have good reason for doing so (if it is outside the limits as you know them). You are not justified in rejecting the whole individual because of a certain bit of behavior, and you are not even stating your own real feelings accurately if you do so."

She reminded Billy of his real feelings—of his general liking for this Negro child and of their general congeniality. But she was holding up before Billy's eyes an *individual* child, and not a Negro child, and suggesting that individuality and behavior are the important things about people.

So much for Billy, and how his side of the name-calling incident might be handled. But Harry is involved in this too. Harry and his grown-up might also have a chat after the impact of the incident has worn off a little.

We shall assume that Harry is a high-awareness child. In this case he has probably heard before those words which

Billy leveled at him, and has learned that they have particular meaning for him and for people of his color-kind. He has learned too that the meaning is unfavorable—an insult and a challenge.

This being the case, Harry's hurt feelings in the name-calling episode are largely accounted for. But he was especially hurt because Billy, who was his friend, attacked _him_ _in_ _this_ fashion.

Harry's grown-up might explain to him, in the same fashion in which it was explained to Billy, about hurting words and how they get their meanings through use. It would be important to emphasize for Harry two facts: (1) the fact that people express their anger and unkindness through _many_ kinds of hurting words—not just those to which he (as a Negro) is especially vulnerable, and therefore that his discomfort is shared by many people who are not Negroes— that it is in some sense a universal problem; (2) the fact that racial epithets may be actually used, as they were by Billy, to say "I don't like what you're doing this minute," though they may seem to say "I don't like _you_, or anything about you, at any time"; therefore the victim may have in fact less cause for hurt than he may think he has.

To know that one's own kind is not alone among victims may be cold comfort, but it at least says to the child, "you are like everybody else in the kinds of troubles you can have." Harry very much needs to be told, and told often, about the ways in which he is _like_ other people who may not resemble him physically. His racial status is very likely to have the effect of making him feel different and isolated, and hence insecure. He needs a great deal of reassurance of an indirect sort concerning the number and kinds of his similarities to people whose physical characteristics may be different. Then, too, Harry, like any other child, needs to know that degrees of physical difference tell nothing about degrees of difference in social characteristics. He needs to learn to see social characteristics first, and to make social ratings on a basis of these.

Harry's grown-up must acknowledge the reality of the fact that Harry, as he grows up, may meet name-calling troubles more often than the average child. Still, he is like other people in that he needs to learn how to meet this kind of trouble, whether it be frequent or infrequent. Harry should know that there *are* techniques for meeting and dealing with name-calling trouble. And a *beginning* (and only that) can be made in introducing him to such techniques.

The first step is to decide what was really meant—how much real cause for hurt there is in being called "out of your name." Billy was really criticizing Harry's behavior at the moment of their clash. Harry's first move should have been to size up the situation.

His grown-up might put it to him this way:

"Billy did not mean that he doesn't like *you*. He was angry because he thought you were not playing fair just then. If you had thought a little about what happened maybe you could have figured that out. Then your feelings wouldn't have been hurt so much, because Billy really thought he had a pretty good reason for being angry with you. If you weren't playing fair, then Billy *did* have a good reason for not liking what you were doing. It wasn't a good reason for calling you names, but it makes a difference. You could still feel hurt because he called you names, but not because he called them without any reason.

"When you know you have given somebody a reason for being angry with you, the best thing to do is to say so. You might have said to Billy, 'I'm sorry I grabbed your book. That wasn't playing fair. I won't do it any more.' And *then* you could have said to Billy, 'and please don't call me names any more. Because that's not playing fair either.'

"When you think you *haven't* given somebody a reason for being angry with you, then you can say so, too. You might have said to Billy, 'I didn't grab your book—I didn't do anything to you. You made a mistake. But you called me names. *You* did something to me. You weren't playing fair.'

"You could say the same thing to Billy if he hit you with a block.

"Whether he hits you with a word or with a block, he's not playing fair, and you can tell him so. That's better than hitting back. Because if you hit him back, you give him a good reason for hitting you, and the hitting goes right on. Everybody gets hurt. Anybody can hit. That's an easy thing to do, and it's a silly thing to do. It isn't quite so easy to stop the hitting, but if you are smart you can do it."

Harry needs to be helped to see that other people make mistakes and fail to play fair, even as he sometimes does. He needs to see name-calling as a kind of unfair play, to be treated as such. Then its power to hurt him will be lessened, because it has become an instance of a kind of silly and unfair behavior of which anybody can be guilty, and a kind for which anybody can be held responsible and corrected. Furthermore, the correction for name-calling can be made like correction for other kinds of hitting. Since you have to be smart to stop the hitting, Harry can be helped to a sense of justified satisfaction in his growing techniques for controlling it in himself and in others.

The special problems of the Negro child do not stop with his need to cope with epithets. His most central special problem is one of self-rejection, arising out of a learned set of values which make his person and his kind unattractive to him. The child who feels this, as so many of our four-year-olds do in varying degrees, badly needs help. He has a problem which threatens his ability to like himself or the people who are in fact most important to him. Without a certain healthy degree of self-regard and regard for those in his own little world, he is in a bad way. He can hardly be happy himself, and he is very unlikely to make a contribution to the better racial world.

Interested grown-ups will find, or they can create, opportunities to help. They can help, and do it without deepening the child's sense of separateness and difference, and without making him feel self-sorry or defeated. They can help by working through with the child the answers to each of his questions, each of his concrete problems. They will try to provide him with knowledge of the *facts* about race, just as the white child must be provided with them. What causes differences in color and other features? How intrinsically important and meaningful are they? How important and meaningful are they in the eyes of other people here and now? How does one deal with these people of here and now who are in error about the importance and intrinsic meaning of physical characteristics?

The Negro child is like the white child in his need for help with these particular questions and with particular situations. The two are alike also in their need for specific help which adds up gradually to a body of general facts about race, and to habits of reacting to it rationally, calmly, accurately, and with social and psychological insight. There is no basic dissimilarity in the *needs* of the white and Negro child. The dissimilarities lie rather in the uses to which each will put the help he gets.

The white child will not have to use the help he gets for purposes of defending his own ego and his respect and admiration for the We-group. The Negro child will have to use the help he gets *primarily* for such purposes. The white child's problem is to avoid an inflated and hence unrealistic sense of the worth he has *because* he is white. The Negro child's problem is to avoid a deflated and hence equally unrealistic sense of the worth he has *because* he is a Negro.

So the task of guiding either child becomes twofold: (1) to serve their common needs for facts and constructive habits, (2) to teach the child how to use these facts and habits for appropriate purposes in the structuring of his own personality and social outlook.

We have listened to some guidance efforts in which there was work under way on both these kinds of tasks. Let us listen to just one more. Then we shall have finished our consideration of possible ways and means of giving our children some tools for the building of "America for everybody."

This time the guidance effort has been triggered by Jane, who is "colored," who knows it, and who has a sense of affinity with whites, of preference for them, and a sense that whites are somehow superior. Jane has just told her grown-up, rather more explicitly than Negro children usually tell it, "I don't want to be colored."

Jane's grown-up does not ask Jane *why* she does not want to be colored. She knows the general reasons, and she does not want to be drawn into a weak defense of the advantages of being colored. It would have to be a weak defense if Jane's grown-up were honest with Jane. In view of the present realities of American life, it is distinctly no advantage to be colored (save under rare and special conditions). Jane's grown-up has to be honest if she is to be helpful, but she need not dwell upon the disadvantages of Jane's position. She can take a more constructive tack, and it might run something like this:

"All right, you don't want to be colored—so let's pretend. Let's pretend that you could make yourself look like somebody else. Who would it be? So it would be your friend Mary, at nursery school. If you looked like Mary, how would you look? Yes, you would have light brown hair and it would be straight.

"And do you know what would happen then? If you had straight hair like Mary's you would want it to be curly, the way Mary does. You would beg your mother to curl it for you, or give you a permanent. If she didn't, you would be cross and she would be cross. If she did curl it, you would have to wear curlers to bed at night, they would hurt and pull your hair when your mother took them out in the morning. Or you would have a permanent. That would be a lot of trouble. You wouldn't like the trouble, and the curls you got would grow out pretty soon and have to be done all over again. The easiest way to wear your straight hair would be in braids—the way Sally and Mildred wear their straight hair, and the way you wear your curly hair.

"Now, if you had light brown hair like Mary's, some people would think it was a very pretty color. Some other people wouldn't think it was so pretty. They would like blond hair or red hair or black hair, like yours. People have different ideas about what hair color is prettiest.

"But everybody likes hair that looks shiny because it's clean and healthy, and everybody likes hair that's neat and combed in a becoming way. You don't have to pretend that your hair's shiny, and neat, and becoming. Because that's the way it is.

"But we'll pretend about your eyes. We'll pretend they're blue, like Mary's. Sometimes people say to you, 'what pretty blue eyes you have, Mary.' And sometimes people say to Jane, 'what pretty brown eyes *you* have.' Some people think blue eyes are prettier and some think brown are prettier.

"Now we'll pretend that your skin is the color of Mary's. It's hard to say what color that would be because it's almost *no* color. But some people think your new skin is very pretty. They say, 'what a pretty, fair skin Mary has.' And some other people think Jane's skin is pretty. They say, 'what a lovely color Jane is.'

"Let's pretend that you, looking like Mary, go to the beach in the summer. You love to play in the sand all day long, with the hot sun shining down on you. You love to get a tan, because then you would hear people say, 'what a beautiful tan you have, Mary.' But you come home from a day at the beach and you have *no* tan! Instead you're a bright pink color that doesn't look very pretty to you or anyone else. And it *feels* anything but pretty. It hurts! You have a sunburn. After it has healed and your burned skin has peeled off, you still have no tan. You're just about the way you were before.

"But Jane goes to the beach and plays all day in the nice warm sand under the bright sun. She comes home with a little tan—it doesn't show very much—but it doesn't matter, because she had a lovely tan before she ever went to the beach. Jane doesn't hurt from sunburn, and her skin doesn't peel off and look funny doing it. Jane keeps her lovely tan all year round too, but if Mary ever does manage to get tanned, she doesn't stay that way. As soon as she stops going to the beach or playing in the sun, she begins to lose her tan. After a while people may say to Mary, 'why Mary —how pale you look!'

"So maybe it wouldn't be so easy after all for a wise little girl to choose whether she'd like to look like Jane or like Mary. Either way she would have some troubles. Either way *some* people would think her very pretty.

"But let's pretend again. Let's pretend that *nobody* ever cares at all what Jane or Mary look like. That's not a whole pretend. It's only a part-pretend, and I'll tell you why. It's a part-pretend because there really *are* some people who don't care at all what Jane or Mary look like. If nobody cared, then do you think Jane or Mary would care? They probably wouldn't, because Jane and Mary are learning to care about what they think other people care about.

"Sometimes Jane and Mary get mixed up. Sometimes they think that *everybody* cares what they look like, and cares a lot. But that's not the way it really is. The way it really is some people *do* care a lot about what Jane and Mary look like. Some other people care, but they don't usually pay very much attention. They're more interested in how Jane and Mary *act* than in how they look. And some people care about very little besides how Jane and Mary act. Those are pretty wise people.

"Those people who care a lot what Jane and Mary look like are not very wise—they are mixed up. They have some funny ideas about what looks mean. They think they can tell, just from how a person looks, how he's going to act. They really can't, of course—nobody can, because people who look quite a bit alike don't act alike. And people who act alike don't look alike. So the people who think looks are terribly important have no good reason for thinking so. They've made a mistake.

"Everybody makes mistakes sometimes, but that's a pretty bad mistake to make very often. The people who make the mistake of thinking looks are terribly important go around making other people unhappy. The mistaken people tell the other people whether they have the right or wrong kind of looks. And that's making mistake number 2, because there's no such thing as a right or a wrong kind of looks. There are just *different* kinds.

"When the mistaken people say 'looks are *very* important,' and 'you have the wrong kind of looks'—they don't always say it in words. Sometimes they say it by not wanting to make friends and not wanting to do things with people who don't have *their* kind of looks. No matter *how* they say it, they're mistaken people. They're not the people Jane and Mary want to be like, or to pay a lot of attention to. Jane and Mary will be much wiser if they copy the wise people—the ones who know that how people *act* is much more important than how they *look,* and the ones who know that there aren't any 'right' or 'wrong' kinds of looks— just different kinds.

"Those wise people are glad there are differences in looks, because it makes people more interesting. Besides, how could you tell Jane from Mary if they looked exactly alike? And they aren't exactly alike, of course. They really are, on the inside, as special and as especially 'Jane' and 'Mary' as they are on the outside. Each of them can grow up to be very wise, and then each of them will be very beautiful *inside,* where it counts."

Chapter 12

Epilogue

THE children who are the central characters in our story are in the early stages of a complicated process of development. The grown-ups around them are likely to think in terms of an arbitrary line between "children" and "grown-ups"—even between "little children" and "older children." And these adults hold fairly standardized ideas about what the minds and feelings of children, as compared with grown-ups, are like. They have standardized ideas too about the minds and feelings of little children as against older ones. It is a standardized idea that "little children pay no attention to race." Evidence to the contrary does not fit the patterned expectations. Hence such evidence is likely to remain unnoticed, or to be forgotten, ignored, denied, or misinterpreted.

Among adult Americans ideas and feelings about race are highly standardized too. Standardization of this kind does not suddenly emerge full-blown at some biologically predetermined stage, nor is its development necessitated by some innate qualities of the human animal. There is plenty of proof that the adult generally manifests the race attitude common in his time and his society, and that he would have manifested quite different ones had his time and society been different. So we know that the standardized American ideas and feelings about race are "transmitted" from one generation of Americans to the next, but not as a biologically determined inevitability or at any given point in the formative stages of the oncoming generation.

244

Getting acquainted with our 103 children has taught us something about the timing and the mechanics of that so-called transmission process. It has taught us that "little children" sometimes pay a startling amount of attention to race, that they are ready to pay attention to race just as soon as they pay attention to other physical—and socially significant—attributes (like age and sex), and that the amount and kind of attention paid by different children vary as a function of certain interrelated factors.

The high degree of race awareness we have seen in many of these children is startling, and not only because it does not fit our adult expectations. The fact is that mere intellectual awareness of the physical signs of race is not all of the story. There is another part which is not merely startling but quite shocking to liberal-humanitarian sensibilities. It is shocking to find that four-year-olds, particularly white ones, show unmistakable signs of the onset of racial bigotry.

So here is a grim, hard fact to be added to the growing collection of grim, hard facts about race relations in America. It is all too clear that the race prejudice which flourishes among us like the green bay tree sends its taproots deep, and even into early childhood.

As an equally grim corollary we have another fact. It is all too clear that Negro children not yet five can sense that they are marked, and grow uneasy. They can like enormously what they see across the color line, and find it hard to like what they see on their side. In this there is scant comfort or security, and in it are the dynamics for rending personality asunder.

It is possible that the personalities of some of our Negro children are already significantly affected. We have observed higher levels of activity, emotionality, sensitiveness, gregariousness, competitiveness, and aggressiveness among Negro children as compared with their white schoolmates. The differences are striking in one of our four groups. Conversely, our Negro children are not distinguished by the apathy and lethargy popularly supposed to be prevalent among Negro adults. (Our personality studies, and their implications, are discussed in Appendixes C and D.)

The thoughts and feelings of our four-year-olds, white or brown, do not come out of the blue. Neither do they come simply and directly from parent to child. They rather *grow* in each child, a unique result of a unique combination of conditions. Each child grows his own set of thoughts and feelings about race, and he achieves them out of the materials at hand. The materials can be sorted into types and labeled personal, social, and cultural.

In operation these types of materials are, of course, elaborately interwoven. Still it is possible to see something of the basic design. Although no two designs are identical, it is also possible to see striking similarities. The child picks up the cues given by other (and usually older) children and by adults (his parents and others). These people he knows or hears about, and the relations between them, are his social materials. The things these people say and do, or fail to say and do, provide him with his cultural materials—with those standardized ideas and feelings about race, about what makes people "nice" or "not-nice," and the multitude of other matters an American child learns in becoming an American adult.

But the social and cultural materials are all filtered through the personal ones in the process of taking root in our child. He will pick up certain cues and ignore others, depending upon his capacity and readiness to see, remember, and put two and two together. Temperament, mentality, and learned thought-ways all work together to determine his capacity and readiness. And even more is involved—his own physical make-up. Whether he is brown or white, handsome or not-handsome, strong or weak—these and other such personal factors can affect his responses to other people, and to the cues they offer. There are the facets of his psychological make-up too—his personal needs and interests, which deeply affect his responses.

So the process by which the patterned race attitudes characteristic of adult America get across even to very young children begins to look extremely complex indeed. To call this process a matter of "transmission" is to imply a misleading simplicity, directness, and mechanical handing-over (or teaching). The process is perhaps less a matter of *transmission* than of *regeneration*. This is to say that there begins early and proceeds gradually, in each individual, a process much more complex than the sheer *learning* of someone else's attitudes. It is rather that each individual *generates* his own attitudes, out of the personal, social, and cultural materials which happen to be his. In view of the fact that the variety of such materials is finite—that in a given country and community certain conditions and experiences are common and rarely to be avoided—

our individuals tend to get hold of rather similar materials and hence eventually to generate rather similar attitudes.

This is an unfortunate outcome. It is unfortunate in relation to the achievement of integration and harmony in American society, and unfortunately costly in relation to the psychological health and satisfaction of Americans. It is unfortunate because those similar attitudes tend to be so similarly bigoted where whites are concerned—so similarly ambivalent and anxiety-laden where Negroes are concerned.

It need not be this way forever. There are no inevitabilities here. What is more, there are no monolithic attitudes springing from monolithic sources. Monoliths are massive and resistant. But the very complexity of the process of attitude-generation, as we have seen its early stages in our four-year-olds, is promising. It means that there are a great many possible points of attack, no one of which is necessarily highly resistant. But the further along the process of attitude-generation, the more resistant each point becomes. Hence the sensible thing is to attack while the personality is still malleable, and even before the generation process is well under way.

There are great potentialities in the early attack. The current American system of race relations, which is a function of standardized ideas and feelings about race, can of course be made to change. It *is* changing, in fact, but too slowly. Since so much of the general welfare is involved, the rate of change needs stepping up. So let us go to the roots of the system—to the early stages in that long, gradual, and continuous process through which the child becomes the man. Let us alter—as much and as many as we can—the materials with which the child will make himself the man. If we do this, even perceptibly, we can count upon the man to alter the materials again in his time.

It is heartening to remember that there is an antithesis to the principle of the vicious circle in human affairs. *The benign circle operates too, and we who have young children in our charge can touch the springs to help set it in motion.*

Chapter 13

Race Attitudes in Children:
An Overview of Research*

IN THE COURSE of the last decade we have seen massive and dramatic action affecting race relations. Two historic milestones stand along the way: (1) the Supreme Court decision of May, 1954, which outlawed segregation in the public schools; and (2) the 1957 enactment by Congress of the first federal civil rights bill since Reconstruction. Reviewing these and other significant developments of the decade leads to the conclusion that "something big is happening to us; the *ideal* of true equality is becoming a real and vigorous *idea*"; it is "an idea whose time has come." [1]

Research and Action

The coming of this time has been at least hastened by research.

In a document of major social import—an appendix to the appellants' brief to the Supreme Court of the United States in the cases presented against segregation in the public schools—a group of 35 eminent social scientists . . . summarized the results of a wide range of social in-

* An addendum prepared for this edition.

248

vestigations of the effects on children of prejudice against minority groups. . . .[2]

The case is not unique, nor is it likely to be without parallels. Such utilization of research findings "may in the future play a larger part in the shaping of public legislative policy, and therefore indirectly in the reduction of group tensions." [3]

Research on intergroup attitudes and their genesis has had other practical consequences. Findings have been much discussed by educators, parent groups, and others professionally or personally concerned with children. Popular or semipopular articles by the score have appeared in magazines and newspapers;[4] countless conferences have been convened for the purpose of discussing how prejudice is learned and how such learning can be prevented or retarded.

"Human Rights" constituted a major program emphasis of the 1960 White House Conference on Children and Youth and egalitarian sentiment among the conferees was overwhelmingly predominant. The attitudinal climate was notably different than at the Mid-Century White House Conference ten years earlier. The 1960 Conference produced thirty-six "human rights" recommendations calling for sweeping action to eliminate segregation and discrimination from education, housing, employment, suffrage, religion, community organizations and services. Recommendations called too for the creation of national bodies (e.g., a National Institute of Social Health; a National Human Relations Commission) to further research, "social justice for children and youth," and intergroup communication.[5]

Clearly the decade has been marked by enormous changes in national policy and in public interests and attitudes as well. Knowledge concerning prejudice and its genesis is greater; concern for the realization of democratic ideals is stronger. A great surge toward this realization is in progress. Relevant research has both contributed to and been stimulated by these changes. However, the volume and depth of research accomplished is less than might have been expected under the circumstances.

Intergroup Attitudes in Children: Studies, 1952-1962[6]

Three currents of thought are evident in the spate of studies of the last decade dealing with intergroup attitudes in children.

Most conspicuous is the "neopsychoanalytic" current, set in motion by Adorno and his associates with the 1950 publication of *The Authoritarian Personality*.[7] Productive of endless controversy and fine-spun theorizing, the widening ripples of this massive work are only now subsiding.[8]

The essential contribution of studies in this mold has been the definition of a personality type which appears to correlate highly with prejudice, presumably prejudice of a "pathological" (psychically-caused) rather than a "normal" (culturally-caused) sort. However, just what the "authoritarianism" or "F-scale" *does* measure has been hotly debated. The 1959 *Annual Review of Psychology* reports, for the year under review, no less than eight studies "relating the F+ to acquiescence, and all of them pointed to acquiescence as being a major component of whatever it is that F+ measures." Other studies showed F-scale results to be seriously affected by the behavior of the person using the test.[9]

A second current reflects "social learning theory," in which authoritarianism is often of focal interest, but

> the social-learning theorist finds it difficult to embrace the version of psychoanalytic theory which holds that the authoritarian personality springs full-blown from the anal psychosexual stage, and is a direct function of fixation due to the trauma of early and severe toilet training. However, within social-learning theory, it is reasonable to entertain sympathetically the notion that the mother who is severe in her toilet training also engages in a number of other child-rearing practices that might well make a child an authoritarian.[10]

(Such practices are identified by Sears, Maccoby, and Levin in their massive *Patterns of Child-Rearing*, 1957.)[11] But authoritarianism can be accounted for in terms of culture, as Christie and Garcia have suggested. In their study of attitudes among college students in a town they called "Southwest City" they found authoritarianism and ethnocentrism much higher than in a certain California community. The authors conclude:

> Less psychoanalytically oriented theorists than Adorno and his colleagues might speculate that lifelong immersion in

an implicitly authoritarian subculture establishes the frame of reference underlying one's perception of the world and the value judgments made about human nature, and that this factor would account for the increased evidences of authoritarianism in Southwest City.[12]

Prejudice, too, can be accounted for largely in terms of culture. Pettigrew, in a comparative north-south study, shows that the difference in incidence of prejudice is great and in the expected direction. This difference he finds to be largely a matter of directly *learned* (cultural) prejudice. The investigator concludes that the incidence of "pathologic" prejudice (prejudice which is presumably a function more of personality dynamics than of learned patterns) is about the same north and south.[13]

A third current reflects emphasis on prejudice as a social and cultural—rather than psychological—phenomenon. The view is that "prejudice is mainly sustained by social usages and sanctions"[14]—that it is these "usages and sanctions" rather than pathologic personalities or harsh child-training which primarily "cause" and perpetuate prejudice. This view predominates in the work of social psychologists, as well as sociologists and anthropologists, who have seriously studied the matter. To this writer it seems highly probable that "prejudice based on conformity to the social customs of a group is the most common [type] in our own society and in others."[15] The individual, with his particular psychological make-up, his needs or frustrations, is always subject to these customs, and "the problem of intergroup behavior . . . is not primarily the problem of the behavior of one or a few deviate individuals."[16]

Certainly our New Dublin children were in the process of being shaped to fit the customary molds of racial thought and feeling in American society.[17] From the New Dublin study, together with studies made in other parts of the country—in rural, town, and metropolitan settings—we know beyond doubt that young children everywhere are shaped to the pattern of "white over brown, with the line between."[18] Clearly children everywhere are growing up, like our New Dublin children, seeing and hearing the evidences of this consensus, and—each in his own way—building it into his own little personal system.

The Developmental Course of Awareness and Attitude

"The first six years of life are important for the development of all social attitudes, though it is a mistake to regard early childhood as alone responsible for them. A bigoted personality may be well under way by the age of six, but by no means fully fashioned."[19] These generalizations by Gordon Allport are supported by every relevant study.

The development of race awareness and attitudes is of course a continuous process through childhood, but three essential and overlapping phases are distinguishable. Phase 1: *Awareness*, the dawning and sharpening of consciousness of self and of others in terms of racial identity; Phase 2: *Orientation* (incipient attitude), the learning and synthesizing of race-related words, concepts, and values; Phase 3: *True Attitude*, the establishing of full-fledged race attitudes. Awareness of own racial identity is but one facet of that consciousness of self which is gradually achieved during the first three or four years of life. Consciousness of others, and of their identities, is a reciprocal and simultaneous process.[20]

By age two, or two and a half, children are likely to begin to give evidence of consciousness of own and others' racial characteristics. Mothers of some New Dublin children reported such evidence, as did mothers of seven of the ten Austin, Texas children studied by H. W. and N. G. Stevenson. Although younger at the time of study than were the New Dublin children, these Austin children also occasionally demonstrated awareness as they went about their ordinary nursery school activities. Of their ten subjects (aged two and one-half to three and one-half years), the Stevensons report that "only one (of the five) Negro and one (of the five) white children gave no indication of racial awareness" by spring of the nursery school year. The authors add:

> Goodman's general conclusion that children begin to develop racial awareness at an extremely early age is supported, and as might be expected, the proportion of 3-year-old children in the present study who showed high awareness was lower than the proportion of 4-year-olds in Goodman's study. Many of the ways in which the children expressed awareness were common to both studies, and some of the children in both studies developed a concern about their own racial status.[21]

It has been reported that

> Among three-year-old Negro children in both northern and southern communities, more than 75% showed that they were conscious of the difference between "white" and "colored." These findings clearly support the conclusion that racial awareness is present in Negro children as young as three. . . . Furthermore, this knowledge develops in stability and clarity from year to year, and by the age of seven it is a part of the knowledge of all Negro children. Other investigators (R. Horowitz; M. E. Goodman; Radke, Trager, and Davis) have shown that the same is true of white children.[22]

Landreth and Johnson, questioning whether such findings would appear equally in children of lower and upper socioeconomic status, studied white three- and five-year-olds of conspicuously different status backgrounds (in California). They conclude that the higher status children incline to "perceive skin color in cognitive terms," while lower status children "perceive it in affective terms." But in both groups a majority of children did perceive it, at both age levels, as did the lower status Negro children they studied. In sum: "Patterns of response to persons of different skin color are present as early as three years and become accentuated during the succeeding two years."[23]

Morland, studying three-, four-, and five-year-olds, found well over a third of three-year-olds (Negro and white children averaged) to be either "high" or "medium" in "ability to identify pictures of Negroes and whites." He reports that "recognition ability was found to progress regularly with age and to have its fastest development during the child's fourth year."[24]

By the age of four nearly all normal children will be at least minimally and occasionally aware of the physical marks of race and many will have developed distinct in-group/out-group *orientations* (incipient race attitudes). This we are justified in concluding since it has been found true in each of the groups of children studied.[25] Phase 2 of the developmental process will be well under way. It is in fact quite probable, as K. B. Clark concludes, that

> the child's first awareness of racial differences is . . . associated with some rudimentary evaluation of these differ-

ences. . . . [Moreover], the child . . . cannot learn what racial group he belongs to without being involved in a larger pattern of emotions, conflicts, and desires which are part of his growing knowledge of what society thinks about his race.[26]

Stevenson and Stewart apparently agree. They report, referring to their study of a group ranging in age from three to seven, that "By the ages of 4, 5, and 6 these Subjects were responding in a manner which indicated not only awareness of racial differences but also the use of stereotyped roles."[27]

Upwards of age five, awareness can be expected and incipient attitudes are likely. By age seven true attitudes are not unlikely. Trager and Radke-Yarrow, summarizing their data concerning "social perceptions" of kindergarten, first- and second-graders in Philadelphia, conclude that

. . . concepts and feelings about race frequently include adult distinctions of status, ability, character, occupations, and economic circumstances. . . . Among the older children stereotyping and expressions of hostility are more frequent, and attitudes are more crystallized than among the younger children.[28]

Kutner, studying seven-year-olds in the Boston area, found 12% of his sample (60 children) "clearly prejudiced."[29]

G. W. Allport concludes that by age seven or eight many children arrive at what he describes as a "totalized rejection" which "seems to reach its ethnocentric peak in early puberty. . . . [But] as children grow older they normally lose this tendency to total rejection and overgeneralization. . . . [However] the 'total rejection' is chiefly a verbal matter." This verbal rejection may be accompanied by behavioral acceptance. By about age twelve, however, verbal rejection is likely to have been replaced by the "double-talk" customary among adults who profess no prejudice while in fact demonstrating it. Verbal rejection (accompanied by behavioral acceptance), gives way to behavioral rejection (accompanied by verbal acceptance).[30] White twelve-year-olds studied by Rosner "were [verbally] almost unanimously prejudiced against Negroes"; however, "the prejudice expressed verbally . . . did not usually express itself in the behavior of these same children."[31]

"Ethnocentrism," verbally measured, was found to be both frequent and generalized (toward several minority groups) among the "Gentile" ten- to fifteen-year-olds studied by Frenkel-Brunswik and Havel. Prejudice toward Negroes was greater than toward other minorities (Mexicans, Chinese, Japanese, and Jews). Of the 81 subjects, 27 were classified as "high scorers," 18 as "middle scorers," and 36 as "low scorers," but

> The children's attitudes are usually a mixture of prejudiced and tolerant ideologies. Our high-scoring subjects, on the whole, were freer in expressing prejudice than the low-scoring children were in expressing tolerance. Furthermore, the middle scorers who are more representative of the bulk of the population show great similarity in their responses to the high scorers. Thus the attitudes of the children as a group are predominantly prejudiced ones.[32]

Although prejudice toward Negroes runs higher than toward other minorities, there is little doubt that prejudice tends to be generalized. Frenkel-Brunswik's findings are supported by evidence from other sources and for different age levels. In children of kindergarten through second grade Trager and Radke-Yarrow found prejudice—or incipient prejudice at least—toward Catholics, Jews, and Negroes, but:

> Derogatory stereotypes and reactions indicative of adherence to patterns of social discrimination occur most frequently with respect to the Negro group.[33]

Galtung, who studied 2,000 American youngsters (in 21 cities) of grades 9 through 12, found prejudice toward Negroes, Jews, and Catholics (in that order of intensity). This investigator concludes that, in general, the level of prejudice among these high school students is at least not below current levels in the adult population.[34] A phenomenon of adolescence may be reflected here, however. Helfant reports, concerning "sociopolitical attitudes," that "Adolescents tend to adopt an attitude which (when in the same direction) is somewhat more extreme or emphatic than the attitude of their parents, especially their mothers."[35]

Adorno *et al.*, are of the opinion that the prejudiced individual seldom limits his targets; those prejudiced against

Negroes tend to be prejudiced against Jews and Orientals as well.[36]

Developmental Differences: Negro Children and White Children

It will be recalled that among our New Dublin four-year-olds we identified five types of *orientations* (see pp. 166-200). We found the Negro children to be basically out-group oriented—to share a "sense of direction" *away* from Negroes and *toward* whites. But the white children are in-group oriented; their basic orientation—their "sense of direction"— is *around* within the orbit of the white world and quite without the racial self-doubt and self-concern which is in the Negro children.

The New Dublin Negro children showed their basically *out-group orientation* in an inclination toward out-group affinity, out-group preference, friendliness toward the out-group (coupled with inclination toward in-group neutrality or even antagonism), and inferiority (or neutrality, but never superiority) vis-à-vis the out-group. Our white children presented a strikingly different orientational picture both generally and specifically.

There is reason to conclude that the New Dublin children are in these respects remarkably like their race counterparts in other places. Morland says of his preschool Virginian subjects that the Negro children tend to identify with whites— as do white children themselves.[37] Of his Negro subjects he observed that many who identified themselves as colored "did so reluctantly and with emotional strain." Among the Texan children (aged three to seven) studied by Stevenson and Stewart, the Negroes often gave evidence of out-group preference and in-group disparagement or rejection. Negro children of three to seven (in both Northern and Southern communities) were the Clarks' subjects; when asked to choose between white and brown dolls "the majority of these Negro children at each age indicated an unmistakable preference for the white doll and a rejection of the brown doll."[38]

Landreth and Johnson observe of their California children that, "though living in a democracy, many Negro citizens apparently learn by three years of age that skin color is important, that white is to be desired, dark to be regretted."[39]

Trager and Radke-Yarrow report, of their kindergarten to second-graders in Philadelphia, that the Negro children—like the whites—"ascribe many undesirable stereotypes"

> to Negroes, and . . . Seldom do Negro children give responses of unmixed positive feelings toward their own group. . . . [Among whites] strong expressions of fear and hostility toward Negro people accompany perceptions of inferior status and rationalize acts of exclusion and segregation. . . . Negroes are expected to have low social status, an inferiority seen as "natural" and inevitable.[40]

In a study of third-, fourth-, and fifth-grade children in Minneapolis, Bird, Monachesi, and Burdick report:

> . . . white children express prejudice toward Jews and Negroes in equal degree. . . . The Negro children hold more favorable attitudes toward white children than the latter do toward Negro children. . . . Negro children manifest very little prejudice toward non-Jewish white children but considerable prejudice toward Jewish children.[41]

Kerckhoff and Gould found that fifth-grade Negro children in Detroit prefer racially heterogeneous neighborhoods, a preference which was not paralleled among their white classmates.[42]

Clearly, children in other parts of the United States learn very early those race-related values which lead to a set of racial orientations much like the values and orientations observed in New Dublin. This is not surprising; American children regardless of race or region can hardly escape exposure to the values implicit in pervasive practices. In fact, and at the level of American behavioral as distinguished from ideal patterns, it is true that

> Merely by reason of his membership in the white group, an individual is accorded certain social privileges, and experiences the sense of being "better" or higher class. Conversely, by mere reason of membership in (or assignment to) the Negro group, one is deprived of these privileges and experiences the sense of being "second class."[43]

McCandless, reviewing relevant data, observes hypothetically "that (U.S.) society is so organized as to lead the Negro child to devalue and perhaps even to reject his own ethnic group. The consequences of such rejection for the self-concept of Negro children are serious and should be investigated further."[44]

There is no reason to question either the reality or the seriousness of the phenomenon. The problem is, as J. H. Douglass clearly states it, that the Negro "rejects himself by seeing himself through the eyes of the majority group." Having "accepted as his own the values, norms, and ideals of the majority, the marginal (minority) person sees himself as part of what is rejected. The result . . . may be self-hatred."[45]

The result may be anxiety as well. Mussen compared TAT (Thematic Apperception Test) responses of Negro and white boys (lower socioeconomic groups, ages nine to fourteen). He found that the white boys predominantly perceive the world as a friendly place; the Negro boys, on the contrary, perceive it as hostile and threatening.[46]

We observed, about the New Dublin children, that for the whites growing race awareness and in-group orientation brings a greater sense of security in their racial status. Typically there is a sense of complacency about the racial self. For the Negro children it is quite otherwise; heightened awareness and growing out-group orientation are typically accompanied by a growing sense of insecurity with respect to racial status, a heightened emotionality and a greater sense of personal involvement and personal threat.

Other studies of young children, without exception, produce closely similar findings.[47] Anxiety levels among fourth- to sixth-graders have been shown (by Palermo) to be higher for Negro than for white children.[48] Boyd finds among Negro elementary school children higher occupational aspirations than their white classmates show. He suggests that this inclination among the Negro children represents a defense mechanism—that it results from their greater insecurity.[49]

Martin Deutsch, studying lower-class children (Negro and white, fourth to sixth grade), finds that their total milieu "fosters self-doubt and social confusion, which in turn serves . . . to lower motivation . . . and aspirations." This is particularly true for "the Negro child in a white world," who experiences "progressive alienation" from both work and his fellows.[50]

The Deutsch study of 400 children, in depth, provides convincing evidence of differences in self-concepts as between disadvantaged children white and Negro. Deutsch found self-concepts generally more negative among the Negroes; "a relatively high proportion of the white lower-class children in this sample have negative self-responses, but not nearly as many as in the Negro group. . . . The Negro group as a whole is affected by lowered self-esteem."[51]

The crucial factors appear to be (1) essential separation of the Negro child from the larger community, simultaneously with (2) pressures to conform to the standards of that community. Academic retardation *and* negative self-image result. There is a sex difference involved; Negro boys are more handicapped than are the girls, both because boys often lack a father figure with whom to identify, and because fewer rewarding occupational avenues in the larger society are open to them than to the girls. The school experience is of scant help; it affords little that influences the development of positive self-attitudes. Deutsch concludes:

> . . . the concept of self of the minority group child must be one of the first factors studied in evaluating the effects of segregation, cultural separation, and inferior social status on his personality development and general socialization, including school performance.[52]

In New Dublin we observed among Negro children two inclinations which relate to out-group orientation and negative self-image: (1) their inclination to earlier attainment of high awareness; (2) their inclination toward greater development of certain personality traits.

Our data on the former point are clear-cut: 40% of our Negro children, as against 24% of our white children, showed "high awareness." However, the balance is reversed at the "medium awareness" level, with the result that the two racial groups are even (15% of each) with respect to proportions falling in the "low awareness" category. In two recent studies the findings suggest some inclination toward earlier awareness among whites (Stevenson and Stewart; Morland).[53] However, in neither study does judgment concerning level of awareness rest on the intensive case study which is the basis for judgment of the New Dublin children. It is quite possible that fuller exploration of each case might have resulted in a different judgment; both Goodman and the Clarks have observed that Negro children of preschool age sometimes identify "incorrectly" not because they are unaware of own racial identity, but precisely because they *are* aware and are rejecting that identity. "A child may try to escape the trap of inferiority by denying the fact of his own race."[54] Slightly older Negro children are reported (by Trager and Radke-Yarrow) to avoid the topic of race; "the responses suggest that the Negro children wish to avoid a painful subject. It is not a lack of concern or awareness about race on their part."[55]

It is relevant too that both of these recent studies draw on communities outside the orbit of "northern" subculture (one in Texas, one in Virginia). It is possible that in these milieux Negro children are as alert to race as they are in the north, and that white children are considerably *more* alert to race than they are in the north. It is possible too that Negro children in the south are more guarded concerning expression of awareness than are those in the north. Certainly, northern Negro children are overtly and intensely emotional (and reluctant) when asked to make racial self-identifications (as the Clarks and Goodman have reported).[56] Lacking further data we are not in a position to close the question, but differences of method and of subculture sampled seem quite sufficient to explain a discrepancy which is in fact of no great magnitude.

The New Dublin data relating to personality differences between Negro and white children raise an important question. In one of four nursery school groups the writer found striking differences between the races; the Negro children were relatively hyperactive and strong in leadership; they were comparatively more sensitive, gregarious, competitive, and aggressive.[57] These findings suggest that young Negro children may show traits quite out of line with the popular conception of the distinctive personality traits of Negro adults (i.e., "a quietism, a passivity"). Allport, commenting on this suggested discontinuity, observes that "passivity, when it exists as a Negro attribute, is apparently a learned mode of adjustment." It may be that vigor, gregariousness, etc., in Negro children stem from a stimulation provided by the dawning awareness of race.

They may be excited by a challenge they do not fully understand, and may seek reassurance through activity and

social contacts for the vague threat that hangs over them.
The threat comes not from nursery school, where they are
secure enough, but from their first contacts with the world
outside and from discussions at home, where their Negro
parents cannot fail to talk about the matter.[58]

Relevant data from other studies allow of no firm conclusion concerning the frequency of this discontinuity phenomenon. It is perhaps more likely to mark the life course of the
northern Negro; the five Negro children of a Texas study
(by the Stevensons) are said not to have differed as a group
from their five white classmates. But method of study is of
possible relevance in this instance too; the Stevensons judge
personality on the basis of observation records (15 hours)
rather than against personality rating scales. More pertinent
to the question are findings from the Deutsch study, which
is large-scale, intensive, and focused on Northern children.
It was found that

in general, the Negro group tends to be more passive, more
fearful, and more dysphoric than the whites. Although the
Negro children do show less aggressive content in their
responses, it is of great interest that, when asked to complete
the sentence "If I could be an animal I would most like
to be ———," 31% identified with an aggressive animal as
compared with only 16% of the white children.[59]

The children referred to are, it will be recalled, fourth,
fifth, and sixth graders. There has been time, since they were
four, for the passivity, fearfulness, and dysphoria to set in.
Moreover, these are all lower-class children, while some—
perhaps half—of the New Dublin Negro children came from
rather middle-class homes. It is notable too that aggressiveness
still appears though mainly in an extremely covert form;
Myrdal has shown its prevalence, in this form, among Negro
adults.

The Prejudiced Child: Developmental
Influences and Antecedents

From intensive case studies of our New Dublin children
we deduced generalizations concerning *significant terms* in

the *personal equation,* and their functional relations with awareness-attitude levels (pp. 200-215). We concluded that there is no *single* key to the how and why of race awareness and race orientation in our children. Rather, there are at least six major kinds of keys, each of which has its own varieties. Each case presents a distinctive combination of certain of these factors—a distinctive *personal equation,* whose terms are interdependent.

Equations characteristic of white children who are high in cross-racial antagonisms tend to assume a form quite unlike that of white children who are low in cross-racial antagonisms. The forms in which significant terms are likely to appear in the high-antagonism child are to a degree reminiscent of the "authoritarian personality" and its supposed antecedents. Similarities are of the greater interest because our formulation does not result from interpretation in terms of the Adorno frame of reference. Rather, our formulation represents direct deductive generalizations.

Our *significant terms* embrace antecedent factors broadly, however, and are not limited to personality factors and the presumably causal child training practices. Individual (physical) attributes, for example, and particularly those which are racially identifying, must be regarded as among the *significant terms.* But the *terms* are interdependent; for example, actual personal attributes are evaluated (the *Values term*) and weighed against those of others. The high-antagonism child is given to strong feeling, sharp differentiations and either/or thinking (the action-, feeling-, and thought-*Ways term*). The "others" he therefore tends to conceptualize as polar, and—because he is given to suspicion (*Needs and Interests term*) and to rejecting the different as such (*Values term*)—he directs his feelings, strong as well as negative, toward those whom he sees as different. Cross-racial contacts real or vicarious (*Individual Situation term*) are ego-enhancing because they bring into focus the people whom he rejects and devalues. This child identifies with, communicates with, and is psychologically dependent upon persons in whom these and related elements are strong (*Models term*).

This analysis of the high-antagonism child among New Dublin four-year-olds converges at several points with that of the "high-scorer" in Frenkel-Brunswik and Havel's sample of older children. These investigators find in such children:

. . . a tendency toward dichotomizing, exaggerated adherence to conventional values, the avoidance of insight into the characteristics of the in-group and fear of threats and dangers from the out-group. . . .[60]

Kutner's findings, in a study of prejudice and cognitive functioning, support and add to our "thought-ways" term. Among his second-graders Kutner observed that "the prejudiced children are not only less capable of producing valid conclusions but the invalid ones they *do* produce are *dogmatically* held." Kutner finds prejudiced children less able in forming concepts, more ready to jump to conclusions, poor in dealing with ambiguous problems, less task-oriented in problem-solving, more easily discouraged and perplexed in face of problems to be solved, less likely to show insight and understanding, and—generally—functioning cognitively in a fashion marked by rigidity and by intolerance of ambiguity. In Kutner's group, as among the New Dublin children, such traits are not a function of basic intelligence (as measured).[61]

Suspiciousness and rejection of the different and unfamiliar, as such, appeared in the incipiently prejudiced New Dublin children. These attitudes appear to be common in prejudiced persons, who incline to "perceive the world as a jungle where men are basically evil and dangerous."[62] Some part of the suspicious-rejecting inclination may be learned, as Allport suggests, from early interpersonal experience: "There is some evidence that children lacking basic trust in early life are prone to develop in later childhood a suspiciousness of nature, including prejudice against minority groups."[63] But it is probable that in the prejudiced person this generalized basis for suspicion and rejection is overlain by more specific learnings; by "those subtle forms of learning—not yet fully understood—whereby value-judgments are conveyed to the child."[64]

That we caught glimpses of this process at work in New Dublin there can be no doubt, nor can we doubt the peculiar relevance of culturally patterned negative valuation of dirtiness, darkness, and roughness. Like McFarland, we saw in preschool children a strong inclination to confuse color, or other marks of race, with values.[65] We observed devaluing of non-whites by association of pigmentation with dirt and darkness, of hair form with roughness. It is reported of fifth-grade children (Kerckhoff and Gould) that they "overwhelmingly claimed (with respect to choosing friends) that dirtiness was the least desirable trait in other children." A large majority of the children in this study alleged that skin color was not important to them in their choice of friends, but this declaration seemed hollow in view of their strongly expressed preference for racially homogeneous neighborhoods.[66]

Other values too become "confused" with race. We have seen, in New Dublin families, the relevance of *conventional* and *avoiding* social orientations. To adhere to the conventional standards of "niceness" (set by and primarily associated with middle- and upper-class whites) implies family values which are readily learned by children. Frenkel-Brunswik reports that, typically, people who are high in prejudice come from families whose primary values revolve around social status and standing in the community.

> Parents . . . transmit to their children, not only specific social attitudes, but whatever predispositions to these attitudes lie within the individual's personality. . . . This raises the question as to whether prejudice is transmitted directly, or else indirectly via a more general formation of character.[67]

There are data which support the view that prejudice represents an aspect of "general character." For example: Evans has demonstrated that among college students those who register high anti-Semitism scores (on the Levinson-Sanford Anti-Semitism Scale) stress political and economic values (as diagnosed through the Allport-Vernon Study of Values). Those who make low anti-Semitism scores, on the other hand, stress aesthetic and social values.[68]

The *personal equation* hypothesis derived from the present study accommodates both direct and indirect transmission. We see no justification for an either-or view of the matter.

Though primary and principal, parents are not the sole source of the child's social learning and character development. The New Dublin study documents this fact. Frenkel-Brunswik and Havel report only low positive correlations between parental prejudice and children's prejudices. Bird *et al.* find (in 145 white midwestern families) that parent-child attitudes differ fairly often. They relate this primarily to lack of parental unanimity in attitudes, adding, however:

... it has not been claimed [in this report] that the conditions within the home are the only ones accounting for differences in attitudes between parents and their children.[69]

The Bird study concludes with an observation quite in keeping with what we know of New Dublin parents:

Very few of the families are typified either by vigorous efforts to educate children in democratic attitudes or by vigorous efforts to inculcate in children strong antipathies toward Negroes.[70]

Trager *et al.* report similarly:

Parents' teaching of intergroup attitudes is frequently unconscious and is rarely direct or planned. Only a few parents indicate that they are helping their children to feel respect for differences or are trying to help them resist the social prejudices around them.[71]

With young children, parents and teachers usually avoid or evade questions and discussions relating to race and prejudice. This fact, amply documented in the New Dublin study, is exactly paralleled in the report on the Philadelphia study. New Dublin children clearly sensed a "taboo"; and among the Philadelphia subjects:

Many of the children have learned that race and religion are topics which are not to be explored or discussed openly.[72]

Awareness, Attitude, and Cross-racial Behavior in Children

The relation between awareness, or incipient attitude, and cross-racial behavior in young children is not so unlike this relation as observed in adults. It is reported that "at the adult level behavior patterns may be quite different—even diametrically opposed to—conscious or unconscious attitudes." But the impression exists that in small children there is a "direct one-to-one correspondence between attitude and behavior."[73]

This is by no means true. We observed repeatedly that children whose public behavior was wholly or largely free of racialism provided, in private sessions, unmistakable evidence of awareness and incipiently prejudiced attitude. The Stevensons, most of whose two and one-half to three and one-half-year-old subjects gave evidence of considerable race awareness and some feeling, report:

> . . . no differences in the behavior of Negro and white children or in the frequency and types of intraracial and interracial behavior.[74]

There is, in short, ample evidence that small children do not demonstrate a "one-to-one correspondence between attitude and behavior." The reasons, as inferred from observation of the New Dublin children, are two: (1) even at age four, there is in some children, and to some degree, a reticence about "public" expression relating to race; (2) more important, race, which looms large in "dead" dolls, pictures, etc., recedes from the perceptual fields under the impact of live and immediate persons and their personalities. A third reason—a matter of "superordinate goals"—is suggested by the work of Sherif et al.: the children in the nursery school situation may spontaneously create "superordinate goals"; while attention is fixed on these shared interests race becomes a matter of indifference.

The "Robbers Cave Experiment" (Sherif and associates, 1961) demonstrates the extent to which intergroup behavior in children can be manipulated. The investigators created two carefully matched groups (eleven-year-old white boys), placed them in a summer camp setting, and developed between them "an unmistakable state of friction manifested in hostile acts and derogatory stereotypes." Sherif et al. believe that they could have reduced the friction by (1) introducing a "common enemy," (2) disseminating corrective information, (3) breaking the groups into individual action, (4) developing pleasant and mutual participation contacts, (5) introducing a "series of superordinate goals," i.e., "goals of high appeal value for both groups, which cannot be ignored . . . , but whose attainment is beyond the resources and efforts of any one group alone." This last was the method used in the experiment; the result: "the prevailing friction between the groups was reduced: . . . favorable conceptions of the out-group (were) developed."[75]

Needs in Research

There is no need for further research to document the fact that race awareness and attitude (incipient, at least) are likely to appear in very early childhood. This fact is thoroughly established, and the relation between age and awareness-attitude is fairly clear. However, with respect to such correlated variables as race, sex, socioeconomic status, and region of residence there is conflicting evidence.

It is not surely established whether race awareness is likely to dawn somewhat earlier in Negro than in white children, in girls than in boys, at lower than higher socioeconomic levels, in the North than in the South. In the interest of achieving a tidy and comprehensive body of knowledge these uncertainties should be reduced. But there are more pressing questions to be answered. There is, moreover, a need to direct selectively the always limited research resources toward what Gordon Allport has called "root problems," and to avoid "trivialization" or sterile scientism.

The "root problems" fall into four categories, or so it seems to this writer, and all are of major importance in both theoretical and practical terms. These "root problems" are:

1. What are the conditions and forces (environmental and psychic) most relevant to the "generating" of prejudice attitudes in children? With respect to this problem we know a good deal, have documented a fair amount, and need to know and document much more.

2. What is the functional relationship between race values and the rest of the value system, both individual and on cultural (or subcultural) levels? Objective study of values, and their implications for behavior, has been neglected. This is particularly true with respect to studies of intergroup relations (except for Myrdal's "American Creed" analysis) and to studies of children.

3. What are the social and psychological realities of the desegregation process for those Negro children and families who are its "pioneers"? It seems well-nigh incredible that in research focused on or relevant to desegregation this crucial facet has not been explored. Such is apparently the case,

however; search of Tumin's "Digest of Recent Research" on segregation and desegregation (1957 and supplement in 1960) and of other bibliographic sources reveals nothing relevant.[76] Indeed there appears to be an equal lack of studies focused on white children and families who are experiencing, or have experienced, the desegregation process. Yet surely this "natural laboratory" provides unparalleled opportunities for study of race attitudes and of attitude change.

4. What is the nature and genesis of tolerant attitudes in children? We use the word "tolerant" in the sense in which Allport uses it, and

> because the English language lacks a better term to express the friendly and trustful attitude that one person may have toward another, regardless of the groups to which either belongs.[77]

The literature on intergroup attitudes is nearly lacking in theory, much less data, focused directly on tolerance. Allport (1954, pp. 425-442) is almost alone in explicit attention to this positive. The preoccupation with negative attitudes, like the preoccupation with pathology in medical research, is understandable but unfortunate. There is much to be learned, for social as well as medical practice and for prevention in either area, from study of the state of health. Negative attitudes do not necessarily represent psychic pathology, but in culturally relative terms they do represent—in a contemporary democracy—anachronisms or anachorisms.

In historical perspective a decade is a negligible unit of time. Against the measure of constructive change it can be, as the last has been, an epoch in race relations. The next decade too may be epochal for movement toward humanitarian goals; depth and concentration in research can help to make it so.

Appendixes

Appendix A

The tables which follow show how the 103 children are distributed according to nursery school group, race, sex, age, intelligence quotient, and level of race awareness.

Table A-1

The Four Groups by Race and Sex; the Total Sample by Race and Sex

Rodney I

	Negro	White	Total
Male	9	5	14
Female	6	7	13
Total	15	12	27

Rodney II

	Negro	White	Total
Male	11	11	22
Female	6	8	14
Total	17	19	36

Coleman

	Negro	White	Total
Male	10	—	10
Female	11	—	11
Total	21		21

Dover

	Negro	White	Total
Male	1	9	10
Female	3	6	9
Total	4	15	19

	Negro	White	Total	Percent of Sample
Rodney I	15	12	27	26
Rodney II	17	19	36	35
Coleman	21	0	21	20
Dover	4	15	19	19
Total	57	46	103	100

	Male	Female	Total	Percent of Sample
Rodney I	14	13	27	26
Rodney II	22	14	36	35
Coleman	10	11	21	20
Dover	10	9	19	19
Total	56	47	103	100

	Total	Percent of Sample
Negro	57	55
White	46	45
Total		100
Male	56	54
Female	47	46
Total		100

Table A-2

The Four Groups by Race and Awareness Levels

Awareness	Rodney I				Rodney II				Dover				Coleman			
	Negro	White	Total	Percent	Negro	White	Total	Percent	Negro	White	Total	Percent	Negro	White	Total	Percent
High	4	2	6	22	8	5	13	36	2	4	6	32	8	—	8	38
Medium	10	9	19	70	6	12	18	50	1	7	8	42	9		9	43
Low	1	1	2	8	3	2	5	14	1	4	5	26	4	—	4	19
Total	15	12	27	100	17	19	36	100	4	15	19	100	21		21	100

Table A-3

Total Sample by Race, Sex, and Awareness Levels

Awareness	Negro			White			Total		Female			Male		
	Number	Percent	Percent of Sample	Number	Percent	Percent of Sample	Total Number	Percent of Sample	Number	Percent	Percent of Sample	Number	Percent	Percent of Sample
High	22	40	21	11	24	11	33	32	19	40	19	14	25	14
Medium	26	45	25	28	61	27	54	52	25	53	24	29	52	28
Low	9	15	9	7	15	7	16	16	3	7	3	13	23	12
Total	57	100	55	46	100	45	103	100	47	100	46	56	100	54

High Awareness

		Rodney I	Rodney II	Coleman	Dover
Negro	Male	Quentin 5-5; 96 Sam 5-1; 114 Thomas 4-10; 106 Donald 5-1; 119	Andrew 4-6; 93 Tony A. 4-6; 100 Eddie T. 4-7; 106 Victor 4-9; 109 Tony R. 4-3; 132	Colin 4-11; 116	June 4-11; 95 Anna 5-0; 137
	Female		Viola 5-1; 110 Cynthia 5-1; 112 Joan G. 4-5; 104	Jackie 4-6; 100 Joyce 4-10; 108 Joan M. 4-5; 130 Carol M. 4-5; 111 Karen 4-8; Bright Joanne D. 5-2; 102 Barbara 4-4; 107	
White	Male	Nathan 4-10; 100	Stefan 4-7; 110 Danny 4-7; 119		David J. 4-11; 114
	Female	Wilma 4-4; 110	Vivien 4-6; 122 Debbie 4-7; 138 Elaine 4-5; 95		Jean 4-3; 129 Lorraine 4-5; 118 Sarah 4-10; 106
Negro	Male	Norman 4-6; 131 Ned 4-8; 106 James W. 4-8; 124 John 4-6; 102	Herman 4-9; 121 Herbert 3-8; 80 Charles 4-8; 114	Paul B. 5-1; 107 Gerard 4-7; 107 James S. 3-11; 95 David H. 4-2; Very bright Leslie 4-11; 106 Malcolm 5-0; 90 James M. 5-3; 131	

Awareness	Race	Sex				
Medium Awareness	White	Female	Winona 4-7; 98 Rose 4-11; 108 Irma 5-3; 98 Nan 5-1; 106 Helen 4-7; 124 Brenda 4-5; 109	Gail 4-9; 114 Candy 4-7; 114 Estello 5-3; 96	Nadine 4-6; 113 Janice 4-4; 98	Dianne 5-0; 102
	White	Male	Ian 5-6; 133 Peter 5-0; 110 Roland 4-6; 119 David 5-4; 109	Gerry 4-7; 92 Billy C. 4-6; 106 Eddie R. 5-0; 98 Paul P. 4-7; 112 Paul D. 4-5; 110 Eddie H. 4-7; 106 Burton 4-11; 84		Joseph 4-3; 110 Ronald 4-11; 95 Peter S. 4-8; 120 Carl 3-11; 123
	Negro	Female	Hester 4-11; 90 Yvonne 5-2; 114 Velma 4-6; 97 Vesta 5-0; 116 Patricia 4-9; 108	Lilita 4-7; 120 Diane 5-2; 122 Rosemarie 5-0; 112 Irene 3-10; 115 Pamela 3-10; 145		Patricia S. 4-11; 106 Carol G. 4-11; 126 Nancy 4-8; 138
	Negro	Male	William 4-7; 107	Sam J. 4-2; normal Stephen I. 4-1; 96 Chester 3-8; 106	James F. 4-8; 102 David W. 4-3; 116	Alfred 4-7; 106
Low Awareness	Negro	Female			Sharon 4-4; 93 Jo-Ann P. 3-7; 109	
	White	Male		Peter Q. 4-5; 88 Marvin 4-9; normal		Paul G. 4-5; 100 William K. 4-5; 98 Theodore 4-7; 94 George L. 4-11; 94
	White	Female	Ruth 4-7; 104			

		Below 4-2	4-2	4-3	4-4	4-5	4-6	4-7
High Awareness	Negro			Tony R.	Barbara	Joan G. Joan M. Carol M.	Andrew Tony A. Jackie	Eddie L.
High Awareness	White			Jean	Wilma	Elaine Lorraine	Vivien	Stefan Danny Debbie
Medium Awareness	Negro	Herbert James S.	David H.		Janice	Brenda	Norma John Nadine	Girard Winona Helen Candy
Medium Awareness	White	Carl Irene Pamela		Joseph		Paul D.	Roland Billy C. Velma	Gerry Paul P. Eddie H. Lilita
Low Awareness	Negro	Stephen I. Chester Jo-Ann P.	Sam J.	David W.	Sharon			William Alfred
Low Awareness	White					Peter Q. Paul C. William K.		Theodore Ruth
Summary	High	N's 0 W's 0 Tot. 0	N's 0 W's 0 Tot. 0	N's 1 W's 1 Tot. 2	N's 1 W's 1 Tot. 2	N's 3 W's 2 Tot. 5	N's 3 W's 1 Tot. 4	N's 1 W's 3 Tot. 4
Summary	Medium	N's 2 W's 3 Tot. 5	N's 1 W's 0 Tot. 1	N's 0 W's 1 Tot. 1	N's 1 W's 0 Tot. 1	N's 1 W's 1 Tot. 2	N's 3 W's 3 Tot. 6	N's 4 W's 4 Tot. 8
Summary	Low	N's 3 W's 0 Tot. 3	N's 1 W's 0 Tot. 1	N's 1 W's 0 Tot. 1	N's 1 W's 0 Tot. 1	N's 0 W's 3 Tot. 3	N's 0 W's 0 Tot. 0	N's 2 W's 2 Tot. 4

4-8	4-9	4-10	4-11	5-0	5-1	5-2	Above 5-2
Karen	Victor	Thomas Joyce	Colin June	Anna	Sam Donald Viola Cynthia	Joanne D.	Quentin
		Nathan Sarah	David J.				
Ned James W. Charles	Herman Gail		Leslie Rose	Malcolm Dianne	Paul B. Nan		James M. Irma Estelle
Peter S. Nancy	Patricia		Burton Ronald Hester Patricia G. Carol G.	Peter Eddie R. Vesta Rosemarie		Yvonne Diane	Ian David
James F.							
	Marvin		George L.				
N's 1 W's 0 Tot. 1	N's 1 W's 0 Tot. 1	N's 2 W's 2 Tot. 4	N's 2 W's 1 Tot. 3	N's 1 W's 0 Tot. 1	N's 4 W's 0 Tot. 4	N's 1 W's 0 Tot. 1	N's 1 W's 0 Tot. 1
N's 3 W's 2 Tot. 5	N's 2 W's 1 Tot. 3	N's 0 W's 0 Tot. 0	N's 2 W's 5 Tot. 7	N's 2 W's 4 Tot. 6	N's 2 W's 0 Tot. 2	N's 0 W's 2 Tot. 2	N's 3 W's 2 Tot. 5
N's 1 W's 0 Tot. 1	N's 0 W's 1 Tot. 1	N's 0 W's 0 Tot. 0	N's 0 W's 1 Tot. 1	N's 0 W's 1 Tot. 1	N's 0 W's 0 Tot. 0	N's 0 W's 0 Tot. 0	N's 0 W's 0 Tot. 0

		Below 100	100–104	105–109	110–114
High Awareness	Negro	Quentin Andrew June	Tony A. Joan G. Jackie Joanne D.	Thomas Eddie T. Victor Joyce Barbara	Sam Viola Cynthia Carol M.
	White	Elaine	Nathan	Sarah	Stefan David J. Wilma
Medium Awareness	Negro	Herbert Charles James S. Malcolm Winona Irma Estelle Janice	John Dianne	Ned Paul B. Girard Leslie Rose Nan Brenda	Gail Candy Nadine
	White	Gerry Eddie R. Burton Ronald Hester Velma		David Billy C. Eddie H. Patricia Patricia G.	Peter Paul P. Paul D. Joseph Yvonne Rosemarie Irene
Low Awareness	Negro	Stephen I. Sharon	James F.	William Chester Alfred Jo-Ann P.	
	White	Peter Q. William K. Theodore George L.	Ruth Paul C.		
Summary		N's 13 W's 11 Tot. 24	N's 7 W's 3 Tot. 10	N's 16 W's 6 Tot. 22	N's 7 W's 10 Tot. 17

115–119	120–124	125–129	130–134	135 and above
Donald Colin			Tony R. Joan M.	Anna
Danny Lorraine	Vivien	Jean		Debbie
	James W. Herman Helen		Norman James M.	
Roland Vesta	Peter S. Carl C. Lilita Diane	Carol G.	Ian	Pamela Nancy
David W.				
N's 3 W's 4 Tot. 7	N's 3 W's 5 Tot. 8	N's 0 W's 2 Tot. 2	N's 4 W's 1 Tot. 5	N's 1 W's 3 Tot. 4

Appendix B

The Methods of the Study

I. Data-gathering Methods

The Observer (the writer and two assistants) went into the nursery schools, with the permission of their respective directors, to gather data through (a) nonparticipant observation, (b) participant observation, (c) interviewing, (d) testing, (e) access to school records and incidental assistance from the school's staff. These several methods were emphasized in roughly the order in which they are listed above, but the approach was of necessity extremely flexible. The cordiality and cooperation we met in the school personnel, the parents, and the children themselves enormously facilitated our study. Nevertheless, we of course had constantly to adjust our methods to the school routines and the convenience of everyone involved therein.

We began by emphasizing nonparticipant observation. This meant observing and simultaneously recording the behavior of the children as they went through the nursery school day. At Rodney we observed either from behind a one-way screen or from a corner of the play yard or playroom. As the children and teachers came to take our presence as an unremarkable matter of fact we were freer to move about, following an individual child or a play group. We became fixtures in the nursery school scene, and occasionally we were called upon to take a hand when a teacher needed help or a child turned to us for assistance with a snowsuit, shoelaces, or some other little service. The teachers, of course, knew our purpose and helped to establish our status as "students" with the parents. In the eyes of the children we were perhaps a little more peculiar than the other visitors to whom they were accustomed, since we "visited" so constantly, wrote so much, and occasionally took pictures. But they accepted us as a kind of visitor-teacher-friend composite.

Our recording of the routine activities was done on a semi-systematic basis. We would "sweep" the group, recording who was doing what, and with whom, at intervals of about ten minutes. During the interim periods we concentrated in turn upon one of the clusters of children or upon an isolate, recording in detail the sequence of verbal and motor behavior. Detailed recording was limited by the inability of any of us to take shorthand. We used our private systems of abbreviation and learned to write very rapidly.

As the days and weeks went by we found many occasions for a brief chat with a teacher, a parent, or a child. We utilized these snatches of time for improving rapport, for getting specific bits of information we needed, or for imparting information about our own activities, interests, and plans.

Eventually it became quite natural and simple to explain to a parent that we would appreciate an opportunity for a longer chat. We told the parent of our desire to know the child as thoroughly as possible, and of our need for the parents' help in this. We usually added that our general interest was accompanied by a specific interest in the child's reaction to other people, particularly to people rather different from himself in appearance. We asked when we might pay the family a visit and discuss these matters.

We generally met with cordiality and hospitality from the parents and we succeeded in arranging home interviews in all but a few cases. In these cases the parent pleaded an overcrowded home with no quiet place to sit and talk, or some other condition which made the home visit impracticable. Clearly the reticence was not always based upon such objective grounds, but we did not attempt to force the issue, and suggested a meeting at the school instead. For these meetings we had the privacy of the room in which we did our work with the individual children.

We went to the interview equipped with a list of the pertinent facts we hoped to elicit, but the list was either memorized or out of sight. We asked no standardized questions, and the interviews were conducted in a primarily nondirective fashion. We asked questions or suggested points for discussion only to the degree necessary to orient the informant or to fill out our list of pertinent items. Our usual experience was of a quite ready flow from our informants, and of their eventually touching spontaneously upon many of our points of interest. Interviews tended to run to two or three hours, and not infrequently we were bid good-by only after being served refreshments and urged to call again.

Our approach to the testing of the children followed the same gradual course. Having built acquaintance and friendly relations with the children we began to invite them, one at a time, to come with us to "play with some new things." Each child eventually received four of five such invitations, and in the course of as many "play interviews" we introduced him to four sets of projective materials. The usual order was (1) a set of jigsaw puzzles, (2) a doll house with its furnishings and miniature doll families, (3) a set of pictures, and (4) a collection of dolls of several types.

These projective materials were assembled for this study on a basis of two considerations: (1) they are suitable to the interests and capacities of the four-year-old, and (2) they tend to stimulate verbal and motor behavior which give clues to the child's race awareness and his orientation toward racial attributes and differences.

THE JIGSAW PUZZLES

Puzzles of this type are a familiar and favorite piece of nursery school equipment. The puzzles we used were popular with the children, and their use in the first of our series of play interviews helped to establish a pleasant association around the Observer and his invitations to "come and play."

Our puzzles were designed and constructed for this study. We used two pairs. Pair A consists of puzzles having ten pieces each. Each piece represents a family member—father, mother, large child, medium-sized child, and small child. Each puzzle thus has pieces representing two five-member families. Puzzle A-1 has two animal families (one of horses and one of elephants), and its partner (A-2) has two human families. One of these human families is brown, the other is "white." Apart from the color difference the families are alike, and all are shown in bathing suits so that the skin color differential is maximized.

We presented puzzles A-1 and A-2 (in that order) with the ten pieces removed and lying in a random heap on the table at which the child was seated. Holding the empty puzzle board up before the child we pointed to the appropriate empty spaces, which are arranged in two rows of five spaces each, saying: "Here is a place for a father animal (father), here is a place for a mother animal (mother), and here—and here—and here—are the places for *their* three children." Then, pointing to the spaces in the second row, we continued: "Here are places for *another* father animal (father), and another mother, and *their* three children. *Put together the animals (people) that belong together.*"

We then sat down beside the child and recorded his moves and comments while he assembled the puzzle, and his time at beginning and conclusion.

We gave no help unless it was necessary to keep the child from quitting in frustration. When he had finished we held the completed picture up before him and asked: "Have you put together all the animals (people) that *belong* together?" When he had responded, we said: "Tell me about the picture you have made."

Puzzles A-1 and A-2 are so constructed that it is possible to assemble either homogeneous or heterogeneous families. That is, a given piece can fit into either the top row or into the corresponding space in the bottom row. Hence the child can put all the animals (or people) of a kind in one row and all those of the other kind in the second row (achieving two homogeneous families), or he can assemble in a given row some animals (or people) of one kind and some of another (a heterogeneous or "mixed" family).

This exercise, then, amounted primarily to an attempt to assess the child's consciousness of kind, both animal and human. Secondarily, it provided the child with representations of brown and of white people upon which to focus his attention. This focus of attention sometimes led to spontaneous and revealing comment from the child. Occasionally a child would volunteer: "these people are brown and these are white"; or, "this is my daddy—my mummy—me—my brother (sister)"; or something of these general orders.

Each of our Pair B puzzles consists of two segmented human figures. Puzzle B-1 shows two boys wearing bathing trunks and having a ball (fixed in the board) in passage between them. One boy is brown and the other white, and each figure is completed by putting together seven pieces (hair, face, two arms, body, and two legs). The figures are alike save for color, but the pieces of the one are not interchangeable with the pieces of the other. Puzzle B-2 shows two girls on a seesaw. They wear identical short dresses and, like the boy figures, each girl figure is completed by assembling several noninterchangeable pieces.

The B-1 and B-2 puzzles were presented, in order, with the pieces lying in a random heap beside the empty puzzle board. The child was simply instructed to "put the picture together." The Observer then recorded his moves and comments, timing the process, and asked at the end: "Tell me about the picture you've made." After the response to this question the child was asked: "Do these children like to play together?" and "Which one would you rather play with?" "Why?"

Watching and listening as the child assembled these segmented figures, it was usually clear enough when, or whether, the child caught the color clue. Some of our subjects immediately selected pieces all of a color to fit with the first piece they had happened to place in a given figure. This was done either without comment or accompanied by some such comment as "all the brown ones go together," or "this boy's brown." Other children operated on a relatively simple trial and error and manipulative level. Some responded to our questions with explicit references to color or color differences, and/or with explicit statements, in terms of color, about the play preferences of the puzzle "children" or about their own play preferences. Other subjects made no references, direct or indirect, to the color identity of the puzzle figures.

The puzzle "interview" generally ran to half or three-quarters of an hour. Not infrequently the child would request one or all of the puzzles again at the same or later sessions. We granted these requests whenever time permitted; and we sometimes had from the same child more perceptive and fuller responses on subsequent trials. Maturing awareness was sometimes quite apparent when the two or more trials were separated by a period of weeks or months.

The puzzle technique proved highly satisfactory for our purposes. It allows of infinite adaptation for age and research objectives, and it is to be recommended as a research tool for studies involving children.

"MINIATURE LIFE TOYS" AND DOLL HOUSE

Our doll house "interview" was adapted from Dr. Lois Murphy's "Miniature Life Toy" technique.*

In the early phases of the study (with the Rodney I group) we followed Murphy quite closely. We simply presented the child with a box containing small dolls and appropriately scaled household furnishings. Our dolls represented both brown and white people, and people of both sexes and different ages. We told the child that he might "take the things out of the box and play with them," and then proceeded to record his behavior without further comment.

In studying our three other groups we altered this approach somewhat. We used a doll house of a standard commercial type, and in it we arranged the furnishings ourselves, in advance of the interview. We set the doll house on a table, and in front of it we laid out our dolls in a randomly mixed heap. When the child came into our room we led him to the table and suggested that he put the people (indicating the dolls) in the house and show us what they might be doing there. We had by now dolls which had been made for our use, since the commercial dolls used in the Rodney I study were not entirely satisfactory (the brown people were too black, families were not identical, etc.). Our custom-made dolls represented two families, one medium brown and one white. Each family had grandfather and grandmother, father and mother, two girls, and one boy.

When our child appeared to have finished his spontaneous play (which we had recorded in detail), we asked some questions. First we suggested that he put all the people again on

* Lerner, E. and Murphy, L.B., Eds., *Methods for the Study of Personality in Young Children,* Society for Research in Child Development, National Research Council, Washington, D.C. 1941.

the table in front of the house. When he had done this we picked up a father doll, and said, "Now let's decide who's going to be in his family. Which mother shall we have to go with this father?" When the child had indicated a choice between the mother dolls (and we had recorded the choice and noted any accompanying comments or significant behavior), we placed the chosen mother with the father and asked for children to "go with" this mother and father, and then for grandparents to add to the assembled family.

Having completed and recorded this little exercise we went on to another if we still had our subject's attention (and usually we had). We picked up the two father dolls and held them together before the child. Then we asked, "which father do you like better?" Having recorded that choice we held up the two mother dolls and asked the same question. We repeated the question in respect to each pair of dolls, and if the child did not volunteer a reason for any of his choices we asked him "why" his choice in respect to at least one pair.

Watching our children place and manipulate the dolls in the house gave us clues to their ideas about family life generally and the relevance to it of color differences. The children usually mixed their people quite indiscriminately, putting browns and whites together at the kitchen table, in the living-room, and in the bedrooms. Occasionally a child would put all the whites in one part of the house and all the browns in another, sometimes commenting to the effect that "these people live here, and these people live here," implying separation on a color basis. Sometimes the color difference was noted explicitly, either by the child who made such a separation or by a child who made no separation but simply threw out a casual comment such as "this father is brown."

When we asked the child to choose family members to "go with" a given father we usually wound up with a racially mixed family. But whether or not the children assembled heterogeneous families they sometimes commented upon color difference.

When we asked for an expression of preference as between the brown and the white fathers, mothers, etc., we were usually given by the white children an unequivocal white preference. The white children gave as their "reasons" either resemblance of the chosen doll to self or a member of their own families, or the statement, "this one's prettier." From the

Negro children we frequently had equivocation and other indications of reluctance to state a choice. When a brown choice was made it was often followed by a spontaneous identification of the chosen doll with own father, mother, etc. A white choice was likely to be explained in terms of esthetic preference ("that one's prettier").

The modifications and new procedures which we introduced after the Rodney I study were calculated to make the miniature "people" more realistic, to focus the child's attention upon them rather than upon the household furnishings, and to encourage him to verbalize about the people. We found our "doll house" technique helpful and, for our purposes, considerably more rewarding than the approach modeled more closely upon Dr. Murphy's "Miniature Life Toy" technique.

PICTURES AND CLAY

Our use of pictures was an adaptation of the Thematic Apperception Test.* Some preliminary experimentation, as well as conversations with Dr. Henry Murry and others, suggested that young children need something to keep them manually occupied while they are looking at pictures. Hence the writer elected to present the child with a ball of brown and one of white plasticene (commercially prepared modeling clay) at the beginning of the session. The child then could, and usually did, finger and manipulate the plasticene more or less inattentively while he was being shown the pictures and asked about them.

The pictures we used were black and white prints taken from magazines and chosen after pretesting (on children who are not included in this study). Three pictures were used with the Rodney I group, and six with our other groups (or as many as ten if interest remained high). After the Rodney I study we used a standard form for this interview, recording the responses on a prepared blank. The form covered only our Series A set of six pictures, however. When we used the Series B set of four additional pictures we improvised the approach, but it followed the lines established for the Series A pictures.

* Murray, H. A., *Explorations in Personality*, Oxford University Press, N.Y., 1938.

We began by presenting the clay and checking on the child's readiness to name brown and white as such, and to express a preference for one of these colors, as such. Most of our children "know their colors," brown and white included. Their expressed color preference had no necessary significance in relation to race, yet it was another little "straw in the wind" when we came, eventually, to reviewing and evaluating the tenor of a given child's whole sequence of responses.

Picture 1 shows a white girl of nursery school age walking across an open space which is clearly outdoors, but the murky background tells nothing more. The child is "tow-haired" and "tousle-haired," and wearing medium weather clothes of no more than medium quality. Her open-mouthed, squint-eyed face can be read as registering a variety of emotions. In short, the picture was used because it shows a young white child about whose activities, emotions, etc. it conveys very little, leaving the subject to supply the "story" out of his own inclinations and resources. The principle that the picture should convey racial identity, age, sex, and very little more, was basic to the selection of our other pictures as well.

We showed Picture 1 and suggested that the child use the clay ("let's make the little girl out of clay"). This allowed us to make an oblique approach to the question of the racial identity of our Picture 1 girl ("which clay shall we use to make the little girl"). We soon learned to follow the answer with "why," although this question was not on the blank. The why question brought some curious explanations, rationalizations, afterthoughts, etc. Sometimes these responses suggested that the clay color chosen was irrelevant to racial considerations, at least if the response were taken at face value. For example, the subject says he will use the white clay "because the little girl in the picture is wearing a white shirt," or the brown "because she's wearing a brown sweater and brown pants." But when the subject chooses the white clay "because it will make a better girl," racial significance is strongly implied, particularly when many other responses from this same subject have explicit racial content.

The remaining pictures in our Series A are: Picture 2—a brown boy (of about nursery school age) walking downstairs; Picture 3—a racially mixed group of children (of various ages and types) playing "London Bridge"; Picture 4—a man and woman (of about middle age) sitting side by side; they are clearly but not extremely Negroid in appearance; Picture 5—a man and woman (again of middle age) looking together at a card or letter which the woman holds; they are clearly white; Picture 6—a Negro woman and a white woman, the first sitting at a table or desk, the second standing beside her.

Our Series B pictures include: Picture 7—a young couple, clearly Negroid, smiling down upon their baby in his crib; Picture 8—a young white couple smiling upon their small son and daughter; Picture 9—a white man and a Negro man standing together, arms thrown across each other's shoulders; the Negro is smiling but his face is cut and bleeding; Picture 10—a Negro man and a white man sitting side by side at what might be a work bench.

The questions we asked about the pictures were designed to elicit several types of response. First we encouraged spontaneous story-telling. Thereafter we asked questions leading toward (1) self identifications and identifications of others—members of the child's family, his teachers, his friends (questions such as: "does he/she look like you/your brother/sister/mother," etc.); (2) expressions of feelings about the people in the pictures (such questions as: "do you like him/her," "would you invite him/her to your house," "is he/she good-looking or pretty," "would you like him/her for your friend," "would you like to play with him/her," etc.); (3) the testing of the child's concepts in respect to race and family membership (such questions as: "could he/she be your brother/sister," "is this little girl the sister of this little boy," etc.); and (4) the testing of the child's readiness to use group labels (such questions as: "what kind of people are they," etc.).

We should have preferred to use fewer questions and to rely more upon spontaneous and less directed responses to the pictures. However, young children are not easily persuaded to the spinning of extended phantasies upon being presented with a picture. Such at least was the writer's experience, and such appears to have been the experience of others who have tried picture tests of one sort or another with young children. Hence the adapted TAT, as used in this study, becomes so highly adapted as to have little resemblance to the technique as used with adults. Nevertheless, the adapted form preserves some of the advantages of the original in that the pictures are so nondefinitive as to allow of self-revealing storytelling, and the subject has at least the opportunity for such storytelling and is encouraged to try it. We found our Picture-and-Clay interviews richly rewarding for our purposes, but they would have been much less rewarding had we failed to ask so many questions.

DOLLS

The use of dolls in research involving children is no novelty. The only novelty in their use in this study lay in the uniqueness of the collection of dolls presented to the children and in the patterning of the situation in which they were presented.

We used commercial dolls of a variety of types and sizes. First we laid before the child a "double-doll" whose long, reversible skirt conceals either the white face which is at one extremity or the brown face at the other. Next came a pair of eight-inch baby dolls dressed in diapers. One is a medium brown, the other white; apart from this color difference they are identical. This pair was followed by a pair of babies identical save for color. This pair is small (about four inches), and dressed in diapers and jackets. The next of our doll groups was a trio of diapered babies. These are about three inches long, and they are white, very light brown, and dark brown, respectively. Last we showed our subjects four dolls dressed to represent children of nursery school age. There are two boys, one medium brown and one white, and two girls, one medium brown and one white.

Our procedures with the dolls were akin to our use of the pictures in that we tried first for a spontaneous, storytelling response. Then, when we had apparently exhausted the possibilities of getting this type of response, we went on to questions. We used no form sheet, but our question sequence was standardized. As with the pictures, we departed from or elaborated upon the usual sequence only as the nature of the child's responses gave us leads and cues.

As was the case with our use of the pictures, we were attempting to gather evidence concerning (1) the child's awareness of his own physical attributes and the attributes of others, (2) his feelings about these attributes and the people (real or represented) who manifest them, (3) his concepts concerning social situations involving people differing in what the adult would call "racial" features, and (4) his readiness to categorize people (real or represented) in color-kind terms or in terms of what adults would call "race."

In pursuit of such evidence we asked, in respect to each of the sets of dolls, "which looks more like you when you were a baby/child," "which is prettier,"* "which would you rather play with" (of the child dolls), "which is the brother/ sister of this one," etc. In addition, we used the child dolls to dramatize simple social situations (posed in an incomplete story). Some of these involved a limited commodity desired by both the brown child and the white. We asked the subject to finish the story, and in doing so he was forced to delegate the limited commodity (e.g., one lollipop) to the brown child or the white, unless he could work out an equalitarian solution. The responses were most interesting. Not infrequently the solution appeared in the form of "taking turns," but when our children were pressed concerning "who gets the first turn" it nearly always turned out to be the doll of the subject's own color. We dramatized social situations involving the home—a brown child visiting at a white child's home, or the reverse, depending upon the racial identity of the given subject. Is the visitor invited to come in, invited by mother to stay to supper, etc.?

We concluded the doll interview by moving from the question "which of these, if they were real children (the four "child" dolls) would you invite to your birthday party," to the last question: "which of the real children here at nursery school would you invite," and "which of the nursery school children do you like best to play with."

The dolls served our purposes extremely well. We garnered a rich return on the time invested in these interviews. As with the pictures, however, the yield would have been significantly less had we depended wholly upon the nondirective approach. But, again, as with the pictures, we should have deprived ourselves of some extremely valuable material had we not allowed time for spontaneous responses and kept our procedures flexible.

Consideration of data-gathering methods takes us finally to the use of school records and the assistance we received from the staffs of the three nursery schools.

The schools do not keep precisely the same kinds of records

---

* These two questions were not juxtaposed, however.

nor are their records uniformly full for all the children. Nevertheless the records were an invaluable resource in this study. They gave us our initial body of facts about our subjects—name, birth date, birthplace, birth dates and places of parents and siblings, address (present and sometimes one or more previous addresses), telephone (if any), a record of at least the major events in the child's physical history (e.g., whether breast fed, when weaned, when toilet-trained, illnesses or operations, etc.), periodic evaluations of the child's personality and his adjustment and progress at school, comments on the child's home, family, and family relations (made by his teacher or by the school's social worker, sometimes after a home visit), and still other varieties of data.

At Rodney the school records included a score and commentary for the child's performance on an intelligence test (Stanford-Binet, Form L). For the children at Dover and Coleman we did this testing as a part of our own study, using the same Stanford-Binet test.

Some of our subjects were younger siblings of "alumni" of the nursery schools. In these cases we had access to all the data concerning the older child and the family as of the period of the older child's attendance. It is not at all unusual for two or more children of a given family to follow one another into the schools. This is true because once the doors are opened to a family they tend to stay open, barring events such as a shift of residence to a point outside the school's roughly defined "district" or a major disagreement between school and home. Hence we often found a very illuminating historic dimension in the records.

Much more difficult to define, but no less important, was the incidental and entirely voluntary assistance we received from the directors, the regular teachers, and the student teachers in each of the schools. Once they understood what we were about they usually fell into the habit of reporting to us any observations or bits of news which they thought might be useful and we might have missed. Not unnaturally they became rather more perceptive of evidences of race awareness as the nature of our investigation became clear to them and their interest in the whole matter grew. Because we spent so much time at the schools we were inevitably "around" at some of the times when the director, the social worker, or the teachers were temporarily able to relax and chat—and very much in the mood to do so. So it was hardly by design or appointment, but rather as a "natural" result of the kindness of these people, of mutual interests, and of sustained proximity, that we gathered innumerable and invaluable items and insights.

One service, however, was performed for us in a more formal fashion. This was the making of personality ratings (see Appendix D). We asked most of the regular teachers, and a number of the student teachers, to make these ratings for us upon the ten (or thereabouts) children whom the given teacher felt she knew best. This was no small favor we asked, but again we were met with remarkable interest and readiness to help.

By way of summary and evaluation concerning the data-gathering methods of this study it seems fair to say that: (1) we utilized a variety of approaches to our subjects and their social contexts, (2) this variety added up to a time-consuming method such as few people would find either feasible or congenial, (3) the slow and multiangled type of study provides opportunities for the gathering of a wide range of data concerning rather few subjects, (4) this type of study allows for a sustained and personalized relation between observer, subjects, and persons in regular interaction with the subjects, (5) the methods of this study are therefore suitable only under special conditions and when the problem under investigation is not likely of resolution via more simple, speedy, and objective methods.

Certainly the methods of attack should be tailored to one's definition of a problem. The core of the problem here was— how do race attitudes begin? But the writer, trained in the holistic traditions of functional anthropology, could not comfortably accept the core alone as an adequate definition. To do so would have demanded an arbitrary amputation of a segment of personality and of the social and cultural systems in which it develops—so the problem was and is seen by the writer, at any rate.

This is not to say that a retrospective view suggests no alterations. On the contrary, it is now possible to see that this investigation might have been considerably more efficiently and more effectively conducted (e.g., by the elimination of the personality ratings, which did not pay dividends proportionate to their cost in time and effort).

But, even in retrospect, the writer remains convinced of the fundamental soundness of race attitude studies holistically conceived. Other types of studies can and do cast light on the same core problem (for example, the studies by E. Horowitz, K. Clark and M. Clark, H. Trager *et al.*). There is no one "right" approach, no one wholly adequate study. Many more race attitude studies, varied as to both method and subjects, are still needed. Some of these, it is to be hoped, will proceed from a holistic definition of the problem. These will cast a light which, if more diffuse, may be expected to illumine a circle, while studies differently conceived may cut a swathe.

II. Data-ordering Methods

The data accumulated as described above were finally ordered on a case study basis. For each child two forms (see pp. 296-309) were filled out from the various notes and simultaneous records kept by the observers, and from the observers' personal and subjective impressions.

The data for each case were summarized and evaluated under two major headings: (1) "Criteria for description and definition of awareness-attitude level" (see pp. 296-301), and (2) "Possible causes and correlates of awareness-attitude level" (see pp. 302-309.) Each of the three observers filled in these forms for the children he had studied.

Each observer also supplied (1) personality ratings for each of his subjects, (2) general data concerning the neighborhoods in which his subjects were living (these data were drawn from school sources, the United States census for 1940, and other and more recent statistics prepared by the United Community Services of New Dublin), and (3) conclusions concerning the levels of race awareness and incipient attitude, and the major determinants thereof, as represented in the entire group he had studied.

The writer then worked with the total accumulation of case studies and supplementary data in preparing the research report which is presented in Chapters 1 through 10 of this book. Chapter 11, which sets forth some suggestions for the education of young children in matters of race, represents the indirect results of the writer's experience in research and as a parent.

CRITERIA FOR DESCRIPTION AND DEFINITION
OF AWARENESS-ATTITUDE LEVEL

Subject's name:
Comprehensiveness of data for this subject:
Age span (period under observation):
Race (and/or national origins):

1. *Group labels and descriptive terms:*
    What abstract color terms does the child command?

    What simple descriptive terms (e.g., dark, light) does
    the child command?

    What associational terms does the child command?

    What group labels does the child command? When and
    where has he actually used these labels?

Awareness: Low, Medium, High
Incipient attitude: Yes   No   Of what nature?

2. *Identification:*

What is the nature and accuracy of his self-identification? (Note: *in re* "nature" consider whether wishfulness may be involved, the degree of wishfulness, and hints as to the meaning of it):

What is the nature and accuracy of his identification of others?

What is the nature and accuracy of his concepts in respect to color and family members?

Awareness: Low, Medium, High
Incipient attitude: Yes   No   Of what nature?

3. *Social relations:*

What type and degree of racial partisanship are suggested?

What type and degree of resistance to "free" social participation are suggested?

What type and degree of racial preference or rejection are suggested?

Awareness: Low, Medium, High
Incipient attitude: Yes   No   Of what nature?

4. *Personal esthetics:*

What type and degree of esthetic preference are suggested?

Awareness: Low, Medium, High
Incipient attitude: Yes   No   Of what nature?

Summary:

Over-all level of awareness indicated: Low, Medium, High
Kind of awareness:

Does child have a consistent idea of kind or race?
Are his ideas restricted to piecemeal perceptions?

Other salient aspects of this child's awareness:

Over-all incipient attitude indicated: **Yes   No**
Degree of present incipient attitude: **Weak, Medium, Strong**
Nature of present incipient attitude:
  In-group affinity; out-group affinity; **none**
    If affinity, how intense?
  In-group preference; out-group preference; **none**
    If preference, how strong?
  Superiority; neutrality; inferiority
  Friendly (positive); indifferent (neutral); antagonistic (negative) toward *other* group
  Friendly (positive); indifferent (neutral); antagonistic (negative) toward *own* group

Do you feel that race perception has ego-reference for this child?

  In what manner is the ego-reference expressed by this child?

Under what conditions?

In what directions? (i.e., with what aspects of the ego structure does the expressed ego-reference seem to be related?)

How significant a factor in the total dynamics of personality are race perceptions and learnings?

Are such perceptions and learnings themselves significant motivations or merely the end result of other motivations?

Is race perception seeming to function either to promote or to disturb personality integration?

What effect, if any, do racial identity and/or perception appear to be having upon the subject's system of social relations (social integration)?

a) with members of his family

b) with friends of own race

c) with others

Is progression indicated (in development of awareness and attitude through observation period)?

Further comment:

POSSIBLE CAUSES AND CORRELATES
OF AWARENESS-ATTITUDE LEVEL

Subject's name: Sex: I.Q.:
Birthday: Age span:

Race (and/or national origins):
Pigmentation:
    Objective: Light, medium, dark
    Relative: a) to members of his family:

        b) to own group generally:

Birthplace:
Place or places of rearing:

Siblings: Number, sex, color, age positions in relation to
    subject:

        Interracial experiences and attitudes:

What is the "tone" of the relations between subject and older siblings?

Living conditions: Quality of home (physical, and *in re* intellectual stimulus):

Type and racial-national composition of neighborhood:

Nature of family standards and degree of interest in personal appearance (cleanliness, clothing, grooming):

Nature of subject's neighborhood play-group relations (restricted by parents or entirely free, races and nationalities represented, race or nationality of favorite or favorites, age range represented, interracial friction or friendship, etc.):

Parents: Birthplaces:

Race (and/or national origins):

Pigmentation: Light, medium, dark

Place or places of rearing:

Educational attainment: Grammar school, high school, college:

Religious affiliation and nature of participation: Occupation:

Marital relations (living together, congenial or not, separated, divorced, etc.):

Approximate present income of family:

Social class level of family:

Upward (or downward) mobility indicated?
How?

Interracial experiences (any close friendships past or
present, conflicts, etc.):

Attitudes (degree of intensity, essentially friendly or
antagonistic, probability that parent is consciously
or unconsciously deluding himself or Observer or
both, what may be major motivation for his expressions, etc):

Other intergroup experiences and attitudes:

Extent and nature of clique and/or associational relations:

Other significant adults: (item as under parents)

Parent-child relations:

Discipline: Harsh, firm and reasonable, unconsciously lax
or deliberately gentle?

Protectiveness: Degree, conscious or unconscious, forms
it takes, etc.

Ambitions (goals) for subject:

Child's attitude toward parents: Primarily affectionate
and responsive, resentful and contrasuggestible, etc.
(the "tone" of the parent-child relationship):

Is there fundamental parent-child similarity, sympathy
and closeness of relationship?

Parent and child attitudes:

To what extent are parent attitudes, their quality, intensity, etc., being transferred to subject?

To what extent do older siblings reflect parent attitudes?

What is the *policy,* and what has been the *practice,* of the parents in the "race education" of the child?

Subject's personal history and salient characteristics: e.g., serious illness, physical handicaps, motor development, physical and social attractiveness, etc.:

Nursery school influences: Adults (including Observers) and other children:

Personality of subject:

Quality of cognitive processes (degree of intellectual acuity with respect to observation, inference, and logical synthesis, and of disposition to exercise these facilities):

Emotional tone (degree of manifest intensity, proportionality (to stimulus), and consistency of emotional responses):

Orientation toward people (degree of positive or negative quality in the child's motivation toward social contact: degree of satisfaction usually derived from such contact):

Dominant striving:

Characteristic defenses:

Child's tendencies *in re* fancifulness, curiosity, emotionality, liveliness, negativism, spontaneity, interests, etc., as indicated by his responses to the Diagnostic Situations:

How "secure" is this child? What are his assets and liabilities in this respect?

Comment:
   Which of these variables appear to you to be the most significant "determinants" of the awareness-attitude level you find in this child?

With what aspects of his personality do you feel his race perceptions and learnings to be most closely integrated? How (needs or defenses)?

Appendix C

Cross-racial Interaction in a
Biracial Nursery School

SIMULTANEOUS RECORDS of the behavior of 26 children at the Rodney School have been intensively analyzed. The behavior recorded was that of the children going through the normal nursery school routines. The protocols cover a total of 169 hours of observation distributed over 69 observation days, with an average of 2 hours and 27 minutes of observation per day.

Analysis of the protocols was made by reducing their interaction items to diagrammatic form. The diagrams carried a column for each child, and his every recorded interaction was indicated by drawing a line between his column and that of the child or children with whom he interacted. The nature of the interaction was indicated by symbols identifying the child who provided the stimulus and the child or children who responded. The nature of the response was also indicated by symbols for positive, accepting, or neutral responses, and for negative, or rejecting responses.

A total of 3,025 interactions (stimulus-response units) were diagrammed. Of this total 8% were found to involve white children interacting with other whites, 40% involved Negro children interacting with other Negroes, and 52% involved both Negro and white children. (See Table C-1.)

Table C-1
PERCENTAGES OF INTERACTION AMONG NEGRO
AND WHITE CHILDREN ($n = 3025$)

	Actual Interactions	Chance Expectation	Difference
W ← → W	8	17	9
N ← → W	52	51	1
N ← → N	40	32	8
	100	100	

Negroes were therefore involved in 92% of the interactions, as compared with a total of 60% involving whites. On a basis of chance alone, 83% of the interactions might have been expected to involve Negroes and 68% to have involved whites.

This follows because the group was composed of 11 white and 15 Negro children. The chances of random interaction are therefore

(1) white-white interaction: $\dfrac{11}{26} \times \dfrac{10}{25} = \dfrac{110}{650} = 17\%$

(2) Negro-Negro interaction: $\dfrac{15}{26} \times \dfrac{14}{25} = \dfrac{210}{650} = 32\%$

(3) white-Negro interaction: $\dfrac{11}{26} \times \dfrac{15}{25} = \dfrac{165}{650} = 25.5\%$

(4) Negro-white interaction: $\dfrac{15}{26} \times \dfrac{11}{25} = \dfrac{165}{650} = 25.5\%$

That is, of 100 entirely random interactions between pairs of children, the Observer should see 17 involving two whites, 32 involving two Negroes, and 51 involving a Negro and a white. Hence $32 + 51$ or 83 out of 100 random interactions should involve Negroes, and $17 + 51$ or 68 should involve whites.

Our records therefore show Negro children involved in interaction at a rate 9% *above* chance expectation and white children at a rate 8% *below* chance expectation. They show, too, that the excessive Negro involvement is a matter of excessive Negro-Negro interaction (40% actual as against 32% chance), with Negro-white interaction at chance level (52% actual as against 51% chance), while the under-involvement of whites is accounted for by their low rate of interaction with one another (8% actual as against 17% chance).

Since Negro-white interaction shows a *chance* frequency, we conclude that we have no evidence for either avoidance or seeking of cross-racial contact as such. The high rate of Negro-Negro interaction and the low rate of white-white interaction must therefore result from the operation of variables of a nonracial order.

We conclude that these variables are personality traits which are unequally distributed between the Negro and the white children in this particular group.

Personality data drawn from systematic ratings on 30 "traits" (see Appendix D) show marked differences between the two racial groups. On the average, the Negro children appear to be relatively vigorous and more frequently involved in gross activity, more aggressive, more competitive, and more inclined to leadership; the Negroes show a higher level of emotional excitability and of intensity in emotional response, and more humor, cheerfulness, curiosity, and fancifulness; the Negro children are found to be relatively friendly, kind, and gregarious, and yet somewhat more quarrelsome, cruel, jealous, and "sensitive." Negroes and whites average essentially alike on originality, resistance, and suggestibility, but the whites average higher on social and physical apprehensiveness, and on patience, tenacity, planfulness, emotional control, conformity, obedience, and affectionateness.

It seems reasonable to suppose that the more aggressive, vigorous, gregarious, etc. children would appear more frequently in interaction sequences, and more frequently with one another than with children less conspicuous in respect to these traits. Hence the above-chance level of Negro-Negro interaction rate, the chance level of Negro-white interaction rate, and the below-chance level of white-white interaction rate observed seem entirely consistent with the personality ratings. (Furthermore, the consistency is reassuring in respect to the validity of the personality ratings.)

Appendix D

Personality Ratings

ALL OF THE SUBJECTS of this study were rated on each of 30 personality "traits."* The technique used was that developed and standardized at the Fels Research Institute, Antioch College.† Ratings were made by placing a mark on a 90-millimeter line at a point considered appropriate for a given child on a given trait, in view of the Fels definition of that trait and of degrees thereof. The sample rating sheet for "aggressiveness," which is shown on the following pages, will indicate the nature of the definitions by which the rater was guided. The rating was then converted into a numerical score. This was done by placing an ordinary millimeter scale along the rating line so that the lower end of the line falls at 9.5 millimeters. The score is read on the millimeter scale at the point where the rating mark has been placed on the rating line. Scores can thus range between a minimal value of 10 and a maximal value of 99.

Most of the children were rated on each of the 30 traits by three or four different people. The Observer rated each child he studied, and usually the child was also rated by his regular nursery school teacher and by one or more student teachers. A child's final score on a given trait was obtained by averag-

* While 103 children were studied comprehensively, 105 are included in the personality rating data.

† For complete data on this method see "The Fels Child Behavior Scales," T. W. Richards and M. P. Simons, *Genetic Psychology Monographs*, Vol. 24, 1941, 259-309.

ing these two to four or five separate ratings. The raters had in all cases been in close contact with the subjects for three months or more. A summary of the scores will be found in Table D-1.

The distortions which are likely to be involved in assessing personality in this fashion are too well known to require discussion here. The writer is aware of the probable distortions and also of the fact that the ratings are quite as nonobjective when presented as quantitative "scores" as they would have been if presented as verbal descriptions. The quantification adds nothing to the reliability of the method and serves only to facilitate comparisons and graphic presentation of the fundamentally impressionistic data. The scores should be read with full awareness of these factors. They are presented here primarily as a body of data which may have some value for other investigators using the same or similar rating scales.

The writer has found that, in connection with this study, the results did not justify the time and effort invested in rating and scoring personality traits. Probably such data have their greatest value in connection with extensive studies rather than with intensive studies like this one. Certainly the statistical treatment which quantification makes possible is more appropriate where validity is primarily a function of a numerically large sample. Where validity is rather a function of intimate and sustained investigation of a numerically small sample, as in the case of the present study, the rating scale data can prove a hazardous basis for generalization. The writer's experience of this fact is perhaps worth reviewing.

As we have noted earlier (in Appendix C), the ratings made for the children in the Rodney I group suggested striking differences between the Negro and the white children. These findings raised important questions concerning personality development in the two groups. Has the Negro child of four to five already begun to respond to the subtle pressures of minority status with hyperactivity, emotionality, sensitiveness, etc., and with compensatory gregariousness, competitiveness, aggressiveness, etc.?*

* The hypotheses suggested by the Rodney I data were discussed by the writer in her *Genesis of Race Awareness and Attitude,* unpublished Ph.D. dissertation, 1946, and in subsequent articles based upon that report. It is now clear that the writer tended to overestimate the significance of the Rodney I findings relating to personality traits of Negro children.

Subsequent study of a second Rodney group, and of the Coleman and Dover groups, must leave these questions still without a conclusive answer. The total sample of 61 Negro and 44 white children is quite inadequate to provide answers to questions of such breadth. It is indeed reasonable to suppose that adult Negroes wear "the mark of oppression,"† and it is not impossible that a good many young Negro children wear it, too, in a fainter form. But we cannot certainly distinguish the mark of racial oppression from the marks left by other kinds of oppressions without studies of numerically large samples of both Negroes and whites.

The writer is keenly aware of the sampling problem as it has been illustrated in this study. Reference to Table D-2 will show that the picture of personality differences between Negroes and whites in Rodney I was not reproduced in Rodney II. Where R-I Negroes averaged 6 to 22 points higher than R-I whites on 18 traits, in R-II the Negroes averaged but 2 to 5 points higher on only 4 of these same 18 traits (frequency of gross activity, vigor of activity, quarrelsomeness, sense of humor). Where R-I Negroes averaged lower than R-I whites on 9 traits, in R-II they averaged lower on but 3 of these 9 (tenacity, planfulness, and emotional control) and again the differences are small (2 to 6 points).

The sampling error which the small group can reflect is also illustrated here in the range shown by average scores as between one nursery school and another (see Table D-3). In respect to "frequency of gross activity," for example, the averages for the four different W groups range from 49 to 68, and on "vigor of activity" these W groups range from 49 to 67. It is of interest that the N group averages on these two traits are much less variable (60 to 68, and 64 to 71, respectively). It is perhaps also worth noting that on these 9 traits noted in Table D-3 the N range is greater than the W range for only 2 traits—"tenacity" and "emotional control." On both of these the N range is notably greater than the W (16 and 17 as compared with 7 and 5).

The differences between the final averages for N's and for W's (Table D-1) are not demonstrably significant. For the N average on "frequency of gross activity," for example, the standard deviation is 18.8, while the difference between N

† As suggested by A. Kardiner and L. Ovesey, in *The Mark of Oppression*, W. W. Norton, N.Y., 1951.

FELS CHILD BEHAVIOR RATING SCALE*

Aggressiveness

The behavior of the aggressive child is characterized by attempts to dominate social situations, to take the initiative, to plan activity of the group. He need not be successful as a leader; he attempts leadership.

Serial Sheet No.

Number	1	2	3	4	5	6	7	8	9	10
Period of Observation										
Age in Months at End of Period										
Child										

* The rating scale blanks, of which this is a sample, were supplied by the Fels Research Institute of Antioch College for use in this study.

FELS CHILD BEHAVIOR RATING SCALE (*cont.*)

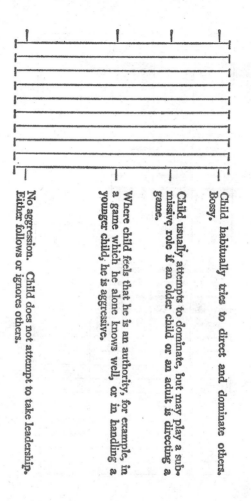

Child habitually tries to direct and dominate others. Bossy.

Child usually attempts to dominate, but may play a submissive role if an older child or an adult is directing a game.

Where child feels that he is an authority, for example, in a game which he alone knows well, or in handling a younger child, he is aggressive.

No aggression. Child does not attempt to take leadership. Either follows or ignores others.

FELS CHILD BEHAVIOR RATING SCALE (*cont.*)

Consistency: How variable is the child from one situation to another? Enter rating at left: Very predictable 5 4 3 2 1 Very irregular

Saliency: How important is this trait in the total pattern of the child? Enter rating at left: Highly characteristic 5 4 3 2 1 Negligible

Certainty: Do you feel that your rating is based on adequate evidence? Enter rating at left: Very adequate 5 4 3 2 1 Pure guessing

	1	2	3	4	5	6	7	8	9	10
Score										
Tolerance										
Range										
Number										

Rater

Date of Rating

Scored by .... Date
Checked by .... Date
Tabulated by .... Date

Rater's Remarks: (continue on back of sheet)

and W final averages on this trait is only 6.* The N-W differences on final averages are, in fact, remarkably small, but both the N and W ranges for individual scores are remarkably great and largely overlapping (see Table D-2, in which ranges for R-I and some R-II scores are given).

Graphic representation of the individual scores for the total N and W samples suggests the nature of the distributions within these wide and overlapping ranges (see Figures 1 and 2). On "frequency of gross activity," for example, the W scores show bimodal distribution, as do the N scores. Both W modes are lower, however, than are the N modes. On "emotional control" the W distribution tends less toward bimodality than does the N. These tendencies might prove significant if tested against a larger sample.

We must conclude that this study does not *establish* significant personality differences between the members of the two racial groups. However, our data do *suggest* that such differences *may* be real. The question whether differences are real, and the related questions concerning their specific nature, intensity, or frequency, are properly matters for another and major investigation. Here we have at least raised what seems to us an important issue, and indicated the possibility that Negro children of four to five show some distinctive personality traits—traits quite out of line with the popular conception of the distinctive personality traits of Negro adults.

* Standard deviation was not calculated throughout, since the measure was clearly unnecessary to demonstrate lack of statistical significance. It is of interest that the Sigma figures reported by the Fels Institute for their sample of 40 W children (see Table D-1) run very high, indicating the same wide range of individual scores found in the present study.

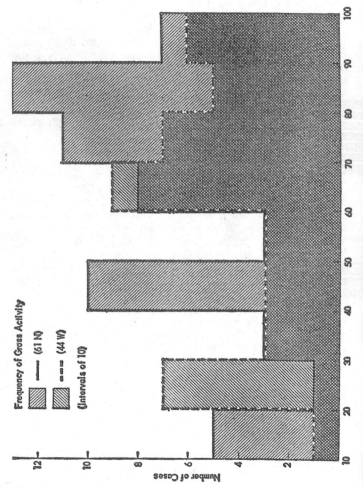

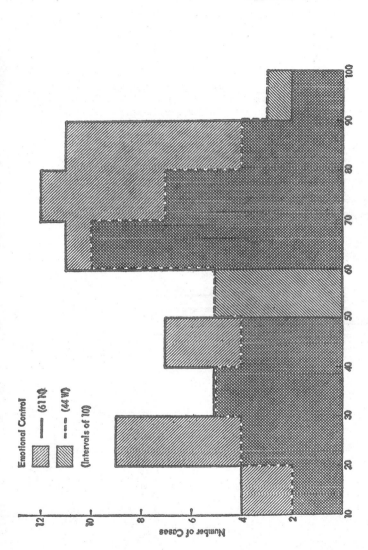

TABLE D-1

Personality Ratings (105)

Traits	Rodney I (26)		Rodney II (34)		Coleman (26)		Dover (19)		Average		Fels Institute Subjects *	
	N(15)	W(11)	N(16)	W(18)	N(26)	W(0)	N(4)	W(15)	N(61)	W(44)	Average W(40)	Sigma
Aggressiveness	62	40	62	62	59		61	60	61.	54.1	53	20.6
Competitiveness	63	45	56	57	58		54	61	57.6	54.2	52	19.3
Leadership	56	43	52	59	58		40	61	51.4	54.2	48	21.4
Vigor of activity	71	49	64	60	64		64	67	65.7	58.7	64	19.0
Frequency of gross activity	68	49	65	62	62		60	68	64.1	59.6	60	19.2
Planfulness	50	54	50	52	54		50	55	51	53.7	47	17.8
Originality	52	51	48	54	44		56	53	50	52.7	45	10.9
Fancifulness	69	61	56	60	58		54	56	59	58.9	45	13.9
Gregariousness	74	55	62	63	64		55	68	63.5	62	62	17.5
Friendliness	76	64	74	77	69		52	70	67.6	70	70	13.8
Kindness	59	53	58	57	67		55	66	59.8	58.7	43	18.1
Sensitiveness	73	61	60	58	64		75	66	67.9	61.7	57	13.6

Trait												
Tenacity	58	62	55	61	54		70	65	59.4	62.5	58	21.1
Patience	53	62	58	48	52		57	57	54.9	55.9	60	23.4
Emotional excitability	71	58	66	67	64		71	65	68	63.3	61	15.8
Intensity of emotional response	72	64	69	69	67		72	67	69.8	66.9	66	13.1
Emotional control	56	60	57	60	61		44	55	54.3	58.2	58	19.5
Jealousy	49	43	45	47	56		73	61	55.7	50	43	19.2
Cruelty	41	31	32	36	46		43	40	40.6	35.7	40	16.4
Quarrelsomeness	62	46	60	58	58		69	60	62.2	54.6	53	20.8
Resistance	50	47	53	54	58		60	60	55.1	53.6	48	18.0
Conformity	64	71	66	63	66		58	60	62.5	64.7	67	14.7
Obedience	58	64	66	60	60		56	56	59.9	60	69	15.1
Suggestibility	65	63	60	58	63		60	60	62.1	60.3	60	12.5
Social apprehensiveness	38	54	48	37	51		61	52	49.5	37.6	49	13.3
Physical apprehensiveness	51	62	56	52	62		60	50	56.7	54.7	54	14.1
Curiosity	75	62	62	66	67		59	60	63.7	64.5	60	16.5
Cheerfulness	70	63	71	74	66		59	70	66.5	68.8	72	15.5
Sense of humor	76	61	65	60	68		66	71	68.6	64.1	57	15.9
Affectionateness	63	71	63	57	64		64	60	63.5	62.5	48	15.5

TABLE D-2

Personality Data—Rodney I and Rodney II

Traits on which R-I N's average higher than R-I W's	Rodney I					Rodney II				
	N range	W range	N average (15 cases)	W average (11 cases)	Difference	N range	W range	N average (16 cases)	W average (18 cases)	Difference
Vigor of activity	19-96	14-90	71	49	22	23-97	34-96	64	60	4
Frequency of gross activity	13-94	18-79	68	49	19	14-97	21-96	65	62	3
Aggressiveness	12-87	14-63	62	40	22					
Competitiveness	15-90	14-75	63	45	18					
Leadership	11-97	13-82	56	43	13					
Emotional excitability	37-97	14-93	71	58	13					
Intensity of emotional response	35-97	23-96	72	64	8	34-98	30-97	65	60	5
Sense of humor	41-99	30-92	76	61	15					
Cheerfulness	37-98	38-97	70	63	7					
Curiosity	49-92	16-92	75	62	13					
Fancifulness	47-94	27-95	69	61	8					
Friendliness	51-98	18-93	76	64	12					
Kindness	32-90	13-94	59	53	6					
Gregariousness	26-95	17-87	74	55	19					
Quarrelsomeness	17-93	16-93	62	46	16	23-96	17-96	60	58	2
Cruelty	13-90	12-92	41	31	10					
Jealousy	17-76		49	43	6					
Sensitiveness	47-94	33-83	73	61	12					

Traits											
Traits on which R-I N's and W's about same average											
Originality	21-80	14-76	52	51	1						
Resistance	13-90	14-86	50	47	3	19-90	15-96	53	54	1	
Suggestibility	25-90	25-92	65	63	2	25-91	25-85	60	58	2	
Traits on which R-I N's average lower than R-I W's											
Social apprehensiveness	16-61	18-97	38	54	16	26-90	25-87	55	61	3	(2 3)
Physical apprehensiveness	31-88	45-93	51	62	11	23-86	13-84	50	52		
Patience	13-86	22-99	53	62	9	28-86	18-96	57	60		
Tenacity	33-95	32-94	58	62	4						
Planfulness	17-81	31-85	50	54	4						
Emotional control	21-94	18-94	56	60	4						
Conformity	26-94	30-96	64	71	7						
Obedience	14-99	15-94	58	64	6						
Affectionateness	25-97	38-98	63	71	8						

TABLE D-3

Average Scores for 4 Groups of Negroes and 4 Groups of Whites on 9 Traits

	Traits	N Average				W Average			
		R-I	R-II	Coleman	Dover	R-I	R-II	Dover	Fels
R-I and R-II N's higher than W's	Frequency of gross activity	68	65	62	60	49	62	68	60
	Vigor of activity	71	64	64	64	49	60	67	64
	Quarrelsomeness	62	60	58	69	46	58	60	53
	Sense of humor	76	65	68	66	61	60	71	57
R-I and R-II N's and W's same	Resistance	50	53	58	60	47	54	60	48
	Suggestibility	65	60	63	60	63	58	60	60
R-I and R-II N's lower than W's	Tenacity	58	55	54	70	62	61	65	58
	Planfulness	50	50	54	50	34	52	55	47
	Emotional control	56	57	61	44	60	60	55	58

Notes and References

Notes and References

CHAPTER 1

1. Among the 103 families covered in this study there are proportionately fewer people of foreign birth than in New Dublin as a whole (approximately one-seventh as against one-fourth). The countries of origin in the sample are, however, quite representative.

2. Nancy, the one white child in the sample who lives with a parent born and reared in the South, is apparently exposed to a minimum of "Southernism" or invidious regional comparison. Nancy's mother might be regarded as an example of the "prejudiced nondiscriminator." (The term is borrowed from R. K. Merton's "Discrimination and the American Creed," Ch. XI, pp. 99–126, in *Discrimination and National Welfare*, R. M. MacIver, *ed.*, Harper and Bros., N.Y., 1949). Nancy's father is a highly vocal "nonprejudiced nondiscriminator" (Merton, *ibid.*). Her mother, though uneasy with father's views and practices, conforms at least overtly.

3. In fifteen of the Negro families one or both parents are of Southern origin. Virginia, the Carolinas, Georgia, and Alabama are the states best represented.

4. Of these six white and three Negro families whose mobility chances are good (due to the actual or potential training of one or both parents), four of the white families are either temporary or peripheral residents in Dover-Harding. Mr. S., for example, is a temporary resident. He is a World War II refugee now studying for the ministry. Like so many

New Dublin immigrants, past and present, he established his first new-world home in a small tenement flat in Lower Harding. He considers himself and his family lucky for the present, but when his studies are completed he hopes and expects to move on.

Patricia's family (W) is temporary too. Patricia lives in Lower Harding, where her mother runs a rooming house and her father interns in a nearby city hospital. A social worker and a professional artist live in Harding too, but so far toward the southern and western borders of the rectangle as to be peripheral to the distinctive area.

Two of our white families, however, are truly residents. Irene and her mother and father live in the heart of Lower Harding in a small one-family house which they own. Both one-family houses and home ownership are extremely rare in these parts. So, too, is residence in Lower Harding on an apparently free choice basis, and Irene's family could presumably find and afford a more middle-class milieu. Lorraine's family is held in Dover by her father's limited earning capacity and by the adjustment problems facing recent immigrants. Her mother holds a European law degree but does not, or perhaps cannot, yet practice here. They will undoubtedly leave Dover, and move at least as far as Upper Harding or the adjacent Jewish community, as soon as their circumstances permit. A similar "upward" movement is very likely to mark the lives of our three Negro children whose fathers are now college students.

5. The Lower Harding-Upper Dover sections together represent New Dublin's approximation of a "Black Metropolis," as Drake and Cayton put it. (St. Clair Drake and Horace Cayton, *Black Metropolis*, Harcourt, Brace and Co., N.Y., 1945.)

CHAPTER 2

1. The passage is taken from Erik H. Erikson's "Growth and Crises of the 'Healthy Personality'," reprint from *Problems of Infancy and Childhood*, M. J. E. Senn, *ed.*, Supplement II, Trans. Fourth Conference, Josiah Macy, Jr. Foundation, N.Y., 1950, pp. 32–33.

2. Passages from Arnold Gesell, *et al.*, in *The First Five Years of Life*, Harper and Bros., N.Y., 1940, pp. 48–52.

CHAPTER 5

1. Conclusions concerning group preference rest upon the predominant tenor of each child's responses in situations where an N W choice (actual or hypothetical) is made (or strongly implied). The excerpts from protocols (pp. 83-88) will indicate the specific nature of the cumulative evidence upon which a final evaluation was made.

See also Appendix B (Methods) for description of the "play interviews" from which these sample protocols are taken.

CHAPTER 6

1. People like the R.'s show personality configurations reminiscent of those so vividly illustrated by A. Kardiner and L. Ovesey in *The Mark of Oppression,* W. W. Norton and Co., N.Y., 1951.

CHAPTER 7

1. "Niceness," for our children as well as for their parents, represents a generalization from a number of related value judgments. For the children, however, fewer of the value scales (p. 109) are involved. Their "niceness" judgments usually devolve upon the good-bad, polite-impolite, attractive-unattractive, friendly-unfriendly, thoughtful-thoughtless scales.

The children are likely to express their "niceness" judgments in terms of nice:not-nice and good:bad, though in context it is often clear that these general terms refer to more specific qualities. E.g., "she's a nice lady—look at her pretty clothes," "he's a bad boy—he's a messy boy," "she's nice—she always lets me play with her toys," "you're not nice—you didn't say 'thank you' for the candy," "he's a bad boy—he always grabs my crayons."

CHAPTER 8

1. The frequency of "broken homes" in our sample is somewhat higher among the Negroes than among the whites. In 16 of our Negro families (30%) the father of our subject is out of the picture, and apparently permanently so. His absence may be publicly accounted for (e.g., "my husband and I are separated," "I divorced my husband") or it may be publicly ignored. Among the whites there are 8 children (17%) without fathers in their homes.

The higher incidence of mother-centered homes among

Negroes has, of course, been noted repeatedly. (E.g., E. F. Frazier, *The Negro Family in the United States,* University of Chicago Press, 1939.) It has also been observed that, in northern urban centers at least, the mother-centered home is much more frequent among lower-class Negroes than among Negroes of the higher social strata. (See Kardiner and Ovesey, *The Mark of Oppression,* p. 70). In the present sample the higher Negro incidence is in line with what one might predict in respect to difference between Negroes and whites. But it also appears that in our sample the mother-centered home *in association with other presumably "lower-class" criteria* is equally frequent among Negroes and whites. One wonders whether the mother-centered urban home may not be primarily a lower-class phenomenon, and a caste phenomenon largely to the degree that the proportionate size of the Negro lower-class group exceeds that of the white.

CHAPTER 9

1. Catholicism is professed by one or both the parents of 13 (23%) of our Negro children and 21 (46%) of our whites. Judaism is the faith of one or both parents of 11 (24%) of our white children. The remaining 14 (30%) whites and 44 (77%) Negroes have parents who consider themselves Protestants of some variety or, more rarely, who do not concern themselves with organized religion in any form.

2. See Appendix C for full discussion of this interaction study.

3. Here is a section of the Observer's notes on a quite representative incident: Viola (N) kneeling on window seat looking out. Gerry (W) comes up and does likewise on her left and close to her. She runs her hands over his head three or four times, looking intently at his hair meanwhile. (This continues about half a minute.) He ignores it. She says nothing. Her attention is concentrated on what she's doing.

CHAPTER 10

1. See, for example, E. L. Horowitz. "The Development of Attitude Toward the Negro," *Archives of Psychology,* 1936; E. L. Horowitz, "'Race' Attitudes," in *Characteristics of the American Negro,* O. Klineberg, *ed.,* Harper and Bros., 1944; E. Frenkel-Brunswik, "A Study of Prejudice in Children," *Human Relations,* vol. 1, 1948, pp. 295–306; E. L.

Hartley, M. Rosenbaum, and S. Schwartz, "Children's Perception of Ethnic Group Membership," *Journal of Psychology*, vol. 26, 1948, pp. 387–398; B. J. Kutner, *Patterns of Mental Functioning Associated with Prejudice in Children* (unpublished dissertation), Harvard College, 1950; M. Radke, H. G. Trager, and H. Davis, "Social Perceptions and Attitudes of Children," *Genetic Psychology Monographs*, vol. 40, 1949, pp. 327–477 (and other publications stemming from the Philadelphia Early Childhood Project).

Studies of very early childhood, though few in number and differently conceived than our study, generally support the findings we report here. See R. E. Horowitz, "Racial Aspects of Self-identification in Nursery School Children," *Journal of Psychology*, vol. 7, 1939, pp. 91–99; K. B. Clark and M. K. Clark, "The Development of Consciousness of Self and the Emergence of Racial Identification in Negro Preschool Children," *Journal of Social Psychology*, vol. 10, 1939, pp. 591–599 (and later papers by the same authors); J. S. A. Chappat, *'Race' Prejudice and Preschool Education* (unpublished dissertation), Radcliffe College, 1944.

For an authoritative ordering and evaluation of prejudice studies, see G. W. Allport, "Prejudice: A Problem in Psychological and Social Causation," Supplement Series No. 4, *The Journal of Social Issues*, 1950, pp. 4–25.

2. This is not to suggest that the *absence* of such learned values operates to build *favorable* associations around Negroes. In most cases such absence would probably mean that, even though *one* of the possible etiological bases for rejection were missing, a number of others would still be present and dynamic. But, supposing that no others were present, it may be that a high degree of tolerance for dirtiness, blackness, not-niceness, or ugliness would promote receptivity toward Negroes, though probably not selectively toward them.

CHAPTER 13

1. M. E. Goodman, *A Primer for Parents: Educating our Children for Good Human Relations*, Anti-Defamation League, N.Y., 1959, p. 9.

2. Rhetta M. Arter, "An Inventory of Research on the Effects of Prejudice on Children," *Children*, vol. 6, 1959, p. 186.

3. G. W. Allport, *The Nature of Prejudice*, Beacon, Boston, 1954, p. 477.

4. See, for a recent example, Benjamin Spock, "Do Parents Teach Prejudice?" *Ladies Home Journal*, January, 1962.

5. See *Recommendations; Composite Report of Forum Findings*, 1960 White House Conference on Children and Youth, USGPO, 1960, pp. 57–61. Writing on "White House Conference Follow-up Within the States," F. Schmidt and M. I. French, *Children*, vol. 9, 1962, p. 7, report: "The White House Conference made strong recommendations on the subject of human rights, and many State committees and youth councils explicitly express a concern for *all* children in their statements of purpose. No reports thus far have been received of any of the State committees or youth councils devising action programs specifically focused on the elimination of racial or religious discrimination. However, the criteria of equality of opportunity are implicit in many of the projects these committees have developed."

6. Pre-1952 studies focused on intergroup attitudes in children were, on the whole, rather restricted in scale and scope. Bruno Lasker, in 1929, provided an exception, as well as the first serious study of "Race Attitudes in Children," Holt, N.Y. Lasker's anecdotal data served, if not to convince, at least to stimulate; more rigorous studies followed during the 1930s, 1940s, and at the turn of the century, under the names of E. L. Horowitz, R. E. Horowitz, K. B. Clark, M. K. Clark, E. Frenkel-Brunswik, E. L. Hartley, M. Rosenbaum, and S. Schwartz, H. G. Trager, and M. Radke. (See Chapter 10, Note 1, for complete references.) See also R. D. Minard, "Race Attitudes of Iowa Children," *University of Iowa Student Characteristics*, vol. 4: 2, 1931; R. C. Peterson, "Motion Pictures and the Social Attitudes of Children," in *Developing Attitudes in Children*, University of Chicago Press, Chicago, 1933; R. Zeligs and G. Hendrickson, "Checking the Social Distance Technique Through Personal Interview," *Sociology and Social Research*, vol. 18, 1934, pp. 420–430; and "Racial Attitudes of Children," *Sociology and Social Research*, vol. 21, 1937, pp. 361–371; H. Meltzer, "Children's Thinking about Nations and Races," *Journal of Genetic Psychology*, vol. 58, 1941, pp. 181–199; R. Blake and W. Dennis, "The Development of Stereotypes Concerning the Negro," *Journal of Abnormal and Social Psychology*, vol. 38, 1943, pp. 525–531; E. Helgerson, "The Relative Significance of Race, Sex, and Facial Expression in Choice of Playmate by the Preschool Child," *Journal of Negro Education*, vol. 12, 1943, pp. 612–

622; M. E. Goodman, "Evidence Concerning the Genesis of Interracial Attitudes," *American Anthropologist*, vol. 48, 1946, pp. 624–630; G. W. Allport and B. M. Kramer, "Some Roots of Prejudice," *Journal of Psychology*, vol. 22, 1946, pp. 9–39; R. Zeligs, "Children's Intergroup Attitudes," *Journal of Genetic Psychology*, vol. 72, 1947, 101–110; R. Zeligs, "Children's Intergroup Concepts and Stereotypes," *Journal of Educational Sociology*, vol. 21, 1947, pp. 113–126; R. M. Goff, *Problems and Emotional Difficulties of Negro Children*, Bureau of Publications, Teachers College, Columbia University, N.Y., Contr. Educ. #960, 1949; P. H. Mussen, "Some Personality and Social Factors Related to Changes in Children's Attitudes Toward Negroes," *Journal of Abnormal and Social Psychology*, vol. 45, 1950, pp. 423–441; R. B. Ammons, "Reactions in a Projective Doll-play Interview . . . to Differences in Skin Color and Facial Features," *Journal of Genetic Psychology*, vol. 76, 1950, pp. 323–341; D. Springer, "Awareness of Racial Differences by Preschool Children in Hawaii," *Genetic Psychology Monographs*, vol. 41, 1950, pp. 215–270.

7. T. W. Adorno, Else Frenkel-Brunswik, D. J. Levinson, and R. N. Sanford, *The Authoritarian Personality*, Harper, N.Y., 1950.

8. See, for example, J. M. Masling, "How Neurotic is the Authoritarian?" *Journal of Abnormal and Social Psychology*, vol. 49, 1954, pp. 316–318; E. Frenkel-Brunswik, "Social Research and the Problem of Values: A Reply," *Journal of Abnormal and Social Psychology*, vol. 49, 1954, pp. 466–470. B. R. McCandless, *Children and Adolescents*, Holt, N.Y., 1960, reviewing research and controversy relating to authoritarianism and the F (Fascism) Scale developed by Adorno *et al.*, cites thirteen studies between 1954 and 1959. G. W. Allport, in *Pattern and Growth in Personality*, Holt, Rinehart & Winston, N.Y., 1961, p. 434, comments on this rash of studies and upon the "unfortunate error" made "in composing the original scale"; i.e., "the items are unidirectional: an agreement is always scored as authoritarian. This fact has led some critics to claim that there is no elaborate authoritarian syndrome involved, but merely a tendency to acquiesce . . . a simple form of suggestibility. . . . The scale still correlates with ethnic prejudice, but the original elaborate theory of an authoritarian 'character structure' is placed under strain. One author (M. Rokeach) believes that a common trait of *dog-*

matism is a better explanatory concept than the complex syndrome proposed by the original authors."

9. J. L. Gilchrist, "Social Psychology," in *Annual Review of Psychology*, 10, 1959, p. 247. The F (Fascism) Scale was constructed by T. W. Adorno and his associates for the study of "implicit anti-democratic trends" in personal ideologies. It is a device for measuring prejudice "without appearing (to the subject) to have this aim and without mentioning the name of any minority group." The F Scale was a major item among the tools devised for identifying and describing the "authoritarian personality." (See T. W. Adorno, *et al., op. cit.*)

10. B. R. McCandless, *op. cit.*, p. 362.

11. R. R. Sears, E. E. Maccoby, and H. Levin, *Patterns of Child Rearing*, Row, Peterson, Evanston, Ill., 1957.

12. R. Christie and J. Garcia, "Subcultural Variation in Authoritarian Personality," *Journal of Abnormal and Social Psychology*, vol. 46, 1951, p. 467.

13. T. F. Pettigrew, "Regional Differences in Anti-Negro Prejudice," *Journal of Abnormal and Social Psychology*, vol. 59, 1959, pp. 28–36.

14. M. Jahoda, M. Deutsch, and S. Cook, *Research Methods in Social Relations: With Especial Reference to Prejudice*, Dryden, N.Y., 1951, p. 365. K. B. Clark, in *Prejudice and Your Child*, Beacon Press, Boston, 1955, agrees and adds that prejudice needs to be studied in the context of societal, rather than individual, problems or pathologies (p. 71). There is, for example, the problem of middle-class striving for status and success; here—Clark suggests—is a "context in which one should seek for an understanding of the origin and nature of hostile (intergroup) attitudes. . . . Conformity to and success in this competitive striving or in other patterned life-ways, brings such psychological advantages and rewards that the wonder is not that there are many prejudiced persons but that there are a good many relatively unprejudiced" (p. 74).

15. E. A. Suchman, J. P. Dean, and R. M. Williams, Jr., *Desegregation: Some Propositions and Research Suggestions*, Anti-Defamation League, N.Y., 1958, p. 58. M. Sherif, in *An Outline of Social Psychology*, Harper, N.Y., 1948, pp. 340–341, states much the same view: "The average individual member of a group exhibits the degree of prejudice toward the member of another group prescribed by the social distance scale of his group."

16. M. Sherif and others, *Intergroup Conflict and Cooperation, The Robbers Cave Experiment*, Institute of Group Relations, University of Oklahoma, Norman, Oklahoma, 1961, p. 198.

17. There is, in any case, no disagreement concerning the fact that intergroup attitudes are *learned*, rather than inherent or instinctive. K. B. Clark observes that not only have "instinct" theories been refuted by research of the past thirty years, but "social scientists are now convinced that children learn social, racial, and religious prejudices in the course of observing, and being influenced by, the existence of patterns in the culture in which they live." *Op. cit.*, 1955, p. 17.

18. E. L. Horowitz, in "The Development of Attitude Toward the Negro," *Archives of Psychology*, No. 194, 1936, presented evidence that white children in Georgia (urban and rural), urban Tennessee, and New York City (an all-white school) held basically similar attitudes toward Negroes. Subsequently Goodman, Trager and Radke-Yarrow, Morland, Stevenson and Stewart, have demonstrated for two Northeastern metropolitan areas, for a Virginia town and a Texas town much the same attitudes, incipient at least, in preschool, kindergarten, or primary-grade children.

19. G. W. Allport, *op. cit.*, p. 297.

20. See M. E. Goodman, *op. cit.*, p. 625.

21. See H. W. Stevenson and N. G. Stevenson, "Social Interaction in an Interracial Nursery School," *Genetic Psychology Monographs*, 61, 1960, pp. 37–75. The authors report that their "observational records contained many examples showing awareness of the physical differences related to race," p. 60.

22. K. B. Clark, *op. cit.*, p. 19.

23. C. Landreth and B. C. Johnson, "Young Children's Responses to a Picture and Inset Test Designed to Reveal Reactions to Persons of Different Skin Color," *Child Development*, vol. 24, 1953, p. 78.

24. J. K. Morland, "Racial Recognition by Nursery School Children in Lynchburg, Virginia," *Social Forces*, vol. 37, 1958, pp. 132–137.

25. I.e., by E. Horowitz and R. Horowitz, by K. Clark and M. Clark, by J. K. Morland, by H. W. Stevenson and N. G. Stevenson, by C. Landreth and B. C. Johnson and by M. E. Goodman.

26. K. B. Clark, *op. cit.*, p. 23.

27. H. W. Stevenson and E. C. Stewart, "A Developmental Study of Racial Awareness in Young Children," *Child Development*, vol. 29, 1958, p. 408.

28. H. G. Trager and M. Radke-Yarrow, *They Learn What They Live*, Harper, N.Y., 1952, pp. 150, 346.

29. B. Kutner, "Patterns of Mental Functioning Associated with Prejudice in Children," *Psychology Monographs*, vol. 72, 1958.

30. G. W. Allport, *op. cit.*, p. 309.

31. J. Rosner, "When White Children are in the Minority," *Journal of Educational Sociology*, vol. 28, 1954, pp. 69–72. Rosner observed that the white children showed overt prejudice in a group in which they constituted the majority. But even in this group they "accommodated themselves" and "accepted" the situation.

32. E. Frenkel-Brunswik and J. Havel, "Prejudice in the Interviews of Children: I, Attitudes Toward Minority Groups" *Journal of Genetic Psychology*, vol. 82, 1953, p. 135.

33. H. Trager and M. Radke-Yarrow, *op. cit.*, p. 345.

34. J. Galtung, *What High School Students Say. . .* , Anti-Defamation League, N.Y., 1961, 24 pp.

35. K. Helfant, "Parents' Attitudes vs. Adolescent Hostility in the Determination of Adolescents' Sociopolitical Attitudes," *Psychology Monographs*, vol. 66, 1952, #345, p. 15.

36. T. Adorno, *et. al.*, *op. cit.*

37. J. K. Morland, *op. cit.*, p. 137.

38. K. B. Clark, *op. cit.*, p. 23.

39. C. Landreth and B. C. Johnson, *op. cit.*, p. 78.

40. H. Trager and M. Radke-Yarrow, *op. cit.*, pp. 345–346. It should be noted too that Negro children are often keenly aware that "acts of exclusion" and "expressions of hostility" have come their way. Goff, *op. cit.*, found that 77% of her 150 ten- to twelve-year-old Negro subjects had experienced "ridicule" or "indirect disparagement"; 41% had experienced aggression from white children; 11% reported physical ill-treatment from whites. Goff believes these figures to be too low.

41. C. Bird, E. D. Monachesi, and H. Burdick, "Infiltration and the Attitudes of White and Negro Parents and Children," *Journal of Abnormal and Social Psychology*, vol. 47, 1952, pp. 695–696.

42. R. K. Kerckhoff and F. Gould, "A Study of Children's

Sense of Community," Merrill-Palmer Institute (mimeographed), 1961.

43. Committee on Social Issues, Group for the Advancement of Psychiatry, *Psychiatric Aspects of School Desegregation*, #37, May, 1957, p. 18.

44. B. R. McCandless, *op. cit.*, p. 381.

45. J. H. Douglass, "The Effects of Minority Status on Children," *Survey Papers*, 1960 White House Conference on Children and Youth, p. 183.

46. P. H. Mussen, "Differences Between the TAT Responses of Negro and White Boys," *Journal of Consulting Psychology*, vol. 17, 1953, pp. 373–376.

The Thematic Apperception Test (TAT) is a projective technique for the study of personality. It consists of a series of deliberately ambiguous but imagination-stimulating pictures. The testee is asked to tell a story about each. Responses are analyzed in terms of standardized categories. The test has had widespread use as a clinical instrument. See L. Bellak, *The Thematic Apperception Test and the Children's Apperception Test in Clinical Use*, Grune and Stratton, N.Y., 1954.

47. E.g., see K. Clark, *op. cit.*; H. Trager and M. Radke-Yarrow, *op. cit.*; H. W. Stevenson and E. C. Stewart, *op. cit.*; J. K. Morland, *op. cit.*

48. D. S. Palermo, "Racial Comparisons and Additional Normative Data on the Children's Manifest Anxiety Scale," *Child Development*, vol. 30, 1959, pp. 53–57.

49. G. F. Boyd, "The Levels of Aspiration of White and Negro Children in a Non-Segregated Elementary School," *Journal of Social Psychology*, vol. 36, 1952, pp. 191–196.

50. Martin Deutsch, "Minority Group and Class Status as Related to Social and Personality Factors in Scholastic Achievement," *Monograph #2*, Society for Applied Anthropology, 1960.

51. *Ibid.*, pp. 11, 19.

52. *Ibid.*, p. 10.

53. H. W. Stevenson and E. C. Stewart, *op. cit.*; Morland, *op. cit.*

54. K. B. Clark, *op. cit.*, p. 37.

55. H. Trager and M. Radke-Yarrow, *op. cit.*, p. 137.

56. K. B. Clark, *op. cit.*, p. 45.

57. The children were rated on each of 30 traits by three or four different people (the Observer, the teacher, one or

more student teachers) using the Fels Child Behavior Scale (see Appendix D).

58. G. W. Allport, *op. cit.*, p. 303.

59. M. Deutsch, *op. cit.*, p. 11.

60. E. Frenkel-Brunswik and J. Havel, *op. cit.*, p. 134.

61. B. Kutner, *op. cit.*, p. 31.

62. G. W. Allport, *op. cit.*, p. 441

63. *Ibid.*, p. 79.

64. *Ibid.*, p. 303.

65. M. McFarland, "Racial Relationships, A Study of Preschool Children," *Psychiatric Communication*, April, 1958.

66. R. K. Kerckhoff and F. Gould, *op. cit.*

67. E. Frenkel-Brunswik and J. Havel, *op. cit.*, pp. 92, 132.

68. R. I. Evans, "Personal Values as Factors in Anti-Semitism," *Journal of Abnormal and Social Psychology*, vol. 47, 1952, pp. 749–756.

69. C. Bird, E. D. Monachesi, and H. Burdick, "Studies of Group Tensions: III. The Effect of Parental Discouragement of Play Activities upon the Attitudes of White Children Toward Negroes," *Child Development*, vol. 23, 1952, p. 305.

70. *Ibid.*, p. 306.

71. H. Trager and M. Radke-Yarrow, *op. cit.*, p. 349. See also M. Radke-Yarrow, H. Trager, and J. Miller, "The Role of Parents in the Development of Children's Ethnic Attitudes," *Child Development*, vol. 23, 1952, pp. 13–53.

72. H. Trager and M. Radke-Yarrow, *op. cit.*, p. 346.

73. Committee on Social Issues, Group for the Advancement of Psychiatry, *op. cit.*, p. 62.

74. H. W. Stevenson and E. C. Stevenson, *op. cit.*, 1960, p. 60.

75. M. Sherif and others, *op. cit.*

76. M. M. Tumin, Segregation and Desegregation, *A Digest of Recent Research*, Anti-Defamation League, N.Y., 1957, 112 pp.; and *Supplement*, 1960, 32 pp.; also systematically checked were issues of *Annual Review of Psychology*, Annual Reviews, Inc., Palo Alto, Calif., Volumes 5 (1954) through 13 (1962).

77. G. W. Allport, *op. cit.*, p. 425.

Index